GAZZA

THE GARY KIRSTEN AUTOBIOGRAPHY

I dedicate this book to Debs and Joshua,
who are my life now.

GAZZA

THE GARY KIRSTEN AUTOBIOGRAPHY

Neil Manthorp

DON NELSON

Cape Town

COVER PHOTO; Gary walking off the field after his final innings in test cricket

ISBN 1 86806 219 8

First Edition 2004
Second Impression 2005

Don Nelson Publishers
PO Box 18600, Wynberg 7824

Cover photograph: Touchline Photo
Design and Layout: Matthew Ibbotson of PETALDESIGN
Typesetting and reproduction by Virtual Colour, Cape Town
Printed and bound by Tandym Print, 25 Thor Circle, Viking Place, Thornton
Set in 9.75 on 13 pt Times

Contents

Acknowledgements

Gary Kirsten: Rondebosch Boys' High and Prep Schools, WP cricket, UCB, my family, my friends, my team mates, Ali Bacher, SAB, Standard Bank, Puma, County and Neil Manthorp (for helping me write this book)

Neil Manthorp is indebted to the following people for their help in speaking to Gary's opponents, colleagues and team mates and for compiling their thoughts:
Fazeer Mohammed, Anand Vasu, Malcolm Conn, Robert Craddock, Charlie Austin, Steve James, Peter Mitchell, Scyld Berry, Bob Woolmer, Ken Borland and Telford Vice.
  And to Alison and my colleagues at MWP for their necessary patience and understanding during the long hours of writing.

Neil Manthorp grew up on the KwaZulu-Natal south coast after arriving in South Africa as a 12-month old emigre in the company of his parents who sought fresh pastures from the north of England.

South Africa's international sporting exile contributed to Neil starting his sports journalism career in England in 1986 where he worked as a freelance commentator and writer. When South Africa's return to international competition seemed imminent, he returned to lay the foundations for an independent sports news agency - which would become MWP Media.

Since then he has covered more than 30 tours with the national cricket team as well as becoming a well-known commentator and columnist for a variety of media outlets.

He lives in Cape Town with his partner Alison and their two daughters Mia and Ella.

Foreword

Gary Kirsten blows that old cliché out of the water, the one about a leopard not being able to change its spots. I had played some provincial cricket against Gary prior to my selection for the '92 World Cup, and the subsequent tour of the West Indies, a week after our World Cup debut came to a rain-splattered end, but I didn't know much about the man at that stage. Apart from the fact that he spent a fortune on hair products, which as you can now see, was a total waste of time and money. He was one of those unfortunate blokes who had to comb their hair from one side right across to the other, and had to be careful which way he was facing when the wind was blowing.

He and Kenny Jackson (of Boland repute) were good friends at the time, and they scraped some money together to join the boys in the Caribbean, for the one-off Test in Barbados. Having spent their meagre budget on their travel costs, they slept on Peter Kirsten's floor. Although, the pre-Deborah Gary Kirsten probably didn't get home until very late, or early, the next morning and wouldn't even have felt the discomfort of the floor.

However, his competitive nature probably kicked in on that tour and I'm sure that he decided then and there that one day he was going to play for his country - even if it was simply so the UCB could fund his enjoyment of life.

When we toured Australia in '93-'94, we had two key players sustain serious injuries - Kepler broke his hand and Brian McMillan damaged his knee on a bumpy outfield after a Madonna concert at the MCG, so Gary was flown in to join the squad. The Kirsten brothers were selected to open the batting for us in the ODI s and in one match in particular, the game against the Aussies at Perth, both Gary and Peter were peppered by some very hostile bowling. Glenn McGrath hit Peter so badly that he had to go to hospital and have his cheekbone operated on. That episode gave me a really good insight into the strength of character and doggedness of Gary - he was able to put the horrific scene of his brother being felled and stretchered off the field behind him and carry on doing his job for the team.

Gary has broken all sorts of batting records, not only for SA but worldwide. However, I firmly believe that his greatest contribution to SA cricket can't be found by dissecting his stats, impressive as they are. A successful team is usually made up of individuals who each contribute a unique quality to the mix; no prizes for guessing who had the ability to make a lot of noise and keep the boys awake. On the other hand, Gary's powers of concentration, and ability to withstand some fearsome fast bowling without flinching soon became his hallmark, and one always had the sense, especially from opposing players, that as long as Gary was still at the crease, the game was far from over, even if South Africa were staring down the barrel.

Mr Consistency went through a lean patch with the bat, as most players at this level are prone to do (due to the sustained pressure facing them for 10 to 12 months of the year), but true to his reputation as a resilient batsman, he bounced back. The way he ended his career was typical, by playing a mature and calm innings that took his team to the brink of victory. In your last match, you are very emotional, and Gary's effort in the partnership with Graeme Smith was testimony to his ability to put aside all distractions and carry on with the job at hand. He wasn't only the rock around which we played so many matches; he was an example off the field, too. His professional approach helped many team mates reach their full potential, something very few ever achieve without role models as important and impressive as Gary.

Thanks, Gazza, for helping me enjoy my cricket, and play to the best of my limited ability. Your throwing arm can now take a well-deserved break.

Jonty Rhodes

Introduction

On my study wall at home I have pictures of my team mates and me in more than a dozen countries, pictures of me scoring hundreds and pictures of me shaking hands with Nelson Mandela and the Queen of England. There are pictures of me celebrating victories with a Castle and a cigar as well as pictures of Debs and me visiting some of the most famous sights in the world.

There aren't any pictures of the times I was dismissed for nought or when I sat in the change room and cried because I was so disappointed or angry. And there also aren't any pictures of me during a day of winter training, cold, wet and exhausted.

In fact when I look back over ten years of international cricket during which I had the honour and privilege of representing my country, I see some of the happiest and most enjoyable days of my life. I had the incredible opportunity of making a living out of something I loved doing.

There have been highs and lows, however, and for a while it seemed as if there were a few more lows than highs, but I wouldn't swap a single day of the last ten years for anything. Except, perhaps, the day I heard that Hansie was guilty.

In this book I talk about that day as well as the many enjoyable and sometimes exhausting days spent on the road with the South African cricket team. I also talk about the people that have played a major role in my life.

I hope this book provides you with an interesting insight into the world inside the South African cricket team and how I was fortunate enough to have experienced this incredible journey.

Gary Kirsten
September, 2004

1

Cricket in the blood

The great thing about being brought up in the Kirsten household was that we were always exposed to sport. My Dad, Noel, encouraged us to get out on the sports field; any sport would do. It was partly a product of the times – we hadn't quite reached the computer age – and going to the movies or hanging around in shopping malls just wasn't an option. So it was simply sport and more sport.

Dad was a huge influence on me from a team sports perspective. He himself had had a first-class cricket career of note playing wicket-keeper for Border and was one of the holders of the South African record of seven dismissals in an innings.

Dad was convinced that cricket was the only way for me to go. I was useful enough as a tennis player to be offered a six-week coaching scholarship in America at a fancy tennis camp, and Mum (Gayl) was keen for me to go, but Dad put his foot down and said 'No way'. I think it may have been a financial issue, as well, to be honest. It involved a fair amount of expense but he used the issue of team sports as the reason for stopping me. I never regretted it, not once.

Dad had boundless energy and ran us ragged every day, especially Paul and me. He threw and kicked balls with us for hours. Whether it was rugby, cricket or soccer, he never seemed to stop. In the summers it was just non-stop cricket. We actually lived at the Newlands cricket ground for eight years, so there was no problem finding a net between the ages of 10 and 18.

Dad had decided upon a career change and applied for the job as grounds administrator – he'd be called a curator today – after a lengthy period as a civil engineer.

It was an incredible experience living at one of the most famous cricket venues in the world and I'm glad to say I had a strong awareness of how lucky I was at the time, not just in retrospect. I developed a passion for cricket early on and with Peter becoming well established on the first-class scene I had a role model built into my life.

I wasn't the only one looking up to Peter's reputation, however, as Paul (who was called Porky, or Porks, from the age of seven months) and Andy also played cricket to an excellent level.

Cheryl is actually the oldest Kirsten sibling, not Peter as most people have assumed, but she was clever enough to avoid newspaper headlines in her career and consequently doesn't get autograph requests in restaurants. She chose a career in interior design and has been hugely successful. Peter and Andy were the product of Dad's first marriage while Porks and I were 'second time around' children.

Andy is only four years older than me and I'm barely a couple ahead of Porks so the three of us spent a good deal of time together growing up while Peter and Cheryl, at 13 and 15 years older than me, were spending their time being grown-ups.

I used to boast to my friends that I had the biggest back garden in the world. We played sport at Newlands literally the year round. In winter we'd play rugby and hockey and, of course, cricket in the summer. The wetter it was in winter, the better it was. Andy, Porks and I used to play a game called 'Bokke' which entailed full contact rugby (and we didn't hold back on the tackles) with three different trylines to defend and score over. I'm not quite sure how the rules worked but it was a huge amount of fun before, inevitably, ending in tears in one way or another.

Today's curators would no doubt cringe if their sacred turf was used as it was back then but the outfield never seemed to suffer despite the Kirsten brothers and their friends playing numerous games of 'Bokke' - and just about everything else - from dawn to dusk.

Porks and I could a make a competition out of anything – and then we'd fight to the death. There were a few fights, a few bloody noses, and cuts and scrapes, but we were inseparable for weeks at a time just 'being boys' and playing sport. Porks used to become very agitated whenever he lost anything to me but not quite as cross as I would be in defeat – I didn't suffer the indignity of losing to my kid brother with very much grace at all, let alone good grace.

As we advanced into our teenage years our competitive nature needed something more constructive than throwing stones at tin cans and we discovered squash. I'm not sure how talented we were but nothing could curb our spirit or determination and we became competent enough to play WP league, something we continued for a couple of years after we'd left school. It was one thing playing a serious match for your team but quite another when we played each other. We even had to win the warm-up routines. We still try to play squash at least once a week but obviously there'll be much more time for it now we've both retired from cricket. I'm happy to say we've mellowed a little from those early days; but only a little.

There was another very obvious advantage to living at Newlands. I could invite my friends over after school and at weekends and they wouldn't have to pay to get into the ground. This was an extremely effective way to make friends and influence people. I can still distinctly remember several boys who had teased me about being a Kirsten and the unfair advantages it gave me suddenly changing their tune when Clive Rice was bringing the Transvaal 'Mean Machine' down for a Currie Cup game. Then I became a great scrum-half and batsman with a great family…as long as they got the invite. I learnt to pick and choose. There was, understandably, a great demand for invites to the Kirsten family home on match days.

Undoubtedly the worst part of living at Newlands was exam time. Dad was diligent at making sure we studied hard and did our homework but come exam time in

November, whatever level I was at, I had the same old problem. My bedroom overlooked the cricket field and there was virtually nothing I could do to stop myself gazing out of the window and watching the cricket. I tried closing the curtains but that just made it worse because every time there was a smattering of applause I jumped up from my desk to see what had happened. And then I'd just watch the end of the over. And then just one more… The fact that I could see the scoreboard made it even worse. How could I abandon a batsman in the 80s when I could watch him all the way to a hundred?

One day, in desperation, I moved all my books and studies to the other end of the house – the road side – where there was no view of the ground. It was hopeless. I could still hear the cheers and I spent most of the day running from my new desk to my bedroom and back again. Obviously I managed to learn something during the lunch and tea breaks, though, because I passed the exams. Just.

The biggest match of the year during the isolation years was undoubtedly the New Year Currie Cup match between WP and Transvaal. It was a guaranteed sell-out crowd with most of the best cricketers in the country invariably rising to the occasion and playing magnificent cricket. Nobody was qualified to say for sure, of course, but nobody doubted that the intensity of competition and atmosphere was as good as a Test match anywhere in the world.

One year, believe it or not, Dad erected a scaffolding platform in the garden so we could sit and watch the match in comfort over the heads of the people who had paid for seats in the 'Oaks' enclosure. It started with a comfortable, family group of four or five but as word of Dad's handiwork spread amongst extended family members and friends, we finished the three days of the match with people hanging off the sides of the structure like commuters on an Indian train. Not that I'd ever seen an Indian train back then. Or ever thought I would.

It sounds like a line from a bad movie but on non-match days I used to sit on the heavy roller with one of the ground staff, James, chugging up and down rolling pitches and just 'feeling' Newlands. It wasn't a case of gazing at the Oaks and the pavilion and dreaming of playing in front of them one day – and I certainly never dreamt of playing for my country, nobody did. But the atmosphere of the place just did special things for me. It was a bit like being in a beautiful cathedral – I remember feeling calm and peaceful. Maybe it was just because I was a kid with no worries.

I was hanging around at nets one day watching the Western Province players who were practising alongside the amateurs from Western Province Cricket Club, which was a separate entity. I had a junior size bat and I'd watch for hours until they'd finished. Allan Lamb used to throw balls for me to hit at the end of the session and he took a real interest in me. I don't think he thought I was very good, but he was obviously impressed by my determination.

Apart from Dad the greatest sporting influence on me during that period was Kevin Lyons, the former English umpire. He used to spend his English winters as the professional coach at Rondebosch School and he taught me the basics of how to play the game. We've stayed in touch ever since and I think he feels modestly proud that one of his pupils has gone on to play international cricket.

For any sportsman or woman to reach the top of their profession they have to take a lot of selfish time. They need the support of family and friends and they need people to do so many basic jobs and chores for them. I didn't realise it at the time, but playing sport for a living isn't very glamorous for those around you and it wasn't very glamorous for Mum back then, either.

She provided amazing support, both physically and emotionally. She never missed a game of rugby that I played in and she provided a constant, endless supply of smiling, caring encouragement. Naturally I didn't have a clue just how valuable she was to my development, but then how many men only realise everything their mothers did for them 20 years later? Most, probably.

Dad could be tough, too. He was the disciplinarian who instilled in me the attributes I became known for, like determination and the ability to work hard for long periods of time. He had a work-ethic culture and it was natural for him to expect his sons to have it, too.

He never watched school matches with the other parents; he always stood somewhere in the distance and never became actively involved. He preferred just to watch without the complications of parental emotion, and he certainly never became involved in any school activities or decisions, such as practices or selection.

Mum was a bit more 'hands on' but she wasn't just a smiling face in the crowd. When it came to tennis Dad wasn't interested so Mum would hit balls with me for hours and hours, just as Dad did with cricket. From the age of eight to 10 we lived in a house next to St. Joseph's College in Cape Town, which had a tennis court and for at least a year we were on that school court every morning from six o'clock.

But rugby was really Mum's game. She watched every game I ever played, from the age of eight right through to my last league game for Villagers in 1993. She was always prominent in the centre of the crowd of parents on the halfway line, cheering and dispensing almost as much advice as the coach.

As I mention later in this book, she has watched me play in one senior game of cricket. Five hundred rugby games, but one game of cricket. Her approach to cricket was the complete opposite to rugby. She will watch a highlights programme in the evening, or the following day, but has never been able to watch me live, even on television. She says her nerves can't take it. The solitary exception was the 1998 Test match at Lord's. I bought the air ticket and arranged everything. Surely, I reasoned, this experience would turn her around. Sadly, her resolve simply hardened further and after suffering through a mere ten minutes (and four runs) of the first innings, I ended her misery by getting out.

My relationship with Peter throughout these formative years wasn't exactly close because, at 13 years my senior, he was probably caught somewhere closer to being a friendly uncle than an older brother. I was also very aware of being 'Peter Kirsten's kid brother' and that played a huge role in my development as a person as well as a cricketer. Peter was already becoming a major star with Western Province, which, of course, was all we could aspire to in those days.

There were advantages and disadvantages. I spent a large part of my school career, even going into high school, blighted by envy and jealousy in some way or another. It was impossible for me to be selected to any team without a comment or two from people saying it was only because I was a Kirsten.

Even when I was picked for the rugby 1st XV there was one guy who felt strongly enough to give me the whole 'Kirsten name' saga over again. And I was captain.

On the other hand it added to the sense of determination I'd already inherited from Dad. There was a burning desire to prove myself as an individual, to prove that I was Gary and not Peter's little brother and to prove myself as a sportsman in my own right. I spent most of school days trying to prove people wrong and that's probably what I carried on doing throughout my adult career. When people said I couldn't play Test cricket, and there were plenty of them, it came as no surprise. I'd been used to it from the age of eight. I knew I wasn't as good as Peter but that was a bonus because at least I never tried to emulate him. It would not have been a pretty sight if I'd tried to play like him. So I settled for being me but I was very, very determined to prove that Gary Kirsten was worth his place in every team he was selected for.

A part of that determination came directly from Peter, of course. The one innings that stood out for me above all others was played at Newlands in the traditional New Year fixture against Transvaal. Sylvester Clarke had stayed on after the West Indies 'rebel' tour and was playing for Transvaal. He turned Peter black and blue. His ribs were bruised as I had never seen before. One delivery hit him on the elbow so loudly that people in the crowd believed he must have broken his arm.

There were no physiotherapists in those days. The 12th man ran on with a bucket of ice and a towel. Peter held some ice on the swelling and carried on to make an incredible 80. He was quite a role model! It was an innings of such bravery and determination it was bound to have a profound effect on me. At the remotest sign of trouble during my career, when it was hard or difficult or painful, I thought of that day and that innings.

Paul was affected even more than me because he had a double dose. He also had to live in the shadow of Peter but he also had to cope with having an older brother at the same school who was also beginning to make a name for himself and being selected for the major teams. Never mind how hard I was battling to make my name, Porky was left in the terrible predicament of having two reasons to be told he wasn't making teams on merit. If he wasn't Peter's kid brother he was Gary's. The back end of the Kirsten brother queue was a bum place to be.

So when Porks established himself at Province for five years, playing some fabulous and often match-winning cricket, it gave me as much pleasure as anything I achieved myself. Possibly more, in fact.

He hit the ball harder and cleaner than I ever did and won several one-day games in the final few overs with truly dynamic stroke play, again something I wasn't capable of. Unfortunately his glovework was not deemed sufficient to earn a call-up; his immediate rivals to become Dave Richardson's heir – Mark Boucher and Nic Pothas – were both seen as superior batsmen and Porks was overlooked. But he was the genuine article for a good few years and, although I don't have any regrets about my own career, I do wish he had been capped for his country. He deserved it.

But nothing, not even Peter's shadow, could stop us sharing the sheer joy of competing in different sports at school. We were lucky at Rondebosch because they encouraged everyone to find a sport or a physical activity that suited them and the facilities were fantastic. The thrill of waking up on a Saturday morning, summer or winter, and getting myself ready for match day made me the happiest kid in the world.

We were extremely lucky at school. The cricket facilities were fabulous and, as a result, there were a lot of good players. Although I loved the game and desperately wanted to be the best, I wasn't under any illusions. I knew there were many better players than me. I wished I could hit the ball like the other batsmen but I couldn't. So my target became to bat for longer than they did.

One of my best friends, certainly in the early years of High School, was Joel Stransky. We both played `A' level rugby and cricket together until he moved to Mooi River in Natal where his family had bought a farm. Throughout the 1990s I had to continually pinch myself to make sure it wasn't a dream to see what these two school kids, best mates, were doing, playing for South Africa in World Cups.

At under-14 and under-15 level Joel was much bigger and stronger than average with plenty of pace, skill and imagination, as he had throughout his career. And I was always this very slow, boring little scrum-half without much imagination. Joel didn't get along with a few of the teachers and they seemed to move him out of positions he wanted to play in. He was so keen to play centre and they dumped him out on the wing where he scored hundreds of tries, but he was never allowed to play centre. He used to get so grumpy but, in a way, perhaps it taught him to be determined and never give up.

When he moved to Natal we quickly realised that he was going to be the rugby player and I was going to be the cricketer. He used to bowl dibbly-dobbly away swingers, about as slow as I was at scrum-half, in fact. He'd take wickets every now and then, regularly to keep him in the first XI, but I think it's fair to say he made the right choice. And I hope he'd say the same about me!

Joel lived with us for three months while he was finishing his standard eight year after his folks had moved to Mooi River to set the farm up and we had some fun times. I suppose we were no different from most other testosterone-fired teenagers keen to find out what happens in the real world.

We were 16-year-old schoolboys and we were naughty. We lived for the weekends, especially Saturday night after our rugby or cricket match that day. One of the most valuable contacts we ever made was a barman at the Newlands Sun Hotel who allowed us into the lounge and turned a blind eye to a couple of beers. But he would start scowling if we pushed our luck so, feeling suitably fired up after two Castles we headed towards the disco at Techs Mutual cricket club near the Vineyard Hotel.

Inhibitions quickly disappeared as we persuaded the barman to give us another beer and I'm afraid the young Stransky and Kirsten were even seen on the dance floor on more than one occasion.

RBHS vs Bishops

The very keen – some might say bitter – rivalry between Rondebosch and Bishops was another key ingredient of my school days. Being situated right next door to each other contributed to the determination to beat them but it was handsomely fuelled by the fact that we were a government school and they were private. I regularly performed at my best in rugby and cricket against Bishops and most of my strongest memories from my early years were of contests against 'them'. Even as an international sportsman I recalled how much harder we competed against Bishops than other schools. The notion of 'raising your game' against the best was learned early and I'll always be grateful for that.

My first hundred came relatively late in life but it was even sweeter for that. The biggest match of the year in both rugby and cricket was, without question, against Bishops and I was 13 years old when I finally reached three figures, 130 not out – against Bishops. I slept well that night.

In rugby season the derby game of 1985 was the last match of the year. We'd had a fair year – won most of our games but lost a couple, too. Bishops, though, were unbeaten and had thrashed virtually everyone. We went into it as firm underdogs. There was a crowd of 3000 jostling and cheering on all sides of the ground. I've subsequently played in front of 30,000 and not felt even vaguely as intimidated as I was that day. The atmosphere was incredible.

I scored a potentially crucial try which was disallowed and my behaviour left something to be desired. I kicked up a fuss. Under today's ICC Code of Conduct, no doubt, I would have been banned for three matches; fortunately there was no match fee involved. But we managed to win the game, my last for Rondebosch Boys' High. By then I still hadn't seriously considered a career in sport and if that had been the last memory of my competitive sporting career, it would have been as sweet as I could have hoped for.

Ironically the rivalry between the schools was turned on its head in the Kirsten family because Porks crossed the 'great divide' just as I left school and spent his last two years at Bishops. Circumstances just weren't working out at Rondebosch and I'm very happy to say he was much happier boy across the road. (Although I supported him from the touchline and boundary through gritted teeth.)

During my school days ambitious boys measured their chances of future success at Nuffield Week and whether you would make the SA Schools XI that was chosen at the end of the tournament. Obviously I was doing something right at Rondebosch because I was chosen for the WP Nuffield XI three times; I think every school coach tried to pick a few grafters to balance out the hitters.

My first year, in standard eight, was my best. Terence Lazard was captain and it was the start of many happy partnerships.

The following year I was very disappointing. The Rondebosch 1st XV were going on a rugby tour to the UK at the same time as Nuffield Week and I desperately wanted to go, but the issue never even came up for debate. Dad was absolutely adamant that I was playing Nuffield Week and I didn't dare argue.

Mum and Dad together at about the time they produced the little guy on the right. Mum watched every rugby match I ever played - but only one cricket match.

Just one of thousands of days when Porks and I would duel to the death, or at least until it was dark and we were called in by Mum. Right foot well planted next to the ball, good balance. I won, of course.

In serious mood waiting to bat for Rondebosch Boys High, aged 15. The most hair I ever had.

Left: Rare picture of me bowling. The off spinners were painless at schoolboy level because nobody was strong enough to hit me out of the ground. But at Varsity and Club level I was destroyed.

Below: Sweeping the medium pacers judging by the position of the 'keeper. Who said I wasn't an improvisor?

he biggest match of the year, the
Derby" against Bishops. I played
ome of my best cricket against
em. Three Nuffield Weeks followed
it by the time I reached UCT
was batting at number eight and
owling terrible off spinners.

Proud Dad with his boys. Noel, Peter, Andy, me and Porks at Newlands around 1980. Home from home, and it became home, too.

There were all sorts of fund-raising events going on for the rugby team and the prospect of going overseas was almost too exciting to cope with. Although most kids would have been equally honoured and excited to be playing Nuffield Week, I was so disappointed. In all fairness to Dad, we weren't a wealthy family and, despite the money that was raised to subsidise the tour, I suspect there was a financial reason for not going. But, finances permitting, I will always encourage my children to broaden their horizons at every possible opportunity ahead of merely playing sport.

My school career finished at the end of 1985 with selection, as captain, for the SA Schools team alongside Allan Donald. I'd had an ordinary tournament, to be truthful, but I was probably picked for my 'experience'.

After the final match the WP team returned to the boarding house at Selborne College in East London determined to celebrate in style. This was difficult to achieve without a drink, of course, so my great friend Paddy Upton and I decided to pay a visit to the storeroom behind the masters' pub. I confess a certain amount of reconnaissance had taken place earlier that day.

The room was open and everything was going perfectly to plan. We had made it back across the cricket field, into the boarding house and up one flight of stairs, me with a case of beer and Paddy with two bottles of Scotch. We only had to make it past our own master's bedroom and the party could begin. But he was with the other masters in the staff pub, so that was no problem.

Then his door opened, just as we were walking past. I thought my heart had stopped. I was momentarily paralysed. Then, as cool and calm as he has remained all his life, Paddy said: 'Good evening, Sir. Thank goodness you're here. We found these drinks at the bottom of the stairs and we thought we'd better bring them to you for safe-keeping.' And Sir believed us.

We walked back into the dormitory with a strange mixture of relief and frustration. So close, yet so far. Half an hour later we repeated the entire exercise and this time we didn't get caught. We had our party.

The happy, innocent days of school were beginning to disappear very quickly indeed, however. By the start of 1986 I was rapidly experiencing the real world, life away from the comfort zones of home at Newlands and school. It was particularly hard towards the end of the year because Dad died in September. My world changed overnight.

Joel Stransky (Rugby Springbok): *Rondebosch Boys' High under-14 rugby and cricket teams were the best in the world. At least we thought so, though Gary was never satisfied. I lived in the Kirsten family home at Newlands for three months and every single day we'd practise something after school, whether it was kicking at posts, having nets or catching high catches. Gary was absolutely relentless, even at that age. Every spare hour was spent in some sporting pursuit, tennis, squash, rugby, cricket...anything.*

We were a bit naughty, though, that's true. I'm afraid we used to raid my Dad's bar at home and sneak off with a couple of beers into the garden before graduating to the

Golden Spur where we'd get older boys to buy us a Castle.

We used to bunk school to watch cricket, too, especially when the rebel tours were in town. When we were living in Newlands I remember hiding our bikes in the storeroom underneath the main scoreboard so it would look like we'd gone to school and then watching from the Oaks.

The best thing about being childhood mates with Gary, and his subsequent success, is that I have a ready-made topic whenever I'm required to give a motivational talk. He's the ultimate example of what can happen to people who are dedicated, work hard and never give up. He's one of the most committed people I've ever met and there's nothing he won't do or try to make a project successful.

In 2003 I took Gary as my partner to an annual, celebrity golf day in Singapore and he must have asked me a thousand questions about the 1995 World Cup and what we did to win it; he covered everything, from team meetings to practice and meals – everything. The team's subsequent failure certainly wasn't down to Gary's lack of preparation.

We reminisce about the old days whenever we get together. Two little 'okes' running around pestering the girls and playing sport all day long, and one goes on to play 101 Tests for his country and the other wins a World Cup. But the problem with both becoming professional sportsmen is that we've been away at the same time for most of our careers and haven't spent nearly enough time together, and that's something I intend to rectify for the rest of our lives now that we've both retired.

2

A very good time...
but no cigar

Varsity

I had been doing a post-school academic course in something, I can't even remember what. Dad had encouraged me to do it. It was probably a good idea but I hated it. Now the realities of life and death had struck it seemed sensible to stop it.

Mum and Dad were divorced and it was a traumatic time for all of us. I was staying with Dad, who became ill with stomach cancer, and Paul was staying with Mum. I had been living with Dad at Newlands until September 1986 when he passed away; now it was time to get on with life, find a job and do whatever it was that real people did. It was a tough time – how could it not have been? – but it gave me the resilience to cope with adversity that, I think, characterised my career.

The last months and weeks of Dad's life were particularly hard. He had been such a tower of strength to all of us and we regarded him as indestructible. Then suddenly he was gone. I was confused and bewildered, no doubt, but I had clearly inherited or copied his qualities of discipline and privacy and I coped as best I could, probably a little like he would have done. I was 18.

I rented a room from one of my old teachers in Rondebosch East and moved in. I stayed there for about six months and worked in a branch of First National Bank. I was anything but a natural for the job, to be honest, but I was grateful for the job and I needed the money. There was no 'invisible' income stream to keep me going. There were a couple of other part-time jobs, too, but it wasn't a very focussed time of my life, understandably.

My first salary cheque was R620 and, considering my greatest expense was R90 a month rental for my room, I was pretty well off. The return train fare was barely a rand a day. Beer was cheap back then, too.

Then I had a much needed and highly appreciated stroke of luck when I was offered a bursary to move from the Cape Technikon to the University of Cape Town and, more importantly, to start playing as much sport as I had done at school. But even that didn't concentrate my mind and I was heading towards the status of loose cannon; probably not much more than many other guys my age, but I certainly needed people to pull the reins in for me. One of those people was Duncan Fletcher who, at that time, was coach of the UCT 1st XI.

We saw a lot of each other, obviously, and he became one of the greatest influences on my life and career, a true mentor. We had a decent team with some genuinely talented players but, as students tend to do, we were also living life to the full. Too full. Too many parties, too many late nights and too little focus on the game – or anything else, for that matter.

One hung-over day Duncan came to me with his typically straight face and asked, in his typically understated way: 'Do you think you can play for Western Province one day? Do you think you're good enough?'

I laughed at him. I thought he was joking. I said: 'Don't be ridiculous. Look at me. Last year I was batting at number three for SA Schools and now I'm batting at nine for UCT and bowling occasional off-spinners…and you want to know if I think I'm good enough to play for Province?'

Ironically enough, my confidence was so washed out that I'd gone to Duncan about a week before and asked whether it would be worth my while playing 2nd XI so that I could do a bit more. He said 'No, fight your way up the order.' That conversation rekindled all the determination I'd shown at school, fighting to prove myself, fighting my way out of Peter's shadow and showing people that I was good enough. So I decided that batting at nine and being good fun at the bar wasn't going to be good enough any more. As for the off-spinners, I don't think I was ever any good. Actually, I don't think there was anyone else, so I got the job by default.

The decision to fight my way up the order in the 1st team forced me to work harder, and for much longer, on my game. Solitary lonely hours of hard work are a vital part of any successful sportsman's life and they are missing from most international cricketers' lives because of the way the game is scheduled these days. Emotionally that results in a lack of development, never mind the physical and skills side of the game. There's no time to play domestic cricket, no time to be dropped, no time to reflect on your goals and targets and no opportunity to fight back from adversity. You need to have a vision, something to focus on and channel your energy towards. There is a danger of drifting in the game these days, even at the highest level.

Contracts and endorsements appear to come more and more easily as each season passes and the players being awarded them seem to be younger and younger. I have no doubt that cricket – particularly international cricket – has become a young man's game but the result of that is a tendency towards complacency and far less of a need to fight for recognition and success.

Anyway, there I was in the Varsity 1st XI down on the card at number nine and determined to fight my way up the order. The first chance came in an important match against Techs Mutual when the top order had largely failed and I made an unbeaten 70, largely through sheer bloody-mindedness although I do recall keeping the strike effectively, which Duncan would have noticed. I presume…

I was very aware that one innings wasn't going to persuade anyone but I was also aware that people were 'watching' me in the second innings a lot more closely than they had during the first. I'm not sure if I deliberately placed more pressure on myself but I knew I had to do it again. Duncan's words about playing for Province had come back to me a few times in the weeks since he said them and all I could think was: 'Well you'd better move up the UCT order before that happens.' I made another unbeaten 60.

Graham Turner, the captain and number four batsman, was selected for Province shortly before the next game and Duncan asked me if I'd like to bat there. I replied: 'Gladly.' Once again I deliberately put myself under pressure to perform and scored enough runs to stay in the top order.

Those couple of weeks were key to the way my career progressed. It was the wake-up to the real world, the letting go of school and the comfort years and the realisation that, whatever I was going to do, it was going to take hard work. I suppose it was the realisation that the world is a big place with a lot of dogs fighting for the same bone…and that being a Kirsten didn't make much of a difference to anyone.

I also realised, thank goodness, that bowling off-spinners was a highly over-rated occupation and that mine had never, in fact, progressed beyond school level. I always bowled them very slowly and there weren't many schoolboys strong enough to hit me; at club level there were plenty of men ready to hit me into the car park, and they often did. Most players tried to park a bit further away when they arrived if there was any danger of me bowling that day. I was still given the ball every now and then but my confidence was blown early on at UCT and I knew I had to be a batsman, and only a batsman.

I might have been taking my cricket seriously by now, but I was only 20 and the parties hadn't stopped. They just weren't the night before a game…so often.

We had an initiation ceremony for new players that almost ended my career before it had started. It involved downing a beer quickly, and then, blindfolded, holding your forehead on top of a stump in the ground and running around it five times each way. Then you had to run to the middle of the pitch and back again to the pavilion but the level of disorientation made this task impossible. But everybody, naturally, thinks they can do it easily.

I was sure I knew exactly which way to go, so I set off running. And running. And running. Until I crashed into a chicken wire fence at the other end of the ground. There were a few cuts and bruises, but nothing too serious. So I picked myself up and started sprinting back towards the pavilion. I'm not sure why I was running so fast, but it had been made very clear to me before I set off that I should be in a hurry. All part of the initiation, I suppose, and you didn't want to let anyone down.

I could hear the voices getting louder and louder as they cheered me home so I knew I was heading in the right direction and I ran faster and faster, straight into the welcoming embrace of a concrete stand next to the pavilion.

Fortunately, like all the best cricket teams, we had a doctor in the line-up and the privilege of stemming the flow of blood and getting me to hospital fell to Willem van der Merwe. I had stitches in my chin, a hand, my nose and various other places. I think I may have lost a tooth, or two, but the memories are a little faded, for one reason or another.

SA Universities

The UCT team was extremely talented. At the time I was acutely aware of how many players were better than me. From the pure talent perspective, the ability to hit a cricket ball where you wanted it to go, I was nothing special. There were many better players and I spent much of my international career wondering why they never progressed to the next level. Perhaps they just didn't want to. They were talented, academic individuals while I was never troubled with the burden of having alternative career possibilities.

One of those players was John Commins, one of my closest friends at Varsity. He played only a couple of Tests for South Africa although his talent merited many more. We played a lot of cricket together but we also found many, many distractions that prevented us from studying as hard as we should have. Or at all, sometimes.

The SA Universities week of 1987 was particularly memorable. Soon-to-be property tycoon Andrew Golding was in the team as were doctors Michael Austin and John du Plessis, all men who, I believe, could have made it in cricket but chose to pursue 'proper' jobs.

We performed creditably on the field but spectacularly off it. Once again, by a strange quirk of coincidence, the venue was Bloemfontein. One evening we piled into Andrew Golding's car for an evening of investment opportunities at the Thaba Nchu Sun casino. We were pretty thirsty, too. We even persuaded the coach to come along. Both pastimes were problematic without money, but the difficulties were overcome with a clever scheme in which we pretended to be rich, pretended to gamble, and were consequently supplied with complimentary beers.

Andrew was the designated driver that night, but the rest of us behaved atrociously on the way back, having failed miserably in our attempts to say 'no' to free beer.

Sitting at a robot on the outskirts of Bloem on the way home, in the early hours of the morning, we thought it would be amusing to poke fun at the dishevelled state of the passengers in the rusty old Datsun parked next to us. Mistake. The occupants were four army troops on weekend leave.

Our fast getaway when the light turned green was another bad mistake. We were only a few kilometres from the Free State University and the safety of our rooms, but a car chase ensued nonetheless.

Andrew decided that dialogue was the best course of action (which explains his later decision to pursue a career in real estate rather than medicine) despite the screams of John and me who thought that pushing Andrew's old saloon to its limit was clearly the best option. I recall us both yelling for Andrew to hit the highway only for him to reply, calmly, that we were already on the highway.

So we drive into the UOFS car park convincing ourselves that the liberal-mindedness of UCT students from the free-thinking city of Cape Town would win the day and that we could negotiate with our 'hosts' and make them see reason.

As we coasted to a standstill, preparing our defence, we were dragged from the car and introduced to some raw army hospitality. I was hit on both eyes before I knew what was happening and John was being belted all over the car park. I'd never been involved in a fight in my life before, let alone thrown a punch. I was boxing like a man swatting flies away: nothing landed and if it did it was harmless.

In fact, it became pretty serious. Having closed both my eyes and dispensed with me, motionless, they turned their attention to John who was, at least, still moving and making a noise on the ground. One of the guys aimed an almighty, army-boot swing at his head but, thank goodness, missed.

I tried to run but I'd sprained my ankle earlier in the week and couldn't really get away. I was chased by a less-than-charming man called Rikus who would, no doubt, have had plenty of fun with me had he not lost interest in the chase just as I was beginning to experience flashbacks of my life. I was worried.

At that point Duncan realised that his wisdom was required and climbed out of the car. Rikus greeted him with a raised fist but then realised that 'Coach' was a little more mature than the rest of us and stopped short of landing the blow. The issue was settled pretty smartly from there on thanks to Duncan's persuasive skills.

Plenty of valuable lessons were learned. Both John and I missed the next game due to injury and it became extremely apparent to both of us that physical encounters outside of the sporting environment were not our strength. We learned, instantly, to keep our big mouths shut and enjoy ourselves in a low-key manner.

A few months later the 'new' John and I met for a quick and quiet lunch one hot, sunny Friday afternoon, the one day of the week we had a regular evening fielding practice. And the lunch really was quick, too. But we spent the next four hours washing it down with cold beer.

Both of us were particularly well oiled, so much so that we were convinced that by keeping a low profile and sticking to the basics, we could get away with the state we were in and Duncan wouldn't notice. Duncan, of course, was the most observant man in Cape Town.

Not by accident, he decided to break with his traditional routine and started the session with high catches. Johnny and I never laid a hand on a single one between us. Realising that it was only a matter of time before one hit us between the eyes and endangered our lives, Duncan stopped the practice and called us to one side. He wasn't angry; he just calmly said it was probably a good idea if we went home and had a cold shower. I always think of that day when I see Duncan coaching England and read reports about his disciplinarian ways, but I suppose you need to show a little more latitude when you're coaching students.

He was to become a huge influence on me for many years to come. Ironically I started at WP before Duncan, so when he was eventually appointed as the provincial coach I was able to welcome him to the dressing room. Just a couple of years earlier he'd told me I could play for Western Province and I thought he was joking. Then I was welcoming him to the team.

Duncan had faced a couple of extremely tough decisions before that. There were a couple of critical times when he needed to choose between coaching cricket professionally and staying in the business world. It's easy to say now that he made a great career move, but at the time he had to show great courage and faith in his ability. To see him succeed for so long has been a huge source of pleasure for me.

A very good time...but no cigar

The years we were together at Newlands were extremely rewarding and enjoyable. He's one of those coaches who have the ability to make everyone play to their full potential. If anybody wanted to know how good he was, he just had to work with Duncan for a while. The secret to being able to do that, obviously, is being able to identify potential talent, as he did with me. So he always knows when to keep pushing and striving for more, and when to back off and pat someone on the back.

He worked so hard with individuals that you had to measure his input in days and weeks, not hours. By the time you went out to play you felt you were performing for him more than anyone else. If I failed it felt like I was letting him down, not giving him a well-deserved return on all the time he had invested in me. The greatest compliment I can pay him was that he believed in me before I believed in myself, and he gave me the ability to believe in myself. He was such an inspiration.

Another huge influence in those early years was Hylton Ackerman. He was involved in coaching the under-20 WP Colts side. Much of what I learned about the game, both technically and its ethos and culture, came from him. I learned to understand the game's intricacies and subtleties, and of what goes through your mind at various times. The mental side of the game will always be what separates those who succeed and those who fail and Hylton knew more about that than anyone else I'd ever spoken to.

He used to explain what was going on during a match other than the bowler running up and the batsman trying to hit the ball. We can all see that. But what little mental battles are taking place, what little moves and countermoves can be made when the game has reached a critical time. Hylton used to ask me whether I would be the fielder able to raise himself to produce the run-out that turns the game when it's four o'clock in the afternoon, it's hot, the bowlers are tired and we haven't taken a wicket for three hours. Suddenly, when you least expect it, a chance comes to make a difference.

It was a challenge that repeated itself in my mind throughout my career. Whenever I took a catch or featured in a run-out late in the day I'd think about what Hylton had told me – and I always tried to make young players think in the same way.

My rugby career was also prolonged at UCT, though perhaps that was by default. Cricket was obviously my first priority but nevertheless I found myself being selected for the 1st XV. The coach at the time was Alan Solomons, whose later career followed a path not dissimilar to Duncan Fletcher's. Solly went on to coach a very successful Western Province side, assisted Nick Mallett with the Springboks and then went overseas to Ulster.

Alan was very similar to Duncan in other ways, too. If he felt you were prepared to put in the time and effort to make the sacrifices needed to succeed, then he would back you to the hilt. There was nothing Solly wouldn't do for his players as long as he was sure they were giving it everything. He was even prepared to fight 'the system' on behalf of the right player. Many players experienced Solly's 'all for one, one for all' approach at UCT and later on the bigger stage, and it gave everyone enormous confidence and belief.

Also like Duncan, Solly's players ended up playing for him. If Solly had been prepared to stand up to the administrators or selectors on your behalf, even been prepared to take the ultimate fall on your behalf, then you inevitably ran on to the field feeling you owed him a decent performance.

Above everything else, however, Solly stands out as the most positive-thinking man I've ever encountered in sport. We were frequently underdogs, most weekends in fact, yet week after week we'd run out on to the field convinced we were going to win. It wasn't easy against rugby institutions like Stellenbosch or teams with scrums the size of small houses (like the Police XV) but no matter what had happened the week before, or where we stood on the log, we'd run out the next week full of Solly's belief that we could turn it around.

It was a characteristic I associate with the South African cricket teams of the early 90s, a desire to take on the best and almost revel in the underdog status. I don't think we were particularly highly rated as a team or as individuals back then, but we caused a couple of shock results through a determination to beat the odds. We had a lot of individuals prepared to fight.

If Duncan had helped me see the light in terms of late-night partying, I'm afraid the same didn't really apply during rugby season. They were very different situations, as I saw it. Rugby season was rapidly becoming my 'off season' and besides, nothing ever happens on the Sunday after a rugby match, so you've got the whole day to have a lie-in and go for a run. In cricket season you play Saturday and Sunday.

After a particularly satisfying win during a tournament in Bloemfontein, the UCT boys decided to create a precedent, set a benchmark for post-match celebrations. Bloemfontein probably wasn't the best place to do it, particularly with the number of police and army bases in the area at that time, but it was spontaneous and nothing was going to curb us.

After several beers, and walking between bars, it was decided (by the forwards), that the parking meters in the city centre were too close together and needed to be re-arranged. As a 78-kilogram scrum-half I wasn't much use for the heavy stuff, but I may have been involved in the planning of where they were going to be repositioned. (May I just say, immediately, that this sort of behaviour is illegal, irresponsible and childish and should not be condoned under any circumstances…)

Naturally a good, law-abiding citizen of Bloemfontein, having seen what we were up to, called the police. A few minutes later, having uprooted a couple of parking meters, we heard the siren and saw the blue flashing light. The laughter and joking subsided to a bleary-eyed murmur.

We had our identity numbers taken, were threatened with jail and then severely reprimanded before arriving back at the hostel where even worse was waiting for us in the form of the tour management committee. They made us prepare statements accounting for our behaviour and then, the following day, we were fined an astronomical R3000 each to pay for the damage. For many of us this was more money than we could understand, let alone had in the bank.

Crisis meetings followed for many days afterwards in which fund-raising schemes were discussed and other money-making ventures planned. Three thousand rand was probably a whole year's beer money. The UCT under-20s were facing their greatest challenge for generations.

Hard as I think back now, I can't remember how the situation was resolved but, after a week or so of shock we were back in training on the field and life was good again. Perhaps the Bloemfontein City Council did the job themselves and set aside the fine on the basis of the amount of money we'd spent in the city's bars that week.

There were other parties but I wouldn't like many of them to be recorded for posterity here. Besides, I was about to become a professional…

Alan Solomons (UCT rugby coach): *I think about Gary virtually every day of my coaching career. He was the coolest, calmest most composed guy in the dressing room before and after every match and always one of the most influential players on the field, usually the most influential.*

In 1988 we (UCT) played Stellenbosch University at Newlands in front of 20,000 people. It was one of Gary's finest matches – he was simply brilliant. We lost by a couple of points and it was devastating at the time but, once again, the way he handled himself and the effect he had on his older team mates made me think; 'He is something special.' We had a couple of extremely special and successful years.

In 1990 he decided to hang his boots up and concentrate on a cricket career, and it was a decision I agreed with – reluctantly. I have no doubt whatsoever he could have had a very, very successful career in rugby and, depending on what style a coach wanted to play, he could have played for the Springboks.

Soon after the start of the '90 season we were struggling and missing Gary badly. We'd just lost to Villagers and Gary was standing on the touchline, watching. I walked over and asked him whether he'd consider playing again and he said: 'OK, if you need me.' I told him to bring his boots to Monday training. He arrived and then I was sly – I called a trial match. He was still in a different league to anyone else, pure class. The following Saturday he went straight back into the 1st XV and we ended the season by winning the inter-Varsity.

After he'd retired from rugby for the second time I had a conversation with a man very well connected within cricket and told him in no uncertain terms that Gary would play for South Africa. He said Gary didn't have a hope. I said I didn't know much about cricket but I knew a lot about dedication, devotion and discipline, and Gary had more of those qualities than anyone else I'd met. I knew he'd be a success.

Something Gary said to me all those years ago has stayed with me in my coaching career ever since, and I remember it every day of my life. He said: 'Solly, when you tell a player that you believe in him, you give him incredible confidence, you make him believe that anything is possible.' I feel proud and flattered that I may have contributed anything to his career, but he certainly contributed to mine. But apart from his sporting achievements, Gary is one of the most genuine, sincere and kind people I've met in sport. And so well behaved.

Apart from one time, on tour in Mossel Bay, when we stayed in a hostel that was also hosting a touring women's hockey team. And there was also that time in the Port Elizabeth Holiday Inn when a fire extinguisher was let off…

Duncan Fletcher (UCT and WP coach): *Just a couple of years after meeting him I was already using Gary, more than any other cricketer, as an example of what can be achieved with hard work, discipline and organisation. We struggled to bat Gary at number nine in the UCT 1st XI when he started and yet he went on to become one of the best opening batsmen in the world. It was an incredible sporting journey.*

He wasn't very organised and, from what I could see, he hated studying. I think he only earned one credit and that was in Religious Studies. He was having a pretty good time, for most of the time, but he was at least taking his cricket very seriously and making great progress. Occasionally he'd slip up, like the time he and John Commins arrived at evening practice after spending the day in the pub, but when he got something wrong you just wanted to laugh. I was only sorry I couldn't laugh in front of everyone else that day and kept a straight face.

When he was captain he arrived for another practice wearing some horrible brightly coloured shorts. I told him he was supposed to be setting the example but he said it would be fine. The following week about four or five other guys arrived wearing similarly horrible shorts. Gary started to realise that people were looking up to him.

But the real change happened after a couple of years as a professional at WP. He came to me and asked for advice. 'Duncan, I've been offered R20,000 by Stuart Surridge to use their kit. But there's also an offer from (a small local company) Open Championship but it's more complicated…it means getting involved in the business and sharing the profits. What should I do?'

Basically Gary had decided. You have to remember that R20,000 was a fortune to a young man in 1991 and all he had to do was use a very nice bat and make runs with it. He just wanted me to confirm his decision. I don't know what he intended to do with the money, not something very wise, I imagine.

I said: 'Gary, there is absolutely no doubt what you must do – there is no decision to be made.' He was nodding in agreement when I said: 'You must take the Open Championship offer. You absolutely must, no question.' He was staring at me blankly.

He was a bit directionless at the time. Outside his cricket there wasn't much to keep him occupied, especially as he'd given up rugby by then. It was a case of getting him organised and focussed, that was what he needed more than money.

As soon as he started attending meetings, keeping a diary, making appointments, learning about import permits and foreign exchange controls, cash flow – anything to do with business in a context that was relevant, he became a changed man. And he's never looked back.

We won the League at UCT with him as captain, and we won it (with apologies to all concerned) with an extremely ordinary team in terms of cricket ability, but a finer group of young men you wouldn't find anywhere. He was an amazing motivator and decision maker and people just seemed naturally to look up to him, not that he was ever aware of that. I will always look back to those UCT days as amongst the most fun I ever had in cricket, and Gary was at the heart of them. He was, and always will be, a first class individual.

3

Time to show a little focus

Western Province selection

There weren't many teams I hadn't been selected for by the time I was called up for my debut in the Western Province first team. In two and half years of club cricket I'd become more and more consistent and once I'd got rid of the off-spinning albatross from around my neck, people had started taking me seriously as a batsman. My record had been good in all the age group teams, too, but I was always hampered by the 'all-rounder' thing.

I'd been selected at the beginning of the 1987-88 season for the WP 'B' team and had scored three hundreds before the call-up came to the 1st team. Finding my feet took a while, particularly in the first-class game, but finally I made my first hundred and I knew I could make a career doing this.

My debut came in a three-day game against Natal at Kingsmead. The wicket was still very green, which put a smile on the faces of Garth le Roux and Stephen Jefferies, our new-ball pairing. But they were both tough 'old school' cricketers who wouldn't even give a youngster like me a sideways glance until he'd done something for the team, something to prove he was worthy of his place.

I've never been in favour of a strongly hierarchical set-up in which the old boys 'bully' the young boys – and it wasn't like that back in those days. But the WP side in the late 80s carried no passengers. A youngster was treated cordially and was given a chance to display his worth to the team, but I didn't feel entirely comfortable, I must say. I was on edge and nervous, even during warm-ups, but I thought that was very healthy. It made me so determined to make a contribution. If I'd been comfortable and immediately 'accepted' into the team as an equal I would almost certainly have lost the edge off my determination to succeed. Besides, Garth and Stephen were heroes of mine whom I'd watched from the terraces just a few years earlier. It wouldn't have felt right if they'd back-slapped me and welcomed me straight into their brotherhood.

Jonty Rhodes made his debut in the same match and scored a century playing with huge courage. I'd love to say at this point that I matched him but real life is never like they portray it in the films. Down to bat at six, I didn't get to the crease in either innings and we won the match quite comfortably with Adrian Kuiper blazing away hitting the ball in the middle of the bat all day while everyone else seemed happy to hit one delivery in three. He always scored runs at Kingsmead and this innings was one of his finest.

Being the youngest and least experienced member of the team I was, naturally, placed at short leg and it was there that I made one solitary contribution, a pretty useful catch off big Garth's bowling. He was like a bear with a full stomach – he just sort of growled his approval at me but it was enough to let me know I'd started to be accepted.

But yet another harsh truth became obvious; I wasn't going to crack it as a number four or five batsman. I was going to have to create something else for myself, reinvent myself yet again. The Western Province middle order was a place for style and flair, it was reserved for the players who attracted 'bums on seats', and I had the good sense to know I wasn't one of those.

Robin Jackman was WP coach at the time and the seed was first planted by him during a Benson and Hedges match at the Wanderers when I was 12th man. He asked whether I'd ever thought about opening. Just as I'd laughed at Duncan a few years earlier, I did it again. I thought Jackers was joking. I'd never opened the batting in my life.

'Well, if you want to make the team on anything like a regular basis, I suggest you think about it,' Jackers said. An opportunity existed at the top of the order but I ummed and ahhed about it for a few days because, once again, I doubted whether I was good enough and didn't want to ruin my chance of a career with WP at such an early stage. Eventually the prospect of actually playing a game won over my doubts and I asked Jackers whether I could take the chance.

It was the 1989-90 season and it was the first time I'd ever opened the batting for any team, at any level. It was for WP against Natal, once again. I scraped together 20 or so in the first innings and a much better 80 in the second. Crazy Meyrick Pringle took a sackful of wickets and we won the game, which, fortunately, meant a winning team wasn't changed.

What had started as a stop-gap measure carried on for the rest of the season and we reached the Currie Cup final, in which I scored 175 and Peter made 130. We batted for ever and in between deliveries it started to sink in. I stood at the non-striker's end and thought: 'That's it, you're an opener now, Gazza. No more middle order for you, boy.'

World Cup

The thought of international cricket, however, had never entered my head at that stage. There was no international cricket to aspire to.

But even in 1991 when our world was turned upside down – or maybe that should be 'the right way up' – and we re-entered international competition after 21 years of isolation, I never once thought about myself. I had just made it into the WP side and was still coming to terms with that. The idea of South Africa playing in a World Cup was the most exciting prospect in the sporting future at that time.

In 1992 I was sharing some particularly grubby accommodation with Kenny Jackson. Empty pizza boxes and unwashed coffee mugs were our constant companions. And a lot of unwashed sports clothing. I'm not sure I would even walk into a bachelor flat like that today, but it was home at the time and we were comfortable.

We tried to go to sleep early on the day of the opening match, South Africa against Australia, but it was hopeless. The excitement and tension was unbearable. Even if Peter hadn't been there it would have been the same, but he'd initially been left out of the squad and then reinstated through weight of public opinion and media pressure. So South Africa were about to play in the World Cup and my brother was in the team. Kenny and I went to our beds but didn't sleep at all. We both got up an hour later and waited for the match to start which was around three o'clock in the morning.

Perhaps that was when I started dreaming of playing international cricket, right there in our sitting room surrounding by the junk of bachelordom. If there was any young cricketer in South Africa not overwhelmed by the emotion and sense of occasion of that night, then he couldn't really have been a cricketer. It was incredible. Allan Donald having Geoff Marsh caught behind off the first ball of the match and being given not out by Kiwi umpire Brian Aldridge, the presence of Sports Minister Steve Tshwete…just the fact that international cricket was taking place. Even the television pictures were conveniently hazy and intermittent to remind us it was happening on the other side of the world. It was difficult to watch without feeling a strange mixture of joy and hypertension.

The 1992 World Cup may have been the most emotional but it wasn't, in fact, the first time I'd seen South Africa play international cricket.

About six months earlier Kenny and I were between seasons with a few weeks to kill. That's to say between the South Africa summer and the Dutch summer. We'd spent a year playing club cricket in Holland and were on our way back there when we decided, completely on a whim, to see if it was possible to travel via the West Indies to watch some of that tour on which South Africa would play its first post-isolation Test match.   We were so naïve – I don't think we even knew the West Indies was a series of different countries.

International travel for holders of South African passports wasn't always a simple process in 1991, and we certainly didn't have enough money for a luxury package, so we took a flight to Barbados and somehow arrived at the team hotel having handed over a good percentage of our spending money to the airport taxi driver.

Peter was very, very good to me. I slept on his floor and he brought me breakfast back from the dining room for the first couple of days. Jacko was also able to borrow some floor space – from Kuips, I think - and, in a way, we were allowed to become a part of the team because we were young, first-class cricketers and the senior guys didn't mind sharing this incredible experience. As the Test match drew closer, however, Kenny and I were soon being treated as official guests by the hotel staff so we strolled confidently down to breakfast with the team and then lay around the swimming pool sipping orange juice while the 'real' team were busy making history and preparing for a Test match against the West Indies.

But a guilty conscience quickly got the better of us and we were dying to help out. So as the Test drew closer we asked if we could earn our keep by giving the batsmen throw-downs, fetching cold drinks and generally trying to be useful and not getting in the way. During the match, though, we were happily seated amongst the 'unprivileged' masses – not that there were many people there.

It wasn't until the World Cup a few months later that I started thinking in earnest that I could play international cricket, but during that Barbados Test I certainly realised what I would be aiming at for the next few years of my life. International sport. Here it was. I might have been on the outside, but I was very close, close enough to touch it, hear it and smell it. Maybe the rum punches from the night before had something to do with it; my senses were racing every morning.

When I finally returned to Holland, and then again the following season back in Cape Town, I trained as never before. I ran thousands of kilometres if I couldn't have a net, and as long as there was someone to bowl at me or throw balls to me, I would never stop. I batted until the sweat was pouring into my eyes and I couldn't see properly, but I kept thinking back to Barbados, to the 'feel' of international cricket, to the sight of Curtly Ambrose and Courtney Walsh. And to what it must be like to travel and see the world in the name of cricket, something that I could now justifiably call my job. I had first become 'a professional' when selected for Western Province. I was paid something like R600 per month.

Kenny and I watched virtually every ball of the first four days, and what incredible cricket it was. Despite a boycott of the match by the Barbados faithful who were enraged by the omission of Anderson Cummins from the West Indies squad, the slightly surreal atmosphere didn't detract one bit from the quality of the bowling and batting. With Andrew Hudson's magnificent century helping to set the match up for what was going to be a famous fifth-morning victory for Kepler Wessels and his team, Kenny and I agreed that we'd seen the best of the match over the first four days and decided to head on, two days earlier than scheduled, to New York. Having tasted Test cricket, and flushed with the scent of victory, Kenny and I felt we could cope with the Big Apple for 48 hours before our connecting flight to Amsterdam. It was a big town, but we were preparing to hit it.

Then things started to go wrong. A technical fault forced our plane to divert from New York to Cuba. On arrival we were told it would take 'some time' to sort the problem out. Then, in a scene straight from a low-budget, made-for-TV, cops movie, all the passengers were marched off into the terminal and told they could make one phone call, to a family member anywhere in the world, to explain what had happened and that they were safe. Naturally, under the circumstances, we called home – but purely for confirmation that South Africa had won the Test given that there wasn't much our families could do about our predicament from Cape Town.

We were genuinely in a mild of state of shock to hear they'd been bowled out in 90 minutes on the fifth morning and lost. For a horrible second I thought it was a practical joke, that we were being wound up, but then it started sinking in. Kenny and I started talking about the party that both teams had been to on the third evening on the match on board the 'Jolly Roger' pirate ship in Barbados harbour. Even though the next day was actually a rest day, the guys celebrated as though the match was won. In fairness, everyone thought it was won. Nobody had seen a match lost from such a strong position at home, but then nobody had been up against an angry Walsh and Ambrose on a cracked fifth-day wicket in the West Indies.

It was South Africa's first Test back after 21 years, and we came so close to winning it. It was only the inexperience that led to complacency that cost us a famous win. If there is one thing I'd love the country to keep from that match, it would be the legacy of fighting until the last ball has been bowled. It's an over-used cliché, but until you've experienced it from the bitter side you'll never know how true that saying is about the fat lady and her singing…

Daiquiris

The return to the Caribbean, a decade later, was especially satisfying. Having come so far from those heady, dreamy bachelor days, to return to Barbados as a senior player was deeply satisfying. I looked around to see if there were any more young Kirstens or Jacksons who needed a floor to sleep on, but I couldn't see any.

And it wasn't just the series win that made the trip so special in 2000. Debs, my wife, came out to join me in Barbados and Antigua. The resort in Antigua, particularly, was picture-postcard perfect. The beach was white, the sea was turquoise, the palm trees were tall, the waiters wore bright flowery shirts…it was all too good to be true. Inevitably my mind went back to the days I batted for seven hours in the nets 10 years earlier, trying to get there, and now it had come true (except it was better because I didn't have a wife in the original dream, let alone have her with me on the beach.)

Still, I could handle it all fine. The beaches, the sea, the lobster and prawns. But if Debs has a weakness, it is for daiquiris. On the second evening we walked in to the resort restaurant and saw a self-serve drinks machine dispensing mango, pineapple and strawberry daiquiris, on the house. We looked at each other and I thought: "This is getting ridiculous."

But back to the early 1990s. My century in the 1989-90 Currie Cup final was followed by steady progress through the next couple of seasons and a few more hundreds that made the doubters (including me) believe that perhaps I really could do the job.

In the 1992-93 season I had been spoken about as a possible international but I refused to take it too seriously. Maybe it was a self-defence reaction to guard against disappointment, but I found it all a bit strange. At the beginning of the next season, however, it wasn't just speculation. In the weeks before the squad to tour Australia was announced, my name was mentioned a lot. I'd been written into most journalists' 'possible tour party' stories and it was difficult not to feel a flutter of excitement. Occasionally I'd think back to the hotel in Barbados, the atmosphere and mood of a Test match, and the feeling would be almost overwhelming. I tried not to think about it.

I was sitting in a pub with my Province team mates after a match when the squad was announced. I listened carefully as the squad was announced and thought for a second that maybe I had just missed my name being read out. But I hadn't. I wasn't there. The feeling was more dumbness than disappointment. I didn't really feel anything, there was no overwhelming wave of sadness or anger, nothing like that. Perhaps all the doubts I'd always had about my ability served me well that day – maybe it was easy to say: 'Oh well, you're not good enough.' If that was the case, it was equally true that I then set out to prove to anyone and everyone that I *was* good enough.

A few weeks later we were playing Northerns at Centurion in the four-day game, by now called the Castle Cup/Supersport Series. I scored 190 and took six wickets. I dread to think why I was bowling again. Worse still, I was captain of the team for the first time because Craig Matthews had been called to Australia. As I recall, the pitch was turning more than usual but it wasn't unplayable. We had scored 400 on the first day and Northerns, following on, had lost only two wickets on the entire third day. So it was in desperation that a couple of players urged me to bring myself on. I took some time arranging my fielders on the boundary and the Northerns batsmen duly obliged by hitting me straight to them.

As ironies go, the fact that Brian McMillan – widely acclaimed as the best all-rounder in the world - had injured himself in Australia 24 hours earlier ranks as highly as any other irony in my life. Having successfully rid myself of the ridiculous 'all-rounder' label that had attached itself to me at the beginning of my career, I was about to be called into the national team as a replacement for one of the best. The media loved it: 'All-rounder Kirsten to SA rescue' was how I remember the story being written. I cringed.

Still, it was the phone call that changed my life.

I was sitting at home doing something of little consequence like drinking coffee when the phone rang. It was Ali Bacher. He said: 'Do you want the good news or the bad?' I didn't want to think. I couldn't. Not another disappointment. Fortunately he didn't wait for me to answer. 'The good news is that you've been picked to go to Australia; the bad news is that you leave tomorrow morning.' A short time later the convenor of selectors, Peter Pollock, also called to congratulate me.

It was an emotional moment and I was acutely aware of the honour. Fortunately everything happened so quickly that I didn't have time to dwell on what it might mean to me. I had barely 24 hours between the phone call and climbing on the plane. It may not sound very ambitious 11 years later, but if someone had told me I'd end up playing over 100 Test matches, I would have laughed long and hard. As I walked up the stairs of the plane I thought I'd be lucky to play a one-day international, let alone a Test match. Selection to the national squad felt like I'd achieved all I could dream of. Australia, here we come.

Andy Flower (Zimbabwean cricketer): *Western Province came on a pre-season tour to Zimbabwe in the early 90s and played a couple of games against Mashonaland. I wondered who the scratchy opener was and waited for him to pop a catch to gully. I didn't think he looked very good, to be honest. He didn't hit the ball well. He scored a hundred but I still wasn't convinced!*

John Traicos was still playing back then, well into his third decade of first-class cricket. He told me over a beer that night that Gary Kirsten was his name and he would play a very long time for South Africa, and would become a mainstay of the team. I asked him how he could possibly see that from one innings, albeit a hundred, and he said: 'Because he looks like the kind of player that can work out his own game.' And that, of course, was exactly what happened. I never forgot what Traics said and it stood me in good stead, too.

But whether it was a bat in his hand or a beer, Gary struck me as a really, really good bloke. He never became involved in the word game that can be so distracting, and he always respected his opponents. And in turn, everyone respected him.

4

A taste of the big time

Australia `94

I didn't know what to expect. Close as I'd come to international cricket, being with the boys in the West Indies and having a brother in the national team, it had prepared me for nothing. I was excited but extremely apprehensive.

I was sitting at Sydney airport an hour or so after arriving from Johannesburg, waiting for the team to land from Melbourne. They'd beaten Australia by seven wickets in the opening game the night before so the locals were restless. I felt like an autograph hunter waiting for the team to emerge. If only we'd arranged to meet at the hotel...

When they walked through the arrivals hall it felt like I was in someone else's dream. Maybe it was the lack of sleep but it was as though I was watching TV – 'Oh, there's Allan Donald and Kepler Wessels and Dave Richardson and Hansie Cronje...' All the biggest names in South African cricket. It just didn't sink in that I was there to join them.

For the whole of that day the dream continued. I'd watched all these guys on television but didn't know any of them very well. But there was no 'atmosphere' like that I'd experienced on my WP debut. There was obviously a bit of respect and some recognition for the fact that I'd earned my place. Nonetheless, I was awestruck. It was mind-boggling just to be amongst these guys and to think I'd made the national squad, something I never believed would happen.

A couple of television crews filmed us getting onto the bus and leaving the airport and they both made sure they had a shot of me. Or at least, that's how it felt. The television cameras really freaked me out. I'd never seen one close up, never mind been filmed by one. I sat quietly in the bus and kept a low profile. I had a lot to come to terms with. I didn't want to start off on the wrong foot, or say the wrong thing.

As we checked into the hotel Hansie shouted out down our corridor that he was going for a run around the Opera House that evening, and that running partners would be welcome. There were more non-runners in the squad than runners at that stage.

I thought it would be a good opportunity to impress management and team hierarchy, so I jumped at the chance. Adrenalin was still thrashing sleep-deprivation in my body. The senior players smiled knowingly and I'm sure I heard a sarcastic 'Good luck' as they disappeared into their rooms.

It was the first of only three runs I ever did with Hansie in the eight years we played together. He was the fittest man in every team he played in, certainly as far as middle-distance running speed was concerned, and he put me through what remains the hardest four kilometres of my life that evening. He loved his training and never missed an opportunity for a run or a visit to the gym.

I was reasonably fit at that stage of my life though, to be fair, I didn't really know what fitness was. Hansie said the route along the harbour front and around the Opera House would take him about 12 minutes. I thought it would take me about 17. When we arrived at the stairs in front of the Opera House Hansie casually suggested we sprint up and down them a couple of times, just for variation. I was in no position to argue. Actually, I was in no state to speak. My heart rate was about 210 and I was on the verge of total collapse. Eventually I spluttered something about needing a breather and he charged up the 100 or so steps while I waited for him at the bottom.

Having had a rest I was able to carry on the run. We were about half way – two kilometres to go. Hansie said almost immediately that he was going to pick the pace up and sprint home, which suited me fine. I came in about four minutes behind him and vowed never to be so stupid again.

My debut came just five days later, against Australia on a very green looking wicket at the Sydney Cricket Ground. At the team meeting on the evening before the game, Kepler had announced the team in batting order with me due to come in at number five or six. Despite being a full-time opener for the last four years, I felt excited about returning to the middle order. Besides, I would have time to soak up the atmosphere and try to get rid of the nerves.

On arrival at the ground at lunchtime, however, the situation changed. Kepler's face turned several shades paler when he saw the wicket. A couple of hushed conversations with his senior consuls ensued after which the captain decided that he would, after all, be far more valuable to the team a little further down the order when the seam on the ball was a bit softer. Young Gary, of course, was the perfect man to see just how sporty the pitch would be.

It was certainly the right decision, for several reasons, but that did not stop the chuckles and smirks as news of the new batting line-up was passed around. As I walked out to bat it struck me how lonely the middle of a cricket ground could be – 45,000 people surrounding you and most of them baying for your blood. It's the modern equivalent of gladiators fighting to the death in a Roman Colosseum. The same principles apply except, presumably, even the 'bad guy' had some people cheering for him in the days of the Roman Empire.

I didn't last long – and neither did anyone else. The pitch was terrible and we were bowled out for 69. It was a dismal performance from everyone, most notably the groundsman. In retrospect it was so bad we should have laughed a lot more. We needed someone to break the ice afterwards although I would have been the last one to join in. I sat as quietly as I could in the dressing room trying not to say the wrong thing. What a start. The 'dream' had just become a nightmare.

To be honest, I was still amazed and overawed by the international game. The crowds, the officials, the media, the press conferences, the travel and the five-star hotels. Everything was still too 'big'. Speaking to reporters and journalists for the first time is a huge experience for a young sportsman – extremely intimidating. You instantly forget that they are just people doing a job, like anyone else, and you certainly aren't prepared for the fact that a first sighting of television cameras during an interview makes it impossible to talk and breathe at the same time.

My first 'public' net session was at the SCG – it was also my first net of the tour. It had never occurred to me that people might actually watch a net session. It was hard enough getting people to watch matches in my experience, let alone net sessions. The net pitches were 'doing a bit' and Allan was running in at real pace. For much of his career, and certainly during his prime, Al didn't hold back during practice. There was never a question of his preserving or nursing his body.

Mike Procter was coach on that tour and he shouted out 'Last round' to the three batsmen in the nets. I felt ecstatic. OK, I'd played and missed a few times but I'd survived and certainly hadn't disgraced myself. I had five bowlers in my net so I was just five more deliveries away from making a reasonably dignified exit from my first net session in national colours. And I survived them all, too. I was thrilled.

As I started walking out of the net, Allan called out: 'Gazza, I just want one more – a last one.' This wasn't supposed to happen. I'd done my time.

The ball nipped back at great pace and beat the inside edge before crashing into my back thigh. I staggered back before hobbling out of the net in much pain. Despite my best efforts, it was impossible not to show how much it hurt. I quickly became aware that it was hurting far more than it should.

I started de-padding very gingerly and realised that I'd forgotten to put my back leg thigh pad on. I had the very beginnings of a bruise that grew to the size of a lunch plate and went through about six colour changes during the next three weeks. It became a team pet. Guys used to ask how it was and whether it was blue or yellow that day.

My debut Test came later on tour. Boxing Day at the MCG is one of the biggest days of the year anywhere in the cricket world. When you walk out to bat you see the Great South stand which holds 48,000 people on its own. Legend has it that when Allan Border mentioned that to Richie Richardson at the start of a West Indies Test, Richardson replied: 'That's more people than live in my country (Barbuda).'

It took me at least 10 minutes to start breathing properly. I thought I might pass out on the way to the middle. It was an awesome experience, awesome and terrifying at the same time, something I'll never forget. The rain ruined the match as a contest but it did nothing to dampen the spectacle or the enthusiasm of the supporters.

The spectacle, of course, came in the next Test, which remains one of the greatest South Africa has ever played and one of the most exciting of all time. Australia's failure to chase down 117 for victory in the face of Fanie de Villiers' tireless bowling on the final morning earned South Africa a reputation as determined fighters and carried us through many a battle for the remainder of the 1990s.

I was lucky to play at all, let alone be part of such an historic Test. I hadn't scored

A taste of the big time

many runs on tour and I didn't think I'd been convincing. Brian McMillan's fitness hung in the balance and, in the longstanding tradition of 'sod's law' and 'balance', it's almost always impossible to replace an X with an X or a Y with a Y when a player is ruled out at short notice. So when all-rounder McMillan was ruled out, rookie batsman Kirsten got the nod.

Kepler batted at number six to create more depth in Big Mac's absence and I managed to score 67 and 42 which, in many ways, kick-started my career. I batted terribly, of course, and never once felt comfortable, but it added up to 109 runs and in a low-scoring Test they were important. There were to be many times I'd bat terribly in my career, but I think I was especially scratchy in that match.

At one point I think I made the mistake of apologising to the captain for the way I looked out there, and Kepler said something I will never forget. Very calmly he said: 'Gary, it is not how you get them, but how many that matters. That is all that matters. That is what people will remember you for.' Having battled to just 'be me' throughout my career, and having battled as a 'gatherer' in the shadow of Peter's 'rampager', it gave me the confidence to carry on scratching for my runs as I had always done. You don't suddenly have to play a different way just because you are playing for your country. That was a mistake that many young players had made before me and many more will in the future.

To have contributed to that win gave me more confidence and belief than anything else in the early part of my career. The 'Little Kirsten' had done something.

The victory remains the single biggest team highlight I've ever experienced. The physical celebrations, hectic as they were, just couldn't do justice to the level of emotion we felt. We'd come back from the dead to win against all odds, somehow, and we'd done it as a team.

Jonty's batting with Allan at the tail end of the innings was particularly memorable. During the previous evening we had told each other that, with a lead of 120, we had a chance. Maybe only a slight chance, but a chance. When Allan went out to join Jonty, the lead was 80. We knew we were dead and buried at that stage. But Allan made 10, Jonty pulled Craig McDermott for six and together they put on 36 for the last wicket. Jonty finished 76 not out.

Perhaps it was because we'd talked about having a chance with 120, added to the emotion of coming up just four runs short of that target when we'd thought we were finished, but we walked onto the field feeling almost buoyant. I don't think I can honestly say I believed we were going to win, but at least we had a chance. It was difficult not to be swept up by the 'dreamers' of the team, like Fanie, who genuinely thought we were favourites! We'd given ourselves the chance we had spoken about, and that put a smile on our faces. Even if we didn't win, we were prepared to make them fight like dogs for every single run. The other card in our winning hand was our naïvety. We were so new to international cricket that we didn't realise just how useless a lead 116 really was.

Fanie bowled Michael Slater for a single but Mark Taylor and David Boon then settled things down and at 51-1 our hopes had just about disappeared. Then Boon clipped a full-length delivery from Fanie off his toes towards the square leg boundary. It was a fine shot and was worth four. Except that it landed in my armpit at short leg, and stuck there. It was luck, of course, although I did pretty well to stay in position and not turn away. Maybe it was all the glowering I had received from big Garth while doing the short leg job to his bowling at WP.

We picked up another couple of wickets shortly before the close of play that evening and they finished the day at 60-4. Once again, a belief in the 'impossible' returned and we were nervously excited over supper that night.

Allan bowled his namesake, Border, early the following morning and at 63-5 we actually took control of the match. An hour and a half later, during which time Fanie bowled his heart out, we'd won the game and there were scenes of jubilation I'd only ever seen on television after a World Cup final. One of the biggest, most spontaneous post-match parties I've seen erupted on the field and there were suddenly South Africans all over the SCG. I was never shy of a party, I must confess, and I was pouring beer and champagne all over the place.

The most remarkable aspect of the day, however, for a young and naïve boy like me anyway, was visiting the Australian change room a couple of hours after the game had finished. I'd had a few beers by then but that didn't stop me feeling apprehensive about their mood after such a devastating defeat.

I was astonished at how receptive they were to our arrival. It was something we'd heard about for several years but had, perhaps, always doubted. What happens on the field stays on the field and all is well off the field – that was a belief we all shared, but this was surely an occasion where lingering emotions could be forgiven.

But there I was, sitting next to Allan Border, a man with 130 Test caps and a wealth of experience I could only dream about, asking him a thousand questions about anything and everything I could think of, feeding off his knowledge. I can't recall a single thing I asked him now but I have no doubt I became a wiser cricketer as a result.

He gave freely of his time and never once seemed more interested in chatting to our senior players. I might have been the unknown rookie but the great man seemed genuinely happy to spend his time with me. He probably doesn't remember it. Why should he? One of the greatest Test cricketers of all time had given me a couple of hours of his time after losing an extraordinary match his team should have won. The dream was continuing, but now it was becoming a real-life dream.

We left the Aussie changing room about four hours after the match, distinctly wobbly, but no amount of beer or celebration could disguise the fact that we'd created a bit of history. And there was no mistaking the fact that I'd played my part, albeit a modest one. For the first time in my life I began considering the possibility that I might, perhaps, have something to offer above 'good team man' and 'honest trier'.

Glenn McGrath, one of the two banes of my life (Courtney Walsh was the other), also started his career on that tour. He played two Tests against New Zealand just before we arrived and then spent the rest of his life tormenting me. If 'Pigeon' and Courtney had played basketball instead of cricket I could have averaged 60.

Ironically my decade-long battle with McGrath began with a victory to me when I made an unbeaten 112 in the first leg of the World Series final. It was one of the few times that I was able to dominate him. He became a better and better bowler as the years went by and the way he compelled left-handers to play at virtually every delivery made him devastating.

His line was so tight that a left-handed batsman let any ball go unplayed at his peril. You were forced to play. Then, if you worked that out, he had the ability to bowl around the wicket and straighten the ball, making the usual 'angle' redundant. You were simply denied any moment of respite that came with most fast bowlers because he was so close to the stumps at delivery.

He also had an extremely aggressive attitude about him and utilised that aggression very cleverly. His verbal 'skills' would get under my skin but that would have been nothing without the ability to match it with his bowling skills.

Glenn always had a lot to say to me. I was never one for saying much back because I genuinely believed that hanging around and continuing to score scruffy runs was the best way to answer back. He seemed so genuinely angry every time I nicked one down to third man that it seemed logical to keep doing it for as long as possible. I wasn't averse to answering back but every single run past gully wound him up far more than anything I could say, so I decided to keep doing that. Or trying to.

I learnt very quickly in my career that most batsmen are fighting a losing battle by engaging in angry conversation, especially when you start answering back. I believe I'm remembered for being quiet and not easy to provoke on the field, but it wasn't always like that, and certainly not at the beginning of my career.

Eight years later, at Kingsmead in Durban, I was facing Brett Lee in the fading evening light. Life was not easy. Glenn was moved up to leg gully. Enjoying this rare chance to field close to the batsman, he began abusing me about my ability to cope and whether I was brave enough for the job. I was keen to remind him that he would not have won the 'brave heart' award if our roles had been reversed. But then fast bowlers weren't supposed to be brave with the bat in hand, so he'd won again.

Off the field Glenn was fine. Without a Kookaburra in his hand and when his blood wasn't boiling, he seemed like a very pleasant guy. I presume that he evaluated the role his emotions played in his performance and decided that he was better off letting himself 'go' when he was angry rather than controlling the anger and focussing it on his target. But I would like to say that, in my humble opinion, Glenn McGrath didn't need to say a word and he would still have been the best bowler in the world in his heyday. He was that good. But the Aussies will argue that aggressive body language (and language) is 'their way' and necessary to become the best.

Other bowlers irritated me over the years but my anger and frustration resulted in runs. More often than not, a fast bowler 'mouthing off' was in much greater danger of distracting himself than me. Unfortunately that wasn't the case with Glenn.

Warney

Shane Warne. I regard the fact that I was able to play so much against him as a privilege. In nostalgic moments I can look back and relive any number of encounters against one of the best bowlers the world has ever seen. I played a dozen Tests against Warney and came to know him as a mate as well as a brilliant opponent.

What made him so difficult to face was his ability to land every ball in the same place. If you had a weak spot, or he found a weak spot, you'd have to deal with it every ball because he simply wouldn't bowl a bad ball. Which also meant you had to make the running against him if you wanted to score any runs, and that increased the level of risk and your chances of getting out.

In his early days his flipper was deadly. None of us were 'naturals' against Warne, or any spin for that matter, but our best batsman was completely and utterly 'done' by Warne, which caused great consternation in the camp. It wasn't much fun for Daryll Cullinan at the time, but there was plenty of dark humour floating around with regard to our Warne woes.

We formed the 'Flipper Club' and most of us became members although I was – and remain, to my knowledge – the only man ever to be stumped by a flipper. I ran down the wicket and missed a dead straight one! Most people were bowled or lbw, but not me – that would have been far too easy. Craig Matthews used to boast proudly that he could never become a member of the Flipper Club because Warne's normal leg-spinners were far too good for him anyway and Warne never bowled a flipper 'first up' to a new batsman.

The only time Warney ever tore into me verbally was during the Sydney Test. He was on top of his game and clearly thought I'd overstayed my welcome, particularly as I kept playing and missing and failing to read anything. He very quickly worked out who was affected by the verbals and who wasn't and he adjusted his game plan accordingly.

We had a mutual friend in Melbourne, Ivan Wingreen, with whom I'd played club cricket and WP 'B' in Cape Town before he emigrated to pursue his accountancy career, so we always had a point of conversation. He was as friendly and genuine off the field as he was hard on it. He is an extremely proud Australian and was desperate for Australia to do well, and there's nothing wrong with that. Occasionally he went over the top but he wasn't the first and he certainly won't be the last. His intensity made for a great battle every time I faced him but he was the first guy knocking on our dressing room door with a couple of cold beers at the close of play, whatever had happened.

I'd been told a lot about sledging before I arrived in Australia but a lot of it was probably myth and legend because, to be honest, not many people in South Africa had much recent experience of Australia. The team, I was told, were champion sledgers (more of that later) but the real eye-opener for a naïve rookie was the abuse you'd get from the crowd.

Barely half an hour into my debut I found myself fielding on the boundary in front of the old SCG 'Hill'. Everyone gets braver with a beer inside him but these guys were especially willing to call you names from behind the security fence. It was no accident that I was there, of course. Kepler thought it would form an important part of my cricketing education.

'Hey, Kirsten is a girl's name, you poof!' This produced howls of laughter of much, loud speculation about my sexuality and habits. Each verse was followed by a chorus of 'Kirsten is a wanker.' Golf balls and tomatoes were highly favoured objects to be thrown from the crowd and another favourite trick was innocently asking you to pose for a photograph and then holding a sign above your head saying 'Moron' or 'Tosser'. Actually, those were the complimentary ones.

You either join in the fun and accept that you're going to have the mickey taken out of you for three hours or you keep your eyes firmly ahead and try not to watch the crowd at all. I found the second option to be a complete disaster. The longer you refuse to acknowledge them, the harder they will try to make you turn around. Frankly, it was a lot easier to smile, have warm beer thrown at you and join in the fun. Besides, I really did think it was fun – they might be crude but a lot of it involves a puerile but sharp sense of humour. They were clearly all people who would roll around laughing when one of them broke wind, but there are worse offences than that. The most admirable thing was their stamina – phenomenal. Very few people could chant the same thing over and over for two hours. Monks, perhaps, but they certainly wouldn't be chanting the same words.

By the end of my third tour I was an old 'favourite' with the crowds. Actually, no. Pat Symcox was an old favourite. They just hated me a bit less than the rest of the team, so I was routinely assigned to 'Bay 13' at the MCG and the 'Hill' at the SCG. But it wasn't just the big grounds, it was every ground in the country to a greater or lesser extent. From Lilac Hill to Devonport you could guarantee at least one group of guys full of beer and (mostly) good-natured abuse.

Kirsy

My brother Peter arrived midway through the tour, following Kepler's injury. He immediately showed his class. Many people believed he should have been there from the start and he proved them right with innings after innings of sheer quality. In the first day-nighter he played he scored a brilliant 97 before hurting his calf. The next match in Perth brought a moment of family magic that we'll talk about for the rest of our lives when we walked out to open the batting together.

We're both a little reserved in our display of emotions but it was an incredible time for us. Having lived my entire life in the shadow of Peter's genius, it was difficult to come to terms with the fact that we were now walking out to bat together for our country.

Peter was even more reserved than me, but although we didn't say much to each other I could sense his pride and happiness. He was bursting with emotion as we padded up together and prepared to face the new ball – it was just too good to be true. I understand the Waugh brothers used to share their deepest feelings 'subliminally' - Peter and I were the same. As aware of the significance of the moment as we were, there never seemed to be a need to discuss it. We could see each other grinning. We both, obviously, thought of Dad.

But it wasn't all roses. In Perth, in our second game together, Peter was struck badly in the face by McGrath. He went down quickly. I rushed down the pitch to see what was going on and it was obvious that his cheekbone was badly damaged. The physio took him off straight away – bad sign.

Yet again, I was facing a strange, new sensation. A voice was screaming out 'Get the runs for both of you now; you must do the Kirstens proud,' and another voice was whispering 'You've only just arrived, boy, you don't know what you've got yourself into.' Fortunately I did manage to scrape a 50 together in that game but it took me a very long time. Setting the tone for the next ten years...

We won the game, thanks to some spectacular bowling from Allan, and then asked our bus driver to take us straight to the hospital to check on Peter. He'd already had the operation to repair the depressed fracture and was vowing to be back in the nets the following day. Crazy. But at least it reminded me of where I came from. It was the most bloody-minded determination you could ever see.

It actually took him three days to get back into the nets, a feat that left some squad members feeling queasy. Three days after a facial re-arrangement, Peter was back in the nets facing Allan Donald. Preparing for a World Series final at the MCG. It was a little difficult to comprehend.

Peter was as strong on the day of the match as he had been in practice and we built a solid platform (53) which enabled me to make my first one-day international century, 112 not out, which helped us win the game. It was yet another step towards the reality of a career in the game that I'd never thought was possible. It gave me a huge amount of confidence, especially in one-day cricket.

We arrived back at the hotel at around midnight after the game, which was normal, and I went straight to my room still feeling a little dazed by what I'd done. But there was another shock waiting for me behind my door. I'm not sure how many there were – between twenty and thirty, probably. Faxes from South Africa, some from friends and family but many from complete strangers who had sat up through the night watching the game and were so moved by the result they went to the trouble of finding out where we were staying and writing a letter to congratulate me. I was absolutely knocked out by the goodwill of people. I had no previous experience of 'fan mail' and nobody had prepared me. I read them all before going to sleep.

The second final at the SCG was a little less heroic. Peter's calf muscle injury had become worse but his form was still fantastic and he played on through the pain. He smashed a cover drive to the longest part of the ground and I ran for all my life – it was worth four and I was going to do all I could to make sure that four went into the scorebook. Poor Kirsy. We were virtually standing next to each other by the time I'd completed the fourth. It was a relay throw so we still had a chance – Kirsy hobble-sprinted as best he could and dived for the line as the second throw came from cover point. Out. By a centimetre. A 37-year-old hero with a broken cheekbone, swollen eye and a torn calf muscle, lying prostrate on the ground, run out – by his brother - without a semblance of dignity. Having played a magnificent cover drive 30 seconds before. Cricket has a habit of turning heroes into villains quicker than any other sport, and it had done it to me. And I'd done it to my big brother. We lost that game, followed by the decider.

It may only have been a handful of games, but I wouldn't swap our time opening together for anything else in my career. They were very, very special days. Fortunately our playing days together didn't end in Australia. We still had one more tour on which to overlap, and it was amongst the most special and memorable of my life.

Allan Border (Australian captain): *Gary was a player I identified with naturally, for obvious reasons. I took a liking to him on that first tour in 93-94...it must have been something to do with the grittiness, the left-handedness and the determination. He was very gutsy.*

So after a couple of matches, when we headed over to their changing room with a cold beer, he was an obvious bloke for me to sit down next to. I wanted to really meet the next generation of South African players – you have to remember I was still from the generation of Australians who associated South Africa with Graeme and Peter Pollock. I don't remember what we spoke about but I do remember that Gary was an interested listener, as I was.

South Africans and Australians have always been similar in that way – play as hard as you can on the field but don't take any baggage off it. Actually, Gary was very quiet on the field. He went about his work efficiently and without fuss and didn't have words to say to anyone, not like some of the other boys! But I enjoyed Brian McMillan's company hugely; he was great value as an opponent and as a bloke to chat with after a game.

It was clear right from the beginning how important Gary would be. You need players you can trust not to get caught up in the emotions of a game, whatever's happening, and Gary was the perfect quiet achiever. Even then you knew he'd be around for a while because he looked so organised with his game and what he was trying to do. He went about his business without becoming distracted or side-tracked.

I genuinely hope retirement suits him well. Somehow, I'm sure it will. He deserves it.

Dave Richardson (South African wicket-keeper): *We had some interesting times as room mates, notably when Australia came to South Africa in 1994 and we ended up with six of us sharing the room. Our organisational skills left something to be desired and Mrs Richardson had joined me with our two children while Gary had invited his girlfriend along. It was chaos for a while until we could sort things out and arrange another room. It was like the Brady Bunch.*

But the only material difference I can claim to have made to Gary's career was by moaning at him for constantly getting out in the 60s at the start of his career. He used to sit there in the change rooms with his feet up sipping a cool drink some time around tea feeling quite pleased with himself because he'd got another 60. Meanwhile the team was 200-6 and in trouble, again, and I was next in.

So I used to moan at him all the time. I suggested, quite firmly, that if he was good enough to reach 60 then he was good enough to reach 100. That took the smile off his face.

Later, when he was scoring hundreds, he told me that he used to think of me when he reached 60 and that was enough incentive to stay out there, no matter who was bowling or how hot it was. He just didn't want to face me again. I'm glad I could help.

5

And then Lord's...
the dream continues

England '94

South Africa had returned to 'normal sport' only a couple of years earlier and already we'd played the West Indies, India, Sri Lanka and Australia. Isolation was quickly becoming a distant memory – at least it was for us, the lucky ones now able to represent a unified South Africa. Many brilliant Currie Cup players were denied the chance of an international career. The majority of cricketers in the country were denied the Currie Cup, of course, because of their colour.

South African cricket had come a very, very long way in a short space of time. The one-off Test in Barbados had happened just two and half years before but it felt like a different lifetime. But there was something very big still missing, and this – a tour to England – was it. Everyone had a sense of completing the journey, coming full circle from isolated, castigated villains to official guests at Lord's, the home of cricket. There was a huge sense of history in the build-up to the tour.

Romantic notions of English cricket tradition abounded but, like most romantic dreams, they were shattered by reality, and the reality was cold. For the first half of the tour, at least, I remember waddling about wearing three sweaters and carrying hand warmers in my pockets. I don't suppose anyone actually enjoys playing cricket in the cold, but some must surely adapt better than others. I don't think I was able to adapt at all. All my life cricket had felt like physical exercise, I felt I'd extended myself and a trickle of sweat was never far from my brow. In England I left the field feeling like I'd been waiting for a bus all day, in mid-winter.

There were many aspects of the tour that did not disappoint, however, and chief amongst them was the first Test, at Lord's. The weather had taken a turn for the better while we travelled around the country playing about 14 of the 18 county second XIs (at least it felt like it), and the sense of excitement and anticipation was impossible to escape. There appeared to be as much interest in us from the English media as we had in going to Lord's.

Arriving for the first practice was an event in itself. Many of us had seen Lord's before, usually as an anonymous spectator or tourist. But arriving as part of the South African team and driving through the Grace Gates was dreamy stuff. Fanie de Villiers didn't think so, however. Fanie is an explorer and a sign saying 'No Entry' is like an invitation to him.

Having bowled a typically long and determined spell in the nets, Fanie decided to cool down by taking a stroll around the main stadium. He walked across from the Nursery Ground and had barely placed a single foot on the sacred turf when a member of the groundstaff starting barking at him like a army sergeant. This did not please him. A hundred years of conflict between the Boers and the Brits flared up briefly and a brooding Fanie returned to the nets vowing to make the Poms pay for their arrogance.

The atmosphere on the morning of the Test was awesome. Even two hours before the start of play the crowds were flocking into the stadium and gathering on the lawns behind the pavilion with flasks of hot tea (and a nip of brandy, I couldn't help noticing).

There's something very special about seeing so many people dressed up to watch a cricket match. It's an occasion that goes beyond a match, even a Test match. To be a part of it, to be at the centre of it, does amazing things to your state of mind.

I'm often asked to name my three favourite venues in the world, and Lord's is undoubtedly second. Newlands has to be first, not just out of loyalty but because of its beauty, the nature of the crowd and because it has been home for virtually all my life.

In third place is Eden Gardens, Calcutta. A career in cricket without a match at the 'other home of cricket' is surely incomplete. The strange thing about the ground is that, unlike Lord's it has no 'aura' outside match days and unlike the MCG there is no imposing size factor to wow you. I couldn't help wondering how 80,000 or 90,000 people could possibly fit in. But when they do, the place seems to triple in size and atmosphere, and noise probably exceeds anything produced anywhere else.

The point about Lord's, with apologies to Fanie, is that it is an international venue more than an English venue. Someone, somewhere, took the decision to create that vibe and that someone should take a great deal of credit for it. If the home of cricket was to survive, then it had to become the home of all cricket, not just English cricket. At other Test grounds in England it's very clear where the home team belongs and where the visitors go, and the same applies all over the world, but at Lord's everyone belongs equally. The downside for England is the way they have played there for the last couple of decades. While opposition teams are routinely lifted and inspired by the place, it probably feels like a neutral venue to the England team.

As you walk into the dressing rooms you immediately see the Honours Board. It's impossible not to feel moved and inspired by the list of names on it. It reads like a Who's Who of the great batsmen and bowlers of the world. I realise this is probably an ambition shared by every single player who has ever walked through the door, but in 1994 it became a burning ambition to have my name up there. In retrospect, perhaps that was the time I stopped thinking of myself as 'lucky to be there' and starting thinking that I could be around for a while. Not that I ever consciously thought I would play another Test there. None of us did. The occasion of this one was far too big to think of another one.

In the first innings of the Test I had a great chance. After reaching 50 it was impossible not to allow the mind to wander, just briefly, towards the Board and the history that it carried, a permanent reminder to future generations that 'G.Kirsten' could play a bit. Then I played a miserable shot against Graeme Hick on 72 and that was that. I cursed myself for thinking my name could have been up there. I was, after all, lucky to be there at all.

In fact, I literally *was* lucky to have been out there. Kepler won the toss and chose to bat, so Hudders and I duly padded up and prepared to go out to the middle. We walked down the MCC pavilion staircase and headed towards the Long Room. We both realised at about the same time that we'd never actually walked this route before. Being a dozy pair at the best of times, we hadn't done our research.

We took a wrong turn somewhere between the bottom of the stairs and the door for the Long Room and ended up in a small, dead-end room at the back of the pavilion with mops and brooms and buckets. The nerves were flying, the fielding side was out there and the crowd was waiting. And South Africa's opening batsmen were in a cleaning cupboard.

Hudders and I later discovered we had walked straight on at the bottom of the stairs instead of turning right into the Long Room. Just in case anyone finds themselves in a similar situation.

The walk through the Long Room, when we finally reached it, was incredible. I have heard so many stories about the change of atmosphere in that room, about how silent it can be when an England captain is out for nought, or when the opposition is dominating. But this was the beginning of the series and we received a standing ovation such as I had rarely experienced.

It was very obvious that the applause was for the symbolism of the occasion. It was a 'Welcome Back' for South African cricket. It gave both of us goose bumps and heightened the tension and jittery nerves as we finally hit the open air.

The performances of Kepler and Allan Donald, who did earn their places on the Honours Board, were cherries on the top of a brilliant team performance that finished with England being bowled out for 99 to lose on the fourth day. Champagne flying on the dressing room balcony, proudly waving the new South African flag that Mike Procter had earlier been told to remove (flags are banned at Lord's) was one of those rare moments in sport when you experience just one, single emotion. Pure joy.

A few days later we were back on the county second XI circuit. One of the games that stood out for me, for obvious reasons, was the visit to Chester-le-Street to play Durham.

It was a constant source of wonder to us that counties picked such weakened teams to play the tourists but, as an opening batsman, I wasn't complaining. Resting key bowlers was probably understandable in a long season although we would all have preferred to play stronger opposition.

I settled quickly and made a good start before accelerating to about 160 not out at tea. Proccie approached me and asked me to retire as we'd lost only a couple of wickets and there were other batsmen waiting for a chance. I was particularly annoyed because you don't just 'retire' during a first-class game, you treat it with the respect first-class cricket deserves (whoever the bowlers are). So I told him that I understood his point but I'd finish the innings my way.

Fortunately a spinner came on straight after tea and I tore into him. History will show that Gary Kirsten trying to hit 'over the top' usually results in a catch within five minutes, but it was a very small ground and I reached 200 quickly.

Keen to get off the field as soon as possible as per Proccie's request, I neglected to inform the umpires that I was feeling unwell and was therefore retiring hurt. The scorers had me down as 'retired' until our SABC radio commentator, Gerald de Kock, came rushing over to the pavilion to clarify the matter. I told him I was feeling sick, 'dehydrated' I think we settled on… and my career statistics now reflect a not out.

Kirsy's Test

The second Test was, and always will be, my big brother's Test.

Peter scored the century that he so deeply wanted. His very best years were behind him, the years when he would have ranked amongst the best batsmen in the world, but now he'd played a dozen Test matches and had a century. He'd left his 'finger print' on the game. Unlike most of his contemporaries, Peter had stayed fit, strong and hungry enough to be around when isolation ended. His own biography, *In the Nick of Time,* says all you need to know about how much international cricket meant to him.

His century came in difficult circumstances at Headingley. Conditions were absolutely normal – it was grey and overcast for five days and the pitch was doing plenty for the seamers. We were in a bit of trouble and Peter battled us through it. It wasn't his prettiest innings, to be honest. In fact, it was probably as close as he ever came to batting like me. The match was drawn.

Afterwards we gathered in the pub of the Leeds Holiday Inn to have a couple of drinks and to toast Peter's century. It meant so much to him and everyone else knew it. He was accepted by everyone on tour as a virtual living legend – one of the best South Africa had ever produced – and now he could bow out with a century.

Peter was late arriving – he'd probably been doing his hair. The pub was full. When he walked in a couple of people started clapping, then everyone else followed and the reception quickly became a standing ovation, not just from the players but everyone there. It was an amazing moment and I don't think Kirsy would mind me saying I spotted a tear in his eye.

A cold beer calmed Kirsy down and he had a conversation with a couple of our travelling journalists that I didn't hear about until years later. 'My time has come, boys, but look out for my boet, he's going to be a great. He may not look much now, but he's got it up here,' he said, pointing to his head. 'He's got guts and determination, more than I ever had. Believe me, he's going to be around for a long, long time.'

If I had heard about his comments at the time I would have laughed them off immediately. Although I was no longer intimidated by the international game, I was still very much finding my feet and unashamedly thrilled still to be a part of the ride.

Actually, Gerald de Kock had the good grace to admit that everyone thought Kirsy was being a little optimistic about my potential. But they humoured him and put it down to a combination of brotherly love and beer.

Andy, me and Porks in the back garden. A ball was never far from any of us and we could make a game of anything. Porks seems a bit outnumbered in this one.

Above: At 13 years my senior Peter was already well established in his professional career during my schooldays but once I started playing for WP the age gap disappeared and we grew closer with every season. But opening the batting together for our country was still an impossible dream at this stage.

A moderately useful scrumhalf with reliable hands and feet, but little pace. Rugby remained a huge part of my life until 1992. I played most of my rugby at UCT under Alan Solomons and finished off at Villagers.

Right: Inter Varsity week was always an experience. Spinning those old leather balls down the back line was a prospect not faced by too many players these days. Thank goodness.

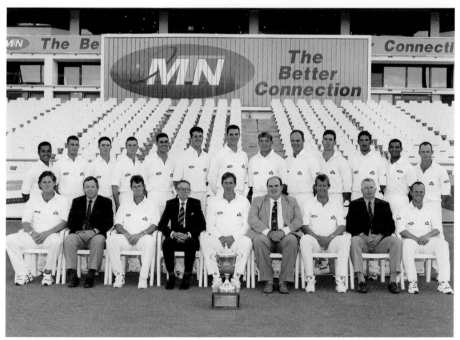

Above: The arrival of big-time sponsorship and confirmation of a new era. What a team, too. Two future international coaches in the front row ... and two Kirstens on the right!

Above: Another winning team. Happy, confident, well supported and well administered by coaches and executives. The joy of fulfilling my childhood dream - playing for WP - never wore off. Every time I posed for a team photograph the smile was real.

Above: Vice captain of the national team. It was naturally an honour but leadership wasn't for me and I never pursued it. The workload expected of international captains is too heavy, particularly off the field.

A couple of hours later and we were still in the bar. The atmosphere hadn't changed much and everyone had a smile on their face. Cricketers can relive every ball of a match if you give them long enough. And enough beer. No doubt we would have been there all night had it not been for a strange moment at about 9.30 pm.

The tour manager, Fritz Bing, came rushing into the bar urging us to get out as quickly as possible. 'Come on, come on, get out – go, now!' he kept saying, waving his arms at us. There was a good deal of confusion but everyone was too mellow to argue, so we moved off and found a new venue somewhere else.

It later transpired that Fritz had spotted a journalist he recognised as being from one of the English tabloid newspapers walking into the lobby of the hotel. He was accompanied by another man with a couple of cameras over his shoulder. We'd already been through several team meetings during which the subject of the tabloids was discussed, and Fritz was understandably concerned that we were about to be 'nailed'. 'Proteas in drunken orgy' headlines the next day would not have pleased Fritz, who had been heavily briefed about the way fact and fiction blurred into one story in tabloid land. It didn't matter that it was only 9.30 and that nothing untoward was happening; Fritz was taking no chances.

Destroyer Devon

The high of the first Test at Lord's was comfortably matched by the low of the third at the Oval when Devon Malcolm destroyed us in the second innings.

I'd never seen fast bowling like it before. He was particularly quick, on a particularly quick wicket, and the result was chaos. As a youngster still fresh to Test cricket, it was an eye-opening experience and one I'll never forget. I've always loved the challenge of fast bowling, any challenge for that matter, and when Devon was thundering in at me I knew straight away that this was one of the greatest bowling challenges I would ever confront, however long I played.

I can honestly say I've never been physically afraid – afraid of being hurt. I have always been respectful of fast bowling, but the only fear I had was that my technique might not be up to the job or that I would lose my wicket. I don't think there's anything wrong with physical fear – no doubt some players can make it work for them. But if I wasn't afraid of being hurt on that day, then I never would. Not even when Shoaib Akhtar hit me in the face in Lahore ten years later.

The reason Devon was so fired up was because Fanie had bounced him when England batted and pinged him on the head. I never ceased to be amazed that fast bowlers bounced each other. All my career I wanted to say: 'Just bowl it nice and straight, and full, and get him out. Don't try to be clever.' On one or two occasions I might even have said it. But fast bowlers rarely feared each other because, by the time they came in to bat, the energy levels of their opposite numbers had subsided and the menace had largely disappeared after bowling 15 or 20 overs.

It was the opening batsmen that had most to fear when a fast bowler was bounced, and hit. When Devon bowled his first ball to me I had absolutely no doubt that he was bowling as fast and as angrily as he had ever done in his life, and I had no doubt it was motivated by the bouncer that had hit him 20 minutes earlier. The looks on the faces of the England fielders confirmed that something extraordinary was happening.

Fanie's delivery had shattered his helmet with bits and pieces spreading all over the pitch. I know – I was at short leg picking them up. I looked into his eyes to see if he was all right but all I saw was deep, burning anger. It wasn't a pretty sight. He didn't say much but one thing I remember went something like: 'You guys are dead.'

I truly believe he would have been half the bowler that day if we'd just bowled full and straight at him. He wasn't much use with the bat anyway. But on such moments do Test matches, and careers, hinge, and Devon Malcolm produced one of the great fast bowling spells of all time to define his career and create his own piece of history.

The innings closed shortly afterwards and we went out to face Devon, no less angry than he'd been 20 minutes earlier. I didn't last long. Not many of us did, for that matter, although Daryll Cullinan showed his class with an unbeaten 94. It became clear during that innings that he was going to be able to reproduce the rare talent – genius, in fact – at international level that he'd shown domestically since he was 16. He went on to play another 70-odd Tests and become one of South Africa's very best. It was a very sad day for all concerned when his career ended in a series of disagreements with administrators.

Daryll and I shared some fabulous partnerships and had a profound respect for each other's games, though they were completely different in style and attractiveness.

But even sport's grim dark moments, there's always something to raise a smile.

It was clear the match was lost and we were witnessing one of the great bowling spells in history. Craig Matthews, who was batting at number nine, was in a hopeless situation. He'd been welcomed to the crease with a couple of deliveries just back of a length that had carried past his nose and almost cleared the keeper. The next ball grazed his thigh pad and flew down the leg side. There was a half-hearted appeal but it was good enough for Craig and he tucked the bat under his arm and started walking without casting so much as a sideways glance in the direction of the umpire. You're not supposed to laugh in the dressing room when you're being hammered but when Craig walked through the change room door it was to the definite sound of muffled giggling.

Earlier on tour we played in a festival match against the Earl of Caernarvon's XI and the Queen paid us a visit to meet the teams. We lined up in our official UCB blazers with Kepler introducing the Queen to the players and Fritz a step behind doing the same for Prince Philip, whose reputation for being a bit different had even reached us.

Apparently the Queen's husband had a habit of putting his foot into sensitive situations, so when he paused in front of me and drew breath for a question, I was hesitant.

'What's happened to the Springbok?' he enquired, eyeing the UCB logo on my blazer pocket. Before I could deliver my patriotic answer describing the new South Africa and the sensitivities regarding the Springbok, the ever-cautious Fritz had leapt to my 'defence'. 'The Springbok, Sir, has jumped,' he said, sounding slightly too eager. It reduced the guys either side of me to fits of giggles.

Perhaps it was the relaxed nature of the game, or perhaps it was the fact that none of us felt like 'colonials', but meeting the Queen of England was fun rather than intimidating. It was an honour, for sure, and one we respected greatly, but there were plenty of smiles. When Fanie called her "Miss, Ma'am, Queen," even the lady herself blushed and laughed.

6

0-6 Time for change

Pakistan '95

We travelled to Pakistan for a one-day tournament involving Australia and the host nation under a new coach, Bob Woolmer. It quickly transpired that we were a finely-tuned, well-preserved, good-looking vintage car amongst a field of sports cars. Imagination and innovation had been almost alien concepts 'till then.

We lost all six games playing one-day cricket in the 'old style' South African way, batting cautiously to a modest total and then backing ourselves to bowl and field our way to victory. Or the other way around. Either way we looked and played like antiques.

We realized half way through the tournament that we needed to alter our sights but it was too late. Two weeks earlier we had arrived in Karachi believing 250 was a monster of a score, something achieved two or three times in a lifetime. Now we realized it was actually par on those wickets.

In the years to come I realized that batting in Pakistan was as close as I could get to cricket paradise. Not only is there no seam movement to speak of, but the ball skids on and rarely rises above waist height, which was perfect for my 'square of the wicket' style. I loved playing there and my record in the country shows how greedy I was – over 500 runs in five Tests. I just wish we had played there more. But none of us really knew what we were doing on that first trip.

We plodded away making 210 and believing we'd win easily, and we lost with 10 or 12 overs to spare. We were still playing a style of cricket that had been the norm in Benson and Hedges cricket for the last decade, a style that revolved around scoring 90 or 100 in the first 30 overs with plenty of wickets in hand and then pushing on towards 200 or 210 with a big slog at the end. It was dreadfully outdated. We saw, for the first time, what it meant to hit over the top in the first 15 overs when the field was up. It never happened for us on that tour, but we learned so much and it paid dividends soon after.

Even in the fifth game, when attitudes had changed a little, we made 250 against Australia but still lost heavily. We had grown up with a premeditated idea of what constituted a good score. We were realizing with every game that a 'good' score could only be gauged while you were actually playing.

Eric

I roomed with one of my best friends and a career-long mentor, Eric Simons. Towards the end, without a win to our name, we were in Peshawar. Harsh terrain, harsh country and, as everyone knows now, active terrain for al-Qaeda on the border of Afghanistan. The centre of the town was a remarkable sight.

From what we could see, it was largely an open-air market catering for the small farmers from the hillsides as far as you could see. Fruit and vegetables traded well but obviously there were farms that grew Kalashnikov rifles, opium and hashish, too. Every morning the traders drew their donkeys and carts into town and set up stall, and every evening they packed up and made their way home again.

The funniest sight I ever saw in the country was one of these tradesmen becoming far too optimistic about the abilities of both his cart and donkey. He was loading up goods on the back of a small cart that most large trucks would have struggled with. As our bus passed on the way to practice, the cart had tipped so far back the donkey was in the air, kicking its legs and making a high-pitched noise that sounded like a combination of hysterical laughter and agony. The attention of the whole bus was immediately drawn to the sight and a very similar noise started coming from the squad.

Driving in the country was yet another experience without precedent for anyone on the tour. The Gautengers bragged that taxi drivers in Jo'burg were the most dastardly of them all, but nobody had seen street manners like those that existed in Pakistan. The bigger the car, the less the rules applied. Single-lane highways favoured the large vehicles because the prevailing logic was that bigger vehicles would smash up less badly than smaller ones. Overtaking took place purely on that basis. If the vehicle overtaking on the other side of the road was smaller than yours, and you were stuck behind something slow, then you pulled out and went for it. That was the way it worked. The squad split into fatalists, who laughed, and self-preservers, who cringed and closed their eyes. Neither group was comfortable, but there was no point fretting. As often as Jonty would ask the driver to slow down, he would shriek with glee and hit the accelerator. We had some journeys of five or six hours. Most of us still believe they took a couple of years off our natural lives.

Vandoid

Eric and I lay awake most nights until well past midnight. We started the tour discussing the problems of the world and how to solve them but near the end we were filling the empty night hours talking such rubbish that we would have been locked up if anybody had overheard us.

One night we decided to invent two new words and apply to the Oxford English Dictionary to have them validated. The first was 'vandoid', which meant 'arrogant' or 'cocky'. The first piece of vandoid behaviour the following day was greeted with its new description and by the end of the tour it was firmly established in our day-to-day language. Actually, it lasted three or four years before dying away with that generation of players.

The second word was 'neophilatic', which was dedicated to Brian McMillan. Having bowled on two or three of the flattest wickets he or anyone else had ever seen, Big Mac managed the spectacular feat of pulling a neck muscle badly enough to keep him out of the final couple of matches. Neck muscles are notoriously pullable, especially for fast bowlers, so it was understandable. Except that Brian did his in bed, asleep.

So a 'neophilatic' was someone with the ability to invent an injury without actually damaging any part of his body or suffering any physical pain. This skill was known as 'neophilaticism'. (Incidentally, it is literally impossible to 'fake' an injury in a professional sporting environment such as the national cricket squad – the 'Fizz', Craig Smith, would have spotted it within 20 seconds. We simply dedicated it to Brian in honour of all the injuries that had saved him from long, hard, hot days in the field on previous occasions.)

We never did write to the Oxford Dictionary people.

One night in Peshawar, when we'd finally fallen asleep, I felt Eric lifting my bed and trying to tip me out. This was completely out of character and not his usual sense of humour, so I tersely told him to get back to bed if that was the best practical joke he could come up with. Then he started shaking my bed, so I sat up and yelled at him. Then I saw him asleep, gently snoring. Weird. Very, very weird. It was about 4 am.

An earthquake had hit town and the whole hotel was swaying like a tree in high wind. I looked out of the window and saw the pond outside the hotel shuddering and sending waves of ripples into the centre. We evacuated the hotel for about 20 minutes and then filed back into our rooms and lay down, wondering whether there'd be another tremor and we'd all die under a pile of rubble.

The last game was in Faisalabad, against Pakistan. We had had terrible problems bowling in all five preceding matches and we had talked until we were blue in the face about where to bowl and where not to, particularly with regard to length. Too short and too full was cannon fodder for the batsmen on flat, lifeless pitches; we had to bowl back of a driving length, and fairly straight. But not all the time – if we became predictable the batsmen would be able to line up and charge the fast bowlers. And that was exactly what happened with Ijaz Ahmed.

Despite batting conservatively yet again, we thought we could defend our modest 222-4 and return home with at least a consolation victory, particularly when they slumped to 76-4. Eric was bowling at the time and there had been some highly mediocre batting. In the light of what transpired in the years to come, this will sound a lot more 'pointed' than it should, but we looked at each other and asked whether they might be 'throwing' the match just so we didn't have to return home empty-handed. It was an innocent, naïve laugh - although I did think about it several times in the coming years. I thought about many games, every strange or surprising result, wondering what might have been happening behind the scenes.

On this occasion, however, there was nothing to worry about. An hour and a half later the match was over with five and a half overs to spare and Ijaz 98 not out from 87 balls. From wondering whether Pakistan were throwing the game, we ended up being given a hiding as severe as anything we'd got in the preceding five matches.

Kepler had not been a certain starter for the tour anyway. Either the Board wanted to replace him or he hadn't been keen to tour, depending on whom you believed. Either way he stepped down from the job as soon as we returned home.

Test hundred

I'd played 16 Tests before the series against England, which came a month or so after our return from Pakistan, but hadn't yet scored the hundred that is such a crucial part of every batsman's 'arrival' on the international stage. It hadn't become a monkey on my back yet, but it was something the press all mentioned in their series previews. The truth was I had made 14 scores between 40 and 70, so it was fair to ask the question.

The first Test at Centurion was all but washed out completely. England batted for the first day and a half with Graeme Hick scoring one of the best hundreds I've ever seen. It rained for the next three days, morning noon and night. On the fifth day, around lunchtime, the skies cleared and the covers came off. The pitch had as much grass on it as the outfield. It was as green as a field in Ireland, and it was damp. Andrew Hudson and I shuddered at the prospect. It was an opening batsman's nightmare. And the match situation, obviously, was hopeless.

We padded up gloomily, trying not to think the worst but finding it hard. Devon Malcolm and Darren Gough on a pitch that had been wet and under cover for three days. We heard the five-minute bell. No turning back now.

Then it starting raining again. Just a few drops at first, then heavy. We were saved. Rain may be the curse of the cricketer's life, but don't kid yourself that it's not welcome sometimes. That reprieve may well have had an impact on the next Test. Instead of arriving with 'caught Hick bowled Malcolm 0', I started with a clean slate and confidence intact.

There were good crowds throughout the Wanderers Test (that's the great thing about playing England, they bring 5,000 people with them) and the atmosphere was as good as we've ever had for a Test in South Africa.

I started scratchily (which was usually a good sign), but started settling after the first hour. It was critical to overcome the doubts that still lingered from Malcolm's performance at the Oval just a few months earlier. We all knew the 9-57 was a once-in-a-lifetime performance but it was critical to prove it. I still had questions about my technique and I needed to have them answered sooner rather than later.

Malcolm bowled particularly quickly that day but I coped well. Two good partnerships with Hansie and Daryll put the innings in good shape and my hundred finally arrived after tea with a cut behind square off Hick. Incredible feeling. I went limp with relief. I probably hadn't realized how much tension had been created by the expectation surrounding the first century, but my whole body was flooded with emotion and happiness. What a moment – never to be forgotten. There are whole months of my career that I don't remember well, but that moment and that day will always be as fresh in my mind as yesterday.

It wasn't just the hundred itself that was special. It was banishing the 'ghost' of the Oval and proving to everyone else that Malcolm wasn't unplayable. I hadn't played the short ball well against him previously and he knew it. We both knew that he was going to come at me hard from the first ball, and everyone else knew it, too. Not often in my career did I attach as much importance to my individual battle with the opening bowler, but on this occasion I felt it could set the tone for the whole match, perhaps even series. And it was for that reason, as much as reaching three figures that I regard it as one of the best innings I ever played.

I hooked once and was hit on the elbow but otherwise I stayed extremely disciplined and left the short balls and those outside off stump really well. For most of the innings I never thought about the hundred. It might be the oldest cliché in cricket, but it's a cliché because of its truth: I played the innings one ball at a time.

That night we went out to a restaurant for dinner and Ian Botham walked over to the table to say 'Congratulations, excellent knock.' Once again, I was stunned. All the previous 'milestones' on the road to establishing oneself as an international cricketer had taken me by surprise – the cameras, interviews, fans, letters of support – and now it was recognition from one of the all-time greats of the game. I didn't know what to say other than 'thank you'. It felt strange, but certainly not uncomfortable. Ian Botham making the effort to say 'well done' to me. It's something I've never forgotten.

Eric Simons (South African cricketer, later national coach): *There are many outstanding characteristics that made Gary Kirsten the cricketer that he was. Much has been documented about him succeeding in spite of the fact that, by his own admission, he wasn't the most naturally talented cricketer in the world. But just maybe the talent he had for critical self-analysis, allied to a fierce determination to succeed, made him one of the most talented cricketers ever to play the game, but that is for another debate. What few truly realized during his career was his unrelenting belief that the team came above all else. When the team won, Gary won, and he led the celebration. It did not matter what his performance had been because the team had won.*

There were times when he asked the selectors to drop him because he was not in the kind of form to do justice to the team. He never considered the fact that, as a senior player, he had the right to regain form by playing through a bad patch.

My favourite off-the-field image of Gary will always be him sitting in a corner of the change room with his dark glasses on, giving us all yet another rendition of Jack Nicholson's 'You want the truth - you can't handle the truth' speech from the movie A few good men'. It always meant we had won and it always meant Gary was happy. At some point during proceedings he would come over to me and give me the familiar instruction – 'Tell my wife I love her because in a short while I will not be in a state to tell her myself.'

Gary represents all that is good about our game.

7

Bandana...are you crazy?

'96 World Cup

We had been playing very good cricket before the World Cup and we were fitter than anyone had known before, but the campaign did not begin auspiciously for me.

The squad had been invited to an SABC launch on the night before we left and the strict World Cup regime had already kicked in. The function was held in a massive hangar in Pretoria and it was a great party. Bars in every corner, snacks, interesting company. As was to happen on many more humorous occasions in the years to come, I ended up in the company of Pat Symcox. And bravado overwhelmed discretion. We felt it was far too good a function to leave early and, besides, it was our last night in South Africa for seven or eight weeks. So we decided to give it a bit of a tonk.

When Bob Woolmer sounded the alarm at about 8.45 that evening to return to the bus, Symmo and I didn't arrive. We had told the others we'd find our own way back to the hotel, and we felt grown up enough to do so. And the party began.

We were absolutely grilled the following day. It had been a very good party, but we paid a price. We were severely reprimanded by Hansie and Bob who both reiterated the new regime of total fitness and total professionalism. I said: 'Well, I am fit. That doesn't mean I can't have a good time, does it?' Anyway, we were given an official warning. If we crossed the line again, we were in serious trouble. Whatever that might mean.

But Bob really had transformed the team and our approach to the one-day game since the 0-6 drubbing we had suffered at the hands of Australia and Pakistan in the triangular tournament in Pakistan two years earlier. The partnership between Bob and Hansie was extremely successful. We had won a lot of games in the build-up to the tournament and we travelled to the subcontinent with a genuine belief that we could do something special. As we discovered on arrival, however, there was a lot of travel in store, most notably with the opening ceremony, before we could actually start playing.

We were based in Pakistan and the gala opening was in Calcutta. It took us a day and half to get there and another 36 hours to get back. Having started our preparations with some success, we had to down tools for four days.

But the will to work was unrivalled. I'll never forget one shuttle session in Faisalabad when everyone was taking enormous strain. It took place on a field adjacent to our hotel but the walls surrounding the area meant it was close to a 20-minute bus ride just to get there. Ever obliging, the local officials knocked a temporary entrance through the perimeter fence which cut the travel time down to approximately 30 seconds.

This particular fitness session was, however, more memorable for a Symmo comment that entered the Hall of Fame for touring quotes. With virtually everyone on hands and knees gasping for breath, Symmo in particular, the old man managed a loud shout of: 'And this will help me get turn and bounce, will it?' Whatever breath we had left was instantly used to laugh with. It was yet another of his famous 'tension-breakers'.

Bandana

Fortunately our first game was against the United Arab Emirates, a match in which I scored 188 not out and made the back pages of several newspapers for my patriotic bandana in the colours of the South African flag. I'm still asked about it, whether it was a display of national pride and how long I'd planned it. The truth is, I never planned it. It was literally two minutes before I went out to bat when several team mates, led by Hansie, all suggested I wore it.

I was fiddling around with the thing until I had to walk out there, trying to see whether it would fit and stay in place. I decided not to risk it but the guys were putting a lot of pressure on me and saying it would look great. Eventually it was just easier to give in to them than protest.

The big score drew plenty of attention to me and I think most newspapers ran a picture of me without my helmet on. If a company had been sponsoring me to wear it they would have had more exposure than they could have dreamed of. It was extremely ironic that it was me causing the fuss. I'd always been a very conservative cricketer yet here I was being portrayed as a patriotic rebel prepared to take on the ICC's strict clothing regulations in order to carry my country's flag on to the field.

Strictly speaking, it did contravene the letter of the law on the ICC's playing conditions but, given that it was hidden from view for 98 percent of the time I was out there, it didn't seem so bad – particularly as I wasn't advertising anything. Except South Africa, of course. Happily, nobody said anything to me and I was able to wear it for the rest of the tournament. I became quite attached to it, in fact.

A few months later, however, we competed in a four-nation tournament in Kenya during which we were required to play in white clothing. The ICC's playing conditions are far stricter in such circumstances, so the tournament referee, Mike Denness, fined me several thousand rand for wearing the bandana. It was paid by someone at home – I never even heard who it was, let alone had the opportunity to thank him. It was a ridiculous decision to fine me, frankly, and I believe it caused quite a fuss at home. Hence the decision by someone to pay it for me. If you happen to be reading this, whoever you are, thank you. It was a couple of thousand rand I would not have enjoyed handing over.

Sultan

The other moment that stands out in most people's minds about that game was the bouncer with which Allan Donald felled the captain, Sultan Zarawani. We realised he was the 'main man' as far as the UAE were concerned but I'm not sure any of us knew that he was the financial benefactor of the team and just about the only Emirates national.

Whoever you were in cricket in 1996, however, you did not stroll out to face Allan Donald wearing a floppy hat. You just did not do that.

The whole team was appalled at this lack of respect although Allan didn't seem overly bothered. Everyone told AD to bounce him – it may not have been important to Al but it was extremely important to the rest of us that the Sultan was taught a lesson. In fairness, there was no malice felt or intended. Every one of us thought he'd duck, catch a wake-up call and then call for a helmet. Nobody, least of all Allan, expected such a perfect bouncer to be bowled.

The rim of his sun hat saved him because it creased up behind the impact of the ball and glanced the blow, flush on the side of the head. It was a horrible moment as he crumpled to the ground. The worst thing is that Allan was suddenly the centre of attention while the rest of us instinctively thought; 'I'm glad I didn't bowl it.' Allan, of course, probably wouldn't have bowled a bouncer if we hadn't pestered him to.

It was a huge relief and a very welcome moment when the Sultan regained his feet, had a drink of water and was able to carry on – with a helmet. Point taken.

Kiwis

The match against New Zealand was also memorable because they'd been spoken about often as a potential force on the slow wickets of the subcontinent because they had the best dibbly-dobblers in the world, guys like Chris Harris and Gavin Larsen.

We were chasing down their total of 180 and the usual rules applied to facing the dobblers – work them around, look for singles and don't take on too much, especially when you need only 180. Then we lost a wicket and Hansie walked to the crease looking even more serious than usual. He took them on almost immediately, slog-sweeping Larsen over deep mid-wicket and belting Harris in the same direction. He reached 50 from 40 balls and about half an hour after he'd come to the crease the match was over. It set an example that we looked back on every time we played New Zealand – and any gentle, frustrating medium-pacer, for that matter.

A sure sign of a confident team is one that finds time to have fun and enjoy itself, and although we had a reputation for being serious and having a workaholic approach to our business, there was always more fun and humour than people realised. There was plenty of time for it, too, with a game every four or five days.

Hansie was the epitome of the apparent contradiction between our image and what happened on a day-to-day basis. Each morning in Pakistan started with the team doctor handing out two malaria tablets. (We couldn't, quite rightly, be trusted to remember to take them ourselves.) One morning Hansie engineered a switch of malaria tablets for sleeping tablets, the kind we use for long haul flights.

The victim was fitness trainer Paddy Upton. By the time we arrived at the ground for training, Paddy was yawning heavily. He stumbled over his feet during a warm-up and continually dropped the rugby ball during a ten-minute game of touch. The whole team was 'in' on the joke but the mass hysteria of the squad was completely lost on Paddy who was shaking his head and slapping himself to wake up. It was clear he was shocked at his own lethargy and highly embarrassed by his exhausted and hopeless attempts to lead the fitness session.

As part of the plan Bob then called for a five-minute 'visualisation session' in which we would focus our energy on thinking clearly and positively about the next game. So we stretched out on the ground under the warm morning sun and Bob made a couple of cursory comments about batting and bowling. Then it was time to resume training. Paddy lay comatose in his original position for the next two hours, not moving even when the local flies crawled up his nose.

Lara plan

Everything remained on course and we were quietly confident a couple of days before the quarter-final against the West Indies. Then we went a fair way to losing the match on the evening before the game was played.

Allan Donald was omitted so we could play two spinners, Symcox and Paul Adams. It was an unbelievable decision. At the time I was in complete shock; most of the team were. Allan was probably our star individual and had the ability to turn a match in an instant. Frankly, it didn't matter what the pitch looked like – you had to play Allan Donald. He was a big-match player and had the ability to produce a match-winning performance at any time. How ironic that eight years later, on home soil again, he was left out of the team that tied with Sri Lanka to exit the 2003 World Cup. Still, the show had to go on.

We had a 'plan' for Brian Lara. It involved Symmo bowling wide and fullish outside the off stump with a heavily packed off-side field including two men fielding behind square. This was going to keep Lara quiet. This was going to frustrate him into making a mistake. And with respect, Symmo had bowled well in the subcontinent previously.

Lara murdered him. It was painful to watch. When you're up against the best batsman in the world you are forced to think beyond conventional plans, and that's why we had formed the plan. At the time it seemed smart and innovative but Lara made it look ridiculous. In hindsight we should have stuck with what we knew and had been doing well, but we all know how many games have been won in hindsight. Before we could think of plan B he'd scored a hundred. A brilliant hundred.

It was Lara's genius that created doubts in the opposition team before you'd even taken the field. Team talks centred on how you were going to cope with him and teams felt they needed to do something special and something different against him.

The Windies had lost to Kenya earlier in the tournament, which resulted in some disbelief but not suspicion, certainly not amongst South Africans. Match-fixing was still a rumour to us. At least, to most of us. I'd heard about it but didn't know whether to believe it. In the case of the Windies-Kenya match, I simply thought it was a clear case of the inconsistent Caribbean temperament being tested by a group of irritatingly accurate spinners, and failing the test. Perhaps that was another reason we decided to play two spinners.

We needed 265 for victory and a place in the semi-finals, and we needed a good start. Every team needs a good start in every innings, I suppose, but this time we needed a good start more than I could ever remember. I was in the best form of my life at that stage. I knew the guys were looking to me for a lead.

I pushed a ball from Curtly Ambrose to the left of midwicket and set off for a quick but very safe single. I slipped as I set off and my foot hit the stumps. Out, gone for three. It was the only time in my entire career, at every level, that I was out 'hit wicket.' What a great moment for it to happen. We lost wickets at crucial times, never caught up with the asking rate and, although Symmo smashed a couple of sixes to get us close, we were never going to win. I'm not a 'what if' kind of person, so I didn't waste energy reflecting on the selection of the team for the game. Once the game had finished my only regret was losing my wicket in the way I did. I'd been in great form and I could have made the difference. I regretted my own mistake, nobody else's.

The build-up to the tournament and the preparation for it had been perfect. We'd won six out of six matches playing powerful, strong cricket, and expectations were high. Before that quarter-final, we had believed we could win the tournament. We might not have started the competition with as many hopes as we had before the 1999 tournament, but we'd reached the stage where we truly believed we could win it. Then we messed it up in one match and that was it. The ending was so sudden. We didn't feel ready to leave. The level of disappointment was intense. Not the anger or sadness that have characterised other losses, but a deep disappointment.

It was difficult to think of any consolations on the trip back home. Even my 188 didn't feel quite so important any more. In retrospect, however, I realise my appetite had been whetted for India on our brief forays into the country from our base in Pakistan. It was the second time we'd toured Pakistan but we still hadn't spent more than a couple of days in India. It fascinated me and the prospect of a full tour there the following year was suddenly a whole lot more appealing than it had been.

8

Just one snap, Jonty!

India 96.

It was an amazing nine weeks. It was difficult to believe that India and Pakistan were once parts of the same country. There was almost nothing the same about touring the two.

The first impression of Mumbai and Kolcatta (or Bombay and Calcutta as they were then) is of an expanse of people, more people than you've ever seen before.

To ride through the streets of the big cities in an air-conditioned bus, seeing people lying on the streets because there isn't enough room on the pavements, was a numbing experience. The poverty was everywhere and I'd never seen it on such a scale before. To see a family of five or six living on tiny patch of dirt between two shacks, to watch them wash in the filthy drain water and to realize that the rags they wore and the blanket they slept on were their only assets, was a shock to the system.

It put South Africa's problems into perspective. Through my involvement with the Foundation for a Brighter Future and other charities I have a very modest understanding of the poverty that exists in South Africa. This was on a different scale. Ownership of the worst shack imaginable seemed to place people pretty well on the social ladder. I have still never seen such a graphic difference between the rich and the poor as exists in India. It's a phenomenon that we experience all the time in South Africa but, once again, I've never seen it so dramatically portrayed as in India.

We stayed in magnificent hotels, five-star in every way, from the food to the phone lines (which were seven star in price), and travelled to the cricket grounds and airports in comfortable buses, yet between the destinations was a never-ending spread of squalor and poverty.

Some players were far more comfortable walking the streets of the big cities than others, but I enjoyed the experience. I had reservations about 'intruding' into this desperate world of hunger and shortage, and obviously I wondered how comfortable I would feel living the life of luxury I was, but a walk through a street market could be one of the most uplifting half-hours of the week.

The same people who had looked so desperate from behind the window of the bus seemed inexplicably contented. The frailty of their bodies seemed much less dramatic when they were surrounding you every time you took a step and they never lacked energy. They may have 'owned' nothing but they still had their spirit, which was phenomenal.

The other phenomenon that completely bewildered us was the widespread knowledge of and passion for the game of cricket. Within minutes of walking down a street in Calcutta with a couple of the other guys, we had a group of three or four hundred people bumping and jostling their way over each other to keep up with us. Of course there were many kids begging for a few coins, but just as many – if not more – were interested in collecting an autograph or just talking about the game.

I walked around with a fixed smile on my face. The atmosphere, the chaos, the poverty and this steady stream of broken conversations about Jonty, or the innings I played against Australia, or my provincial average (seriously) - it was all too weird to take in. Add in the even more constant barrage of stall-holders and shop-keepers trying to sell you everything from fake perfume to roasted peanuts, and the prospect of being barged into the road and knocked over by a moped carrying four people and a goat, and you could understand why some people rarely left their rooms. It was a friendly, well-meaning commotion that wrapped itself around you like a welcoming blanket. But it wasn't for everyone, least of all the claustrophobic.

Often we would be invited to a particular store where we would happily accept a 'present', often an item of clothing, before usually buying several more at a 'very good price'. If it seemed generous on the part of the shop-keeper, he certainly made our visit work for him, too. Word of mouth worked faster than any internet connection yet invented and minutes after we'd arrived, a crowd of 500 had gathered outside the shop. It was important for the impression to be created that we had simply 'dropped in' by chance; that way the shop-owner's kudos would rise significantly and he'd take a step up the business ladder. A picture on the wall with him serving and socializing with 'famous' tourists would be worth its weight in gold, apparently, with future trade guaranteed.

Just one snap

On one of these visits we were driven to a Levi store in downtown Calcutta. Within 15 minutes the crowd outside was so massive it was obvious we just weren't going to be able to get out. Or if we were, it would have taken several hours.

The shop-keeper reassured us, gave us a Coke and promised to release us through a private exit. Jonty was with us that afternoon. Our eventual escape lasted about 200 metres before the crowd discovered the side street down which we were scurrying and a chase ensued that even the best comedy film directors would battle to reproduce. Baskets of fruit went flying, bicycles crashed into each other and entire families wobbled and fell off their mopeds. We quickly gave up the chase and settled for signing and posing for pictures all the way back to the hotel. It took hours.

It's very difficult to understand or even describe the Jonty fervour that existed in India. He was comfortably bigger in that country than he ever was at home. That tour became known as the 'Just one snap, Jonty' tour. The man could not move without someone popping up from nowhere with an ancient instamatic camera and asking, or demanding in fact: 'Just one snap, Jonty!'

He didn't have a single, uninterrupted meal for nine weeks. For breakfast, lunch and dinner Jonty had people walking up and requesting a picture – and an autograph. The man carrying his bags to the hotel room would push his way inside on the pretext of being helpful only to whip a camera out of his pocket once the door had closed. And on the rare nights when Jo would stay in his room and order a club sandwich, the waiter would do the same. Then, when he finally relaxed, there would be a knock at the door. And another one. And another one.

I should clarify my earlier, generous description of the hotels. They were routinely tremendous in the big cities. In some of the smaller venues, unused to coping with back-packers let alone international sports teams, they could be dreadful.

One of the worst was in Rajkot. The bus driver couldn't even find it, and he was a local. The ground floor was a hardware shop. The reception was two floors up. There was a narrow door on the pavement next to the hardware shop which led into a narrow passage. At the end of the passage was an even narrower lift with an iron gate across it. There was a staircase to the hotel, next to the lift, but it also had an iron gate across it and it was padlocked shut. The padlock and chain were rusted.

The lift could take one person and one bag per trip. With management, we were a party of 19. With 113 pieces of luggage. Not being a pushy sort of person, but also no longer the junior member of the squad, I reached my room approximately an hour and 40 minutes after assembling on the pavement outside. The last of my three bags was delivered sometime after midnight, several hours after I'd fallen asleep.

To complete the picture, our new home – described optimistically on a peeling signboard outside as a 'luxury hotel', did not have a restaurant, although it did offer meals. Manager Goolam Raja had become a seasoned traveller in these parts and always knew the best way to investigate. So he ordered a meal, for research purposes.

It transpired that the 'hotel' had an arrangement with a restaurant further down the street and that meals were simply ordered and delivered. This arrangement might even have worked if it hadn't been for…the lift. Whatever was ordered hot arrived cold, and whatever was ordered cold arrived hot, many hours after it was expected. We had a problem.

Everyone reacted in a slightly different way, but to a certain extent it was a case of each man for himself. Fortunately I had Symmo as a feeding buddy and he'd secretly kept a couple of bags of biltong in his coffin – we had been given some by the staff at the SA embassy about ten days earlier. For two and a half days, we ate nothing but biltong and dry toast with Bovril. Breakfast, lunch and supper, that was it. The toaster in the team room at the hotel was operating in overdrive.

In the evenings we would retreat to the roof of the hotel with a six-pack of the sponsor's finest and watch the sun set on the amazing scenery around us. As far as the eye could see, the sprawling urban mass of Rajkot with its clouds of dust and pollution thickening the red and gold sky stretched before us. Half an hour later and a couple of cold Castles lighter, and the world seemed like a good place once again. Symmo always maintained that it was our responsibility to the team to have a couple of Castles. While so many guys were falling victim to bugs, we stayed happily healthy. Symmo said it was the beer that was fighting off the infections. It was a good theory and I was happy to stick to it.

For some guys, like Derek Crookes, it was predominantly the taste of the local food that made it impossible to eat – he just couldn't get curry past his tongue. Others were just plain suspicious of the way it may have been cooked, or not, and occasionally I fell into that category. But most of the time it was simply a professional decision for the good of the team: Was it worth taking a chance on something you were completely unfamiliar with, ghee and all, and run the risk you might spend the next 24 hours getting rid of it from both ends, often involuntarily? Happily, I had only one experience of this process and it lasted less than a day. A combination of caution and strong guts made me a good Asian tourist.

Travel

Domestic travel between cities was also fabulous, in a darkly amusing way. Although it frequently led to huge sense-of-humour failures.

We left Rajkot en route for Guwahati where we were due to play Australia two days later. The travel schedule between the two cities, which are approximately 900 kilometres apart, made for some interesting reading.

We started with a wake-up call at seven o'clock in the morning after the match (in which we beat India by five wickets). A last meal of Bovril toast and biltong. It would not be strictly accurate to say the drive to Rajkot airport was during rush hour because, as in every city, the only time it wasn't rush hour was between 2 am and 5.30 am, but the traffic was certainly as heavy as it could get.

We flew to Delhi and waited five hours there for another connecting flight to Calcutta. We then transferred to an airport hotel for the night. At least, we were told it was the airport hotel but it was a 45-minute drive from the arrivals terminal. Almost all our luggage was nowhere to be seen. Apparently it had been booked straight through to Guwahati. By then we hardly cared. Almost everyone had lost a bag or two at some stage of the tour and just about all had turned up some time later. By now we had all worked out what to carry in our hand luggage. The bare essentials included a few items of spare clothing, two tooth brushes, some emergency rations like biscuits or biltong and whatever else was important (Imodium in some cases). We finally arrived at the 'airport' hotel around 9.30 pm.

The wake-up call the following morning was at 5.30 to catch the 7 am flight to Guwahati. We arrived there an hour and a half later, collected whatever bits of luggage that had actually travelled with us and set off for the hotel, which was another hour's drive. We arrived some time after 10 am.

Our route had taken us 24 hours. The pilot admitted a direct flight, if one had existed, would have taken about an hour and a half. It wasn't always the best way for some players to stay calm.

Just one snap, Jonty!

Brian McMillan was one of the first to 'lose it'. Big Mac wasn't often happy when things went wrong. There was a great moment on arrival back at a hotel from a practice when he needed some quick calming down. It was our first day in whatever city we were in. He asked the man at concierge where our consignment of Castles was. The man replied cheerfully that he would be delighted to help and immediately called for a hotel car and driver. Mac, confused but thirsty, climbed in. A few minutes later he managed to establish what was happening. He was being driven 20 kilometres out of town to a local sight-seeing attraction, which was, indeed, a castle. He was not happy.

Hansie, too, could remain calm for long periods before lashing out in a fit of temper. He did so the evening we arrived in Rajkot. He cursed and swore blue for five minutes. This was not, he said, the way international teams should be treated. The rest of us smiled and kept our heads low. We had learnt quickly that it made no difference to the outcome.

Ghandi

The Ahmedabad Test was awful for several reasons. It was a gruesome stadium consisting of one, huge slab of concrete set in a virtual 360-degree circle of the ground, with hardly anybody in it. The most memorable aspect of the Test was visiting the Gandhi Museum two days before the match started. Not many of us, including me, had any real idea of the time the great man had spent in South Africa as a trainee lawyer. I'd been acutely aware of how often Nelson Mandela and Gandhi were linked as two of the greatest leaders mankind had known, and of how little I knew of the 'other' man. It was an inspiring couple of hours. Strange to think how the bitter miseries of apartheid South Africa had helped create not just Madiba, but Gandhi, too.

I had my birthday during the Test. Our hotel was a little ordinary, unfortunately, but there was a brand new and very pleasant hotel further out of town at which Goolam organized a party. When things are as grim as they were in Ahmedabad, birthdays are no better or worse than other days. We had snacks, drank some Castles and then came the 'cake tradition'.

Wherever we were in the world, Goolam always managed to organize a cake. Sometimes they were delicious and sometimes they were not. Sometimes, they were very undelicious indeed. But whatever the state of the cake, Hansie always engineered a way to get some of it – usually quite a lot of it – onto the birthday boy's head. Once you'd had three or four birthdays on the road you learned to limit the damage, as I did on this occasion, but the new boys invariably ended up wearing a lot of cream and icing.

We had a tuk-tuk race back to our hotel, most with our wives or partners as co-passengers, while the bachelors teamed up in pairs and lost heavily because of the extra weight. I recall Debs and me doing particularly well although we may have been pipped at the post by Jonty and Kate. Tactics for tuk-tuk racing were straightforward and involved regular bribing of our drivers to go faster and faster until their tiny engines sounded like lawn-mowers being thrown off a cliff. I was a year older.

Partners

Thankfully it is now normal for wives, families and girlfriends to visit their partners during an agreed 'window period' on tour, but it wasn't always that way. There was a huge debate on the subject before we left for Bombay and I was very much involved as vice-captain. There was still a strong 'old-fashioned' school of thinking that believed there was no place for the ladies on tour.

Debs and I had met earlier that year and were at the stage of our courtship where every day apart was pretty hard work. I was vociferous at the meetings about what I perceived to be common sense and players' rights. But quite apart from the 'personal' aspect, I knew without a shadow of doubt that I would perform better with Debs at my side. Eventually the motion was passed – much to the disgust of some members of management who believed it was a corruption of all the basic principles of touring rather than a move towards decent, practical and professional conditions.

Once the principle had been accepted, however, there were further problems. Who qualified? There were suggestions that it should be only married partners and that players would only qualify to bring their spouses once they had accumulated a certain number of 'points' earned in Tests and one-dayers. Paul Adams, for example, who had been a part of the SA squad for years but had also performed more than his share of 12th man duties, had a long-standing partner but couldn't earn the points to bring her on tour. To be honest it was messy and upsetting to a number of people and remained that way for several years. Thankfully, it was finally sorted in the couple of years before I retired.

I'll always feel vindicated that I fought for what I believed was right because Debs still remembers the '96 tour of India as one of her all-time favourite experiences, at least as far as her seven years of cricket touring were concerned. The markets, the people, the fabric, the spices, the food...everything. She loved it. Whereas the crushing throng of humanity would intimidate or unnerve most people who weren't used to it, Debs thrived on the atmosphere. It was a very special tour for both of us.

Actually, it was a crucial time for us and our relationship. We were extremely close at that stage – or at least, we wanted to be and we grew together during Debs' time in the country. Seeing India through each other's eyes and sharing experiences that you wouldn't normally have went a long way towards confirming what we knew we felt for each other.

The way international cricket schedules are organized these days virtually denies any professional cricketer the chance to build or even sustain a relationship at home. If spouses and partners weren't allowed to join their men on tour then they would hardly ever see them. It's difficult enough for most young cricketers to develop 'normal' social skills when they are home and amongst 'normal' friends for only two or three months of the year without condemning them to bachelordom as well.

I also happened to score lots of runs on this tour, which was a great relief considering the stance I had taken.

Just one snap, Jonty!

Stadium

The Ahmedabad stadium was diabolical. When the attendant arrived to open things up on match day morning, the locks were so rusted he had to find a hacksaw to let us in. It took a long time. Sadly, despite the honest and sincere efforts of many people, we were in another kitchen hell. The food offered to us would have blown most of us away for a week. Our fitness trainer, Paddy Upton, was a willing guinea pig and tested anything we were unsure of. Even he was unwilling to taste the main dish served for lunch; it was bubbling in a silver bowl and sealed from the outside world by an inch of oil. It was the hottest thing any of us had ever smelt. With the biltong finished, it was back to the Bovril toast, and for five days, not two.

The match was similarly awful. The best thing about being an opener in India was you always had the best of conditions, batting first or second. The wicket was almost always flat and friendly for the first innings before disintegrating on the last couple of days. This pitch looked poor, but we felt we'd be all right – at least for most of the first day. In the third over of the match I received a ball from Javagal Srinath that pitched on a good length and flew over my right shoulder. I didn't even have time to flinch. The ball was going 'through the top' after 15 minutes and we knew were in for a nightmare, especially against the spinners.

We were drilled. Hard town, bad Test, bad loss. Bad.

How things change.

When I first arrived at Eden Gardens I felt as though I was destined to play there. Although it was not exactly what I'd expected, it was still magnificent. Without its stands packed to the rafters, Eden Gardens is emasculated. But its facilities are world-class and I defy anyone who has ever played there in front of 80,000 people to say they have experienced a more intense atmosphere.

The extremes of noise will live with me forever. When Hudders and I were putting together a stand of 200 on the first day there were times we felt everyone in the stands could hear our conversations. When Mohammad Azharrudin was smashing 100 off 80 balls three days later we couldn't exchange three words at a nose-to-nose distance.

Even when the place was full it was difficult to believe there were 80,000 people there. Fortunately I did justice to the occasion and the venue and enjoyed one of my best Test matches, making a century in both innings, something I regard amongst the three greatest achievements of my career, so I had plenty of time to study the crowd in the quieter times of the day. I was convinced they were sitting two to a seat. Before play on the third or fourth morning I went to look at the stands, which were basically concrete benches with painted lines demarcating the seats. Each was about 30 centimetres wide. Scary.

At the end of the match, with Lance Klusener having taken 8-63 on debut after being pounded by Azhar in the first innings, we boarded the bus for the short trip back to the hotel behind huge police barricades erected between the dressing rooms and the bus. It was bigger than a Hollywood premiere night with thousands and thousands of fans pushing against the police lines trying to get a view of Sachin, or anyone, for that matter. It may even have been bigger than a Bollywood premiere. No, probably not.

As we left the dressing room for the final time, the crowd spilt over the line and there was no way through. The police reacted with a typical baton-thrashing session, which seemed to put the fear of death into everyone. The crowd scattered like pigeons at the sound of a gun, trampling all over each other to avoid a beating. As the dust settled and the bus pulled off, all we could see was thousands of sandals lying by the side of the road, abandoned in pursuit of a first-hand sight of their heroes. It made us all laugh, despite what looked like a savage approach. In fact, the canes were mostly beaten on the ground in front of the crowd and nobody seemed to get injured. I guess they just accepted any old pair of sandals when they returned. Share and share alike.

We were staying in the magnificent Oberoi Hotel, and it was, ironically, the only time I'd ever been sick. Having avoided the bug that scythed down a significant number of players and wives in Ahmedabad, both Debs and I fell victim to the most innocent (and popular) meal on the room service menu. As usual I was playing it safe during the Test and ordered the touring cricketer's 'banker', the club sandwich. It was a particularly good one, too, so I encouraged Debs to have a bite. But something went wrong, for once, and I spent the whole night with my head hanging over the toilet bowl. The next morning I felt absolutely fine, if a little tired, but by then the bug had hit Debs. In eight tours to the subcontinent, that was my only mishap. I could say that the touring illness stories told by most cricketers were exaggerated, but there are always two or three unlucky guys that stay sick for the entire tour and they would not agree.

I remember my great friend Johnny Commins arriving as a late replacement for the injured Jonty. He was there for only a week or two before the tour ended but he immediately picked up some dreadful stomach bug and remained sick for at least six weeks after we arrived home. John never carried much weight to start with but he was reduced to skin and bone by the time his system returned to normal.

Kanpur

So we'd squared the series and faced the possibility of creating a little bit of history. No visiting team had won a series in India for over a decade and, although everyone was feeling a bit weary, there was a fair amount of excitement and belief that we could do it. At least, there was until we saw the pitch. It remains the flattest strip I've ever seen. Even when Allan Donald tried to bowl a bouncer the ball didn't bounce above waist height.

We batted poorly, their spinners had a great time, Azhar made a brilliant 160 and we were hammered, well and truly hammered. It was one of those occasions where you got beaten so heavily it almost didn't hurt. Besides, the weather was so cold we were too numb to feel anything.

Nobody in our squad had ever associated India with being cold, but Kanpur is in the far north, nestled in the Himalayan foothills, and we could see snow on the mountain tops. We were not prepared. We sat huddled in the dressing with a couple of electric heaters on full time, not leaving until we had to. The 12th men were sent to a local market to buy hats and gloves.

If we'd felt tired and keen to get home before the Test started, we were now completely beaten up. Beaten up and fed up. Years later, when I heard Hansie had taken $30,000 on the third night of the Test, I was shocked but not surprised at the timing. If the idea was to tempt him at a weak moment, the bookies could not have timed it any better.

This end-of-tour malaise is a difficult subject for cricketers to talk about because it can open us up to fierce criticism. But it exists; it is a fact. After nine weeks, thousands of kilometres travelled, many virtually sleepless nights and a tough time on the field, there is nothing you can do to stop yourself thinking about home. You focus all your energy and resources on playing good cricket and representing your country with pride and honour, but eventually the spirit starts to sag.

Sports scientist Professor Tim Noakes accompanied us to the '96 World Cup and, having observed many different sportsmen in alien environments, tried to quantify the optimum time that a team could perform to its potential while on the road. He says that after six weeks most people will suffer an inevitable and unstoppable decline in form and interest. We certainly experienced it then. In fact, every team I've been in that has toured for longer than five or six weeks has experienced it.

'The Prof' was a legend in those days, as he still was at the end of my career. I had heard about him but had never met him before. He had actually come to Pakistan as our team doctor but his interest in the team, and touring, extended far beyond his medical duties. His intellect might have been intimidating had it not been for his humility and desire to learn as much as possible about us and about cricket – and touring. The moment I met him I instantly enjoyed everything about him and I knew we would stay friends, which we have.

We sat next to each other on the flight from Cape Town to Johannesburg before departure for the World Cup and his desire for knowledge was insatiable. He asked me endless questions about my thoughts and emotions as an opening batsman and what pressures I experienced. He had fantastic ideas about writing a book about that tournament with the input of all the players, but I believe he was denied permission by the Board.

Two days after our conversation he showed me a nine-page article he had written with his own interpretations following our conversation. It was more than just interesting, it was insightful and a valuable aid to the rest of my career. South African cricket would surely benefit from more scientific input from people as qualified as The Prof.

Tim's greatest book, *The Lore of Running*, has sold hundreds of thousands of copies and is regarded as something of a bible for road runners in South Africa and many other countries. Yet, if I may say so, his trademark shuffle around the boundary edge during training was something to behold. He is a man who has run seven or eight Comrades and as many Two Oceans ultra-marathons, and I expect the scientist in him has learnt to conserve as much energy and limit the damage to his bones as much as possible. No doubt I will be seeking advice on the subject in my future years.

At the beginning of the tour I had absolutely no idea whether match-fixing even existed but by the final days it was clear that it did, based purely on the amount of gossip and rumour-mongering going on in the squad. I had absolutely no idea of what was about to happen. I don't think anyone did. Match-fixing was about to explode right in my face.

Rahul Dravid (Indian cricketer)**:** *It was always fantastic to watch someone like Gary play. In a lot of ways I saw myself in him - in the sense that he was more a stable, solid player than a flashy one. His ability to score runs for South Africa in difficult times amazed me. He showed with some of his innings that he was a genuinely big player, someone who could score big. In both one-day cricket and Test cricket he was constantly developing. Every time you played against Gary in a new series he was a better player than the last time around. It was great to just watch him go about his job in a professional manner. I was in Scotland during the 2003 season and I watched on television as he scored that incredible hundred against England at Headingley. I was amazed by the way he batted.*

When Gary batted he looked shaky initially and the bowlers thought they had a chance. But once he got set he was a hard man to get out. In Kolkata he made a hundred against us, and, come to think of it, he always got runs against us. In that sense it was a pain to be on the field when he was playing one of his big knocks. I always remember him as a very tough competitor, and someone who made the best of his abilities.

Venkatesh Prasad (Indian cricketer)**:** *I don't want to sound immodest, but for some reason I always felt I had the mental advantage whenever I was bowling to Gary. There was something in me that made me feel I could get him out. There's no doubt he is a great batsman – the records prove that. To go on and play 100 tests is something that shows his ability, his mental toughness and his physical fitness.*

But then, there are a few players whom you think you have an edge over, and for me Gary was one of them. I think he might have sensed this too. But, this doesn't mean I dominated him. There were plenty of times when he got the better of me. Off the field I had a chance to have a chat with Gary more than once. I found him very approachable, and a fantastic guy even though he keeps to himself. The fact remains that after playing cricket for all this while he was never involved in any controversy.

One thing about Gary that everyone admired was his commitment and attitude towards the game. This is what enabled him to go from strength to strength in his career.

9

Vulnerable cricketers... easy targets

The Benefit Match '96

It was light-hearted banter, almost like teenagers talking about smoking cigarettes, but it had increased towards the end of the tour. Guys were joking that the match-fixing 'thing' seemed rife in India. There was a lot of jesting about throwing matches and how much money there was to be made. It sounds terrible now, but we didn't know any better. At least I certainly didn't and I'm pretty certain most of the guys were genuinely clueless about the reality of the situation. That's why it was easy to be jovial and trivialize the situation.

We had been told by manager Robbie Muzzell that there might be 'shady figures' lurking around the dressing rooms 'up to no good'. He'd caught wind of something and felt duty-bound to warn us, but the vagueness of what he said made it pretty clear that he, too, was simply acting on whispers. As far as I was aware only one of us had been confronted with anything approaching reality and that was Pat Symcox, whose curiosity and bullish approach made him the obvious candidate to discover things first.

We'd had a regular set of functions to attend in every city we visited and there were the usual embassy and consulate cocktail parties to attend. Symmo told a few of us that he'd been chatting to Mohammad Azharuddin and had asked him whether it actually happened. Azhar just laughed and said 'Of course it happens; it's been happening for years.' Then he explained how it worked. Symmo didn't go into the details. So I knew it was real from then on, but it was someone else's nightmare as far as I was concerned. It would never affect me. Or it wouldn't until that fateful afternoon when Hansie called us together for a meeting in his hotel room in Bombay.

What was about to happen was a diabolical moment for cricket although, personally, I still find it more bewildering than anything else. I just didn't know what to think. It was crazy.

Nine weeks in India, 27 domestic flights, beaten in the final Test and the tour was over. At least, nearly over. One crazy, miserable, meaningless fixture remained and we couldn't have cared any less about it. We had no more than nine or 10 fit players. It was basically a benefit match for Mohinder Armanath but several weeks earlier, in a bid to boost ticket sales (apparently), the Indian Board had asked the UCB to agree to an upgrade to full one-day international status. Ali Bacher had agreed, much to Hansie's and the team's frustration and anger.

Now, with the squad in disarray and virtually unable to put a team in the field, Hansie tried to get the match cancelled. No chance. It was going ahead - end of discussion.

So on the afternoon of 13 December Hansie started calling us in our rooms. We were required for a meeting. Some guys had been sleeping, some were really sick with high temperatures and some of us were physically healthy but mentally unable to focus on much more than the flight home in two days' time. It wasn't a big room, but big enough. A few people sat on the bed, others on a couch and chairs, some on the floor. Hansie was very calm.

'We've been offered money to throw the game, a lot of money,' he said. I swear you could have heard a pin drop on to a carpet at that moment. Nobody moved a muscle. In retrospect I think I'd gone into instant shock. Even if I had wanted to speak, I would have been unable to. Nobody said a word. Hansie carried on talking, slowly but clearly.

I listened but it was out of respect for the captain and a strange fascination with what he was saying rather than any intention to carry out the instructions. I knew within a few seconds that I could not become involved. I literally could not. I would rather have given up my career. But I listened.

He had been asked to create the 'perfect fix.' Every single spread had to work out exactly. He spelt out the details of how the match needed to pan out, with a spread of scores we needed to be within every five overs – sometimes even more precise. The details were blurry at the time and they haven't become any clearer in the years since, but one thing I do remember clearly was what I had to do. I had started sweating. It was a bad dream, it just wasn't happening. I kept thinking: 'How do batsmen get out deliberately?' It was ridiculous. After eight overs we needed to be one wicket down – me – and we needed to have under 25 runs on the board.

How would I get out? The idea was absurd. I'd never got out deliberately in my life.

You have to remember exactly what sort of situation we were in at the time before you ask why nobody jumped up and told him to shut up. Hansie Cronje was a seriously respected individual within world cricket, let alone the team that was sitting in his room. He had an exceptional record as a captain and had become a good friend to many of the team. Against that background we sat and listened, almost as though we were displaying our respect, at least hearing him out. His reputation was such that people's minds began wandering, tossing up whether it was actually feasible or not.

He mentioned a couple of times that it would be worth between 60 and 70 thousand rand each. It was a lot of money, make no mistake. It was for a hit-and-giggle game that we couldn't care less about and, although we didn't know anything about match-fixing (at least, the vast majority of us didn't) nobody had been fined, disciplined or even caught for it. Yes, for one second, the first second, as I sat dazed on the floor, I thought about it. But it was a brief second. I knew it was dirty money and, anyway, how could I get out deliberately? I always knew I couldn't do that. What shot would you play that wouldn't look too obvious? Maybe you could ask your partner to run you out. Hudders…? The idea was so ridiculous it made me laugh. Privately.

Vulnerable cricketers…easy targets

The details were staggering. We had to be between 60 and 70 for two wickets after 15 overs and so the list went on, down to the last wicket. And it wasn't a massive score by any means. Perhaps, to some batsmen, it was the skill of manipulating an innings that appealed as much as the money. I still find it very hard to imagine, the whole thing. Apart from anything else, there was a mountain of information to memorise.

Hansie would have had to give us all a sheet of paper with all the spreads and targets on it. Match-fixing is a desperately sad and serious subject these days, of course, but humour can often be found in the gloomiest moments and I couldn't help imagining what would happen if someone forgot what the next target was. What would you do? Send for gloves? Keep the sheet of paper in your pocket and pretend it was something else while you read it?

There was a cold, cold feeling in the room and deathly silence. The cash, as I recall, was in a briefcase in the lobby of the hotel, or perhaps it was in a nearby room. Either way, Hansie said a man would bring it straight away if anyone wanted to see it. He wanted to prove to everyone that it was for real and available.

The whole talk lasted about ten minutes, but it felt a lot longer. Eventually Daryll Cullinan and Hudders spoke out. They both spoke along similar lines and they represented all of our views. If they hadn't spoken I'm sure someone else would have. I think there were a few others ready to speak out. They said we'd be crazy to even think about it and reminded us of what the implications would be if we were caught. They both said they wanted no part of it. Hudders said we were ridiculous even to think about it, let alone talk about it. The same feeling filtered through the room and the meeting was clearly over. There were no waverers or doubters.

Over and Out

After the game, amongst all the resentment and pain, there was more dark humour and irony. About half the spreads had come true naturally. There were a few quiet laughs in corners of the dressing room.

I don't like admitting it, but the fact that we'd said 'No' to fixing the match hadn't made the slightest difference to the way we approached it. We still resented every minute of it and, frankly, didn't care what happened. I was keeping wicket in place of Dave Richardson, who was one of the sick ones, and we played all four spinners, purely on the basis that everyone fit had to play. Fanie de Villiers was the worst hit of all. He stayed in the dressing room until the last possible moment, covered with iced towels in an attempt to control his temperature, which I think was 103. He bowled five overs with the new ball before almost fainting and returning straight to the dressing room.

There were only two great cricketing moments during the game, as I recall. The first was Sachin Tendulkar's century, which was pure class despite the quality of the opposition. The second involved his dismissal. A delivery from Nicky Boje turned and bounced enough to beat the shoulder of the bat, which was quite an achievement against Tendulkar on 114. Not having practised my emergency glovework for many weeks, I was slow to react and was out of position as Tendulkar stretched out of his crease. However, in a flash of inspiration I deliberately chested the ball down towards the stumps and effected a stumping of rare brilliance. I always meant to teach the move to Mark Boucher before I retired but never got round to it.

The match ended in defeat and near disaster for Hansie, who lost his temper with a changing room attendant. He did have sudden mood changes and this was one of them. He was ready to beat the guy up. Nobody knew what he'd done wrong, but it could have become nasty. Hansie had the man by the throat before Robbie Muzzell pulled him off and calmed him down. It pretty much summed up the way the tour had ended. It was the culmination of weeks and weeks of frustration and, in Hansie's case, pressures and contradictions that we simply knew nothing about.

That evening, as we were packing to leave, finally, there was a knock on my door. It was Hansie. Our rooms were next door. We chatted briefly about the tour in general and about going home, but there was clearly something else on his mind. Then he asked if I could help him write a letter. His resignation.

I was almost as stunned as I had been about 'the offer'. I told him he was being ridiculous and that he had the team's full support. I reminded him that everyone was feeling lousy after a tour like the one we'd just had and that he was over-reacting. But he wrote the letter. I don't know whether he gave it to anyone but I had the impression he was quite serious about quitting.

10

Mastering the subcontinent

Pakistan '97

There was an intense, almost obsessive drive to win a Test series on the subcontinent. Having failed in India a few months earlier, the desire to achieve it in Pakistan was immense. Once again, as in India, the local side hadn't lost a series for over a decade – 16 years, in fact.

Positive memories came flooding back. I had made 188 during the World Cup in Pakistan. But the first Test, also in Rawalpindi, started bizarrely when Azhar Mahmood scored a century on debut and added a world record 151 for the 10th wicket with Mushtaq Ahmed. From dominating the match we were suddenly batting to save it, replying to first innings total of 456.

I made 98, which was especially irritating after putting in seven hours' hard work. Jonty Rhodes was the only batsman I ever knew who could say it felt 'almost the same' to score 98 or 100, because it was a team game as far as he was concerned and he wasn't going to allow himself to be upset about two runs. But he was just as pleased to score a century for his country as the rest of us were and when Jo scored his hundred at Lord's to have his name preserved forever on the most famous Honours Board in the game, he was mighty proud. There will, though, always be something significantly different about falling a couple of runs short, and it certainly made a big difference to me when I fell a couple of runs short, despite feeling genuinely happy to have made a difference to the Test.

The 98 in Rawalpindi did much to save the match and keep us in the series – it was probably one of my best innings from a team perspective, but it isn't recorded as a hundred and therefore it's largely forgotten. Even by me. It might have felt like a hundred to Jonty, though.

The match was drawn although it was also memorable for a typical moment of hilarious madness from Pat Symcox. Having had his third or fourth lbw appeal turned down within a very short space of time, Symmo blew a gasket and was leaping about and screaming as though he'd been stung by a wasp. I think the umpire caught a bit of flak, too. Having quickly calmed down and regained his composure, Symmo displayed his knack for quick thinking and started talking into the umpire's walkie-talkie – a direct line of communication to the match referee, Ranjan Madugalle. I can't be sure what he said but it was something like: "Go easy on me, Ranjan, we don't get paid much…"

Ranjan later admitted he couldn't help laughing and there's a very good chance the resultant fine was a few thousand rupees less than it might have been.

Bouch

Dave Richardson suffered just the second injury of his career during the game. A broken finger meant he had missed the '96 World Cup and now a bad hip allowed Mark Boucher to make his debut as a fresh-faced 19-year-old. He was still completely jet-lagged and confused after a 24-hour journey via Dubai the day before the match but he stubbornly maintained a brave face throughout practice.

The second Test was held in Sheikhupura, the first Test to be staged there. The stadium was adequate, but there was no hotel deemed suitable for our purposes so we were driven in a presidential-style motorcade every morning and evening from Lahore, a journey that lasted about an hour and 20 minutes. For the media, who didn't have the benefit of police cars, sirens, flashing lights and motorcycle outriders, the trip was close to two hours each way. By the third day they had 'wised up', however, and paid a brave taxi driver to stick close to our bus and travel in the wake of the debris and destruction we created on the crowded, narrow streets.

Play had to start early because daylight ended at about 5.00 pm. This meant a 7.00 am departure from the hotel in order to be at the ground our customary two hours before play. Most of us boarded the bus with pillows and blankets and carried on dozing, as best we could, while the motorcade bulldozed its way to Sheikhupura.

It had rained heavily overnight and when we finally arrived at the ground it was to discover that the covers had leaked and the pitch was wet. When we saw the groundstaff attempting to dry it with an old mattress and other pieces of torn sponge, we knew immediately we wouldn't be playing that day. An hour later we were climbing back on the bus for the return drive to Lahore.

Everyone was feeling a bit gloomy and there was definitely an uncharacteristically cool edge to the air that we hadn't experienced before, but that didn't explain why Jacques Kallis was wrapped up like a polar explorer, looked as white as a sheet and was still shivering.

That night Jacques deteriorated further and was diagnosed with appendicitis.

Jonty, who was set to be named as 12th man for the Test, took Jacques' place while Jacques recovered from surgery at the famous hospital that Imran Khan campaigned to build in the early 1990s. After the first day's play we visited Jacques and those of us who were nervous and concerned for him could not have been more pleasantly surprised. He was in a magnificently equipped ward and was obviously in exceptionally good hands. He could not have been better looked after or more comfortable anywhere else in the world.

Adam B

Further showers disrupted the game and it ended, inevitably, as a draw. I opened the batting with Adam Bacher and our time as an opening pair will always be one of my favourite memories. The job of opening is unique and bonds the players who do it. We weren't together long but the experience was especially rewarding. Adam has a rare sense of humour and he was immensely popular with the team; on the field he was as gutsy and determined as almost anyone I played with. He also carries the distinction of claiming the most 'impossible' catch I have ever seen, a one-handed grab from short leg at a full-blooded drive to get rid of Graham Thorpe at Lord's in 1998.

But perhaps my most abiding memory of Adam will be the night we spent in Amsterdam a few months later after doing our best to lose a one-day game to Holland. We'd slumped to 80-5, or something similar. Adam was injured and not playing. But I managed to scrape together a hundred and put together a big stand with Mark Boucher. That night was soccer World Cup semi-final night, Holland against Brazil.

My great friend, Wulf van Alkemade, had organized an evening in the most packed, patriotic and atmospheric bar I've ever seen. In truth, every bar in Amsterdam must have been like that on World Cup semi-final night. Wulf had encouraged us to wear something orange to show our support and we were only too happy to oblige. While most of us opted for a scarf or even a shirt, Adam bought an enormous orange hat to go with various other orange accessories. He cheered and shouted throughout the game to such an extent that locals were convinced he was one of them.

At the final whistle Adam was seen face down on the table howling with indignation and misery at the result. You could never have seen a more Dutch South African at that moment, and we were all trying hard that night!

Adam's sense of humour and popularity very quickly won him a lot of friends despite what I imagine would have been a difficult start to his international career in the shadow of his uncle, Ali. I had the perception that people were cautious around him, wary of their language and the target of their complaints. But it lasted barely a week before we realized what a great team man he was and the huge amount of value he added to the team and the change room environment. I'm only sorry he didn't have the opportunity to play more international cricket because he certainly had the stomach for a fight.

All square

So we moved to Faisalabad all square, with the series up for grabs. After my first year of Test cricket I couldn't help setting goals for myself, or at least dreaming of the achievements I thought would be most special, the most I could hope for in what I hoped would be a career of five or six years. I rarely made these target-dreams public, but it was important to push myself. The top three, in no particular order, were to score two centuries in a Test, make 10 Test centuries and carry my bat through an innings. In Faisalabad, I achieved the last one.

A directive had been issued by the Pakistan Cricket Board to spice up the wicket for the last Test after two flat pitches in the previous matches. With Waqar and Wasim in the line-up, they had reason to feel confident. With Donald and Pollock in ours, so did we.

At 98-7 a few minutes before lunch on the first day, however, we were feeling much less confident. It was a disaster.

Symmo came to the crease and was as bubbly as ever. He wouldn't stop talking and, as usual, he had a theory for everything. I was trying hard to concentrate on the crisis we were in, but Symmo was a welcome and amusing distraction – as much for the bowlers and fielders than me. There is no doubt the distraction helped me rather than hindered me because I was forced to relax rather than tense up, but I'm not sure the Symmo batting method could ever be taught. For all the humour, though, he was extremely proud of his batting and very brave. He believed he could make a difference and he often did. It even reached the stage when he was used as pinch-hitter in a couple of one-day games in Sharjah and made an important 60 in the final.

Although Symmo scored a Test century against Pakistan a couple of months later at the Wanderers, in similarly dire circumstances, I don't think he would rate this innings much behind the hundred. In both matches the game situation was difficult and tense. We added 124 for the eighth wicket and I'd gone from about 20 to 92 before Symmo was dismissed.

He had also enjoyed the most outrageous piece of luck I have ever seen, and not just on a cricket field. He played back to a ball from Saqlain that spun into him and kept low. It was dead straight and Symmo missed it. The 'death rattle' was a fraction of a second away. But it never came. Moin Khan, the Pakistani wicket keeper, leapt in the air to celebrate but as he landed he made the same noise as a cat when someone stands on its tail. The bails were still in place. The ball had passed between the middle and off stumps without dislodging the bails. It was a classic, crazy, funny subcontinent moment. Always expect the unexpected.

Steve Dunne, the umpire from New Zealand, walked very slowly down the pitch to see exactly what had happened. He had also, clearly, seen the ball 'hit' the stumps but nothing happen. I don't think he intended it to be a comic moment, but Dunne scratched his head and then slowly took off his glasses and began cleaning them. It was a scene straight from Charlie Chaplin.

Having checked to see that the ball hadn't somehow become squashed out of shape, the umpires ascertained that the groundsman had set the stumps slightly too far apart and he was recalled to fix his embarrassing mistake. At least, that was what most observers believed. Actually, it was the umpires' mistake because they are responsible for checking and declaring conditions fit and ready for play. Symmo added another 55 runs to his total and, although cricket doesn't always work out this simply, the extra runs were enough to win the Test – and series.

Paul Adams did everything he could to stick around and showed what a determined fighter he could be, even at the age of 20. The nervous 90s were even worse than normal because the scoreboard operators weren't the best around and there appeared to be a shortage of certain numbers. It was the original, club-style board with metal plates which hung on rusty nails. For a while my score just read 9 as all the available 8s were being used. There was some confusion in the crowd when I took a single about ten minutes later and the scoreboard showed 100. The applause started, the guys were cheering on the balcony and the congratulations started. I was aware of the confusion but very happy to take the hundred – I wasn't bothered about any nagging doubts. Still,

I waited a few moments so see if anyone was going to spot the mistake, if there had been one, but nobody did. The century was official.

The tension and relief were too much for Paul and he was bowled almost immediately. But my worst doubts became reality within minutes of getting back into the dressing room where I noticed the television scorecard had me on 99 not out and I heard there was a discrepancy in the official scorebook. Two of the three scorers had 99 but the senior man had three figures. A few minutes later, it was finally confirmed – 100 not out. South Africa 239.

The official scorers were extremely discreet, they never actually confirmed what they had done but, in the spirit of the game, I think they reworked the books. There were rumours that they had been seen rubbing away at the leg byes column and adding a single to my score. Did I care? No!

Neither side batted well for the entire match although it was a personal triumph for Symmo, who added 55 as nightwatchman in the second innings to, once again, keep us alive.

Despite Symmo's efforts, nobody gave us a real chance of defending 145 in the fourth innings. But Polly produced his best spell for South Africa at that stage to collect 5-37 as we won by 53 runs. It certainly ranks amongst the three strangest Tests of my 101.

The greatest challenge that evening was how to celebrate appropriately. Even in the most excited moments we were always aware of the conflict of interests between Muslim culture and our preferred method of toasting a victory, and we were careful not to offend.

SA Breweries had once again worked a piece of diplomatic magic through the SA Embassy in Karachi and several (quite a few, to be honest) cases of Castle Lager had been subtly delivered to the hotel. We shut off the team room, made it as noise-proof as possible and – let rip. It was a fantastic celebration and release of tension. We were as strong a unit that night as I ever saw. It wasn't like being at home, or in England, Australia or anywhere else. In those places people have preferred destinations and the team fragments. That night we felt like 14 brothers.

Watershed

In the years since that night, Mark Boucher – who was playing his second Test - spoke to me often about his regret that home victories are not celebrated in a similar style. His belief was that the team should stay together for a reasonable period of time, a couple of hours at least, to savour the moment and cherish the memories. And I think he's right. There will always be 'downs' in the game, but they won't feel as miserable if the good times are properly appreciated.

The whole tour was a watershed for me. I scored runs in every Test and I pushed my average up towards 40, a figure I always believed was essential to prove my worth to the side. I played one of the best pace attacks in the world with confidence and, to be fair, there are many who might say that the spinners in that series were amongst the best, too.

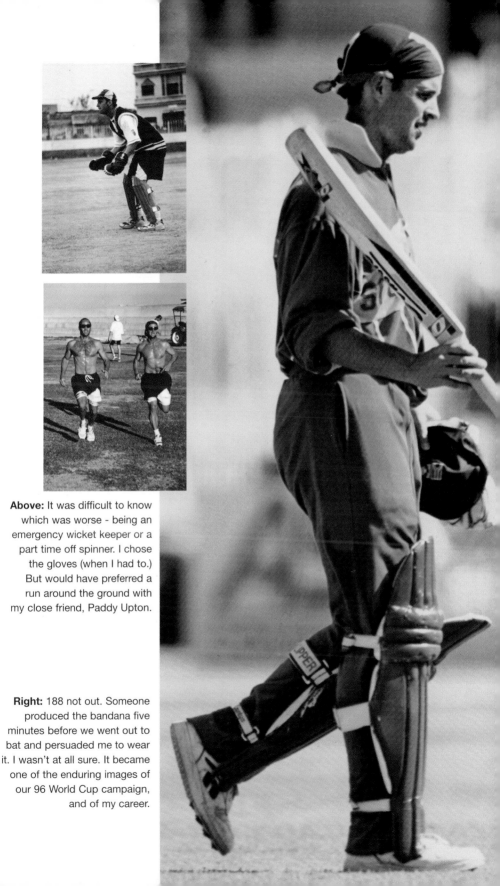

Above: It was difficult to know which was worse - being an emergency wicket keeper or a part time off spinner. I chose the gloves (when I had to.) But would have preferred a run around the ground with my close friend, Paddy Upton.

Right: 188 not out. Someone produced the bandana five minutes before we went out to bat and persuaded me to wear it. I wasn't at all sure. It became one of the enduring images of our 96 World Cup campaign, and of my career.

Above: Where it all began, Australia '93-'94. Wide-eyed and wondrous, happy to be in the picture let alone the team. Unable to believe my luck. If anybody had said then I'd play 100 Tests I would have asked what they were smoking.

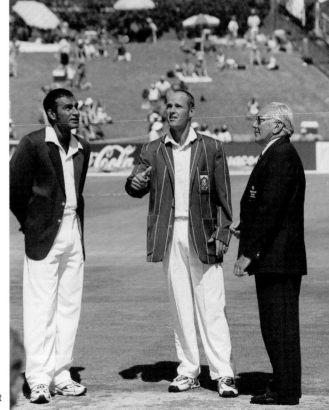

Right: One-Test wonder, as captain. The match was delayed by 24 hours, I lost the toss, Pat Symcox scored a hundred at number ten and Shoaib Akhtar hit me on the head with a bouncer. Then it rained and we drew. At least I'll never forget the game!

Talking tactics with Daryll Cullinan. We thrived on the
competition between us and drove each other forward in the
quest for more runs and hundreds. It was a great shame our
'contest' didn't last longer.

Above: The 'other' team photograph. No doubt Hansie was at the centre of the joke. Kirsten, as always, never far from the shoulder of Goolam (nothing could ever go too badly wrong with Goolam close by!)

Above: No matter what he did and how it finished, it doesn't change the fact that Hansie was a great friend, captain and companion for the majority of his life and my career. Here we celebrate victory over England at Lord's.

I'm often asked why I was so successful on the subcontinent and the truth is that it's easier batting up front in that part of the world. It's actually easier facing the new ball than in any other part of the world and, if you survive until the spinners come on, you've hopefully got 30 or 40 on the board and your eye is in. If you come in at 140-3 against two spinners with four men around the bat you don't have a very comfortable start.

I'd quickly like to add here that green, seaming wickets in other parts of the world – and at home - which flattened out beautifully into 'belters' after the first couple of hours didn't help my average! Having said that, I hope I will be remembered as someone who could also play on the 'greentops'. My best record on home grounds was at Kingsmead, so I wasn't just a flat-track accumulator.

If the final day victory at Faisalabad was strange, equally strange, and only a little less odd, was the day Symmo took us carpet shopping earlier in the tour. As usual, Pat had made all the useful 'contacts' in every city we visited. On this occasion his new friend was a police officer and, in our experience on the subcontinent, anyone connected with security, the government or the law was invariably connected to anyone and everyone connected with anything and everything useful. Symmo was on a significant mission to purchase several of the beautiful, hand-woven rugs that had become a feature of our tours to that part of the world. And a couple of us gratefully accepted his invitation to come along.

We were treated like royalty. It was the policeman's cousin, or brother, or best friend – I can't remember. But it wasn't important. We were offered tea and cool drinks, while the 'showing' of rugs was more of a performance than a sales pitch. Inevitably, after the effort of unrolling 300 carpets, a little heat was applied to the prospective buyers to make sure the effort was worthwhile. And that was when we were most grateful to be in the company of Symmo. He was the ultimate negotiator and deal-maker, and we could happily smile at the salesmen secure in the knowledge that big Patrick was looking after us. We were so confused by the end of the display that we had no idea of what we wanted or why. But Symmo negotiated on behalf of all of us and I have little doubt that the rugs I carried back will last as long as I do. Longer, probably, if the 'knots per square inch' have anything to do with it.

Adam Bacher (South African opening batsman): *From the moment I walked into the South African dressing room for the first time, expecting to be overawed and nervous, Gary treated me as an equal with the same respect as everyone else. It almost made me feel uncomfortable! Our achievements were like chalk and cheese but he believed that if you were good enough to be chosen for South Africa then you were certainly good enough for him. In the two and a half years I was with the team I realised that respect applied to everyone Gary played with and against.*

My only regret is that we didn't share any really big partnerships. We had three century stands but nothing to define our time together, like a 250. For a lot of the time we were at the opposite ends of the form spectrum so we didn't quite 'click' as an opening pair. Which doesn't mean to say I didn't enjoy our time together because they were the happiest years of my career.

I would like to say, however, that I was only celebrating as much as I did in Amsterdam that night because I had a fractured collarbone and wasn't going to be fit for at least two weeks. So the guys made me 'night captain' and all good captains lead from the front.

Gary's greatest innings? No question at all, it was that hundred against Holland. You can forget the 275 and all the other Test hundreds; none could possibly compare to the conditions in which he scored those runs in The Hague. He had a procession of partners who could hardly stand up at the other end and Gary was more than a little weary himself. I can understand how the guys lost the Dutch match four years earlier.

But the best memory with Gary was facing Shoaib together at the Wanderers in early 1998. We'd faced him a couple of months earlier in Pakistan on a wicket so flat we were debating whether we needed to use pads. Shoaib was rapid but he was a youngster.

Then he came to the Wanderers and it was one of the 'old style' pitches, fast and bouncy with a bit of green. After his first over we were staring at each other with wide eyes and half grins, both thinking: 'Are you seeing what I'm seeing?'

Tim Noakes (Sports scientist and UCT professor):
Extracts from the essay he wrote on Kirsten in March 1996:

He considers that he has improved as a cricketer since he began international cricket but he has much still to achieve. He would like to be the first choice opener for South Africa for at least the next five years and to score 10 centuries from 100 balls in international one-day cricket. Aside from personal goals, he identifies strongly with, and is inspired by the goals that the team have set. In his own favourite saying, he 'shocked' himself when he achieved his first one-day century against England at Centurion Park in January 1996. Less than two months later, he had almost added two more. His innings of 188 not out against the United Arab Emirates in Rawalpindi during the 1996 Wills World Cup came off 159 balls and is the record in the World Cup. Kirsten was denied the world record score for a one-day international when a straight drive early in the innings that would have carried to the boundary, was inadvertently 'fielded' by a slow-moving umpire, preventing the certain four that would have carried him three runs beyond the current world record. But satisfied with the one record, Kirsten did not refer once on the tour to the incident that cost him a cricketing world record. Like all great self-motivators, Kirsten sets himself achievable goals. His goal in the recent series against England was to score three centuries; he achieved two.

In retrospect, Gary considers that his father erred in his approach to his son's failures on the cricket field. He was too critical of Gary's failures and was too committed to the belief that the sole measure of a batsman's success is simply the number of runs that he scores in each innings. The undesirable effect of this approach was that it induced a fear of failure in Gary. Modern psychologists would suggest that, in a sport as complex as cricket, the paternal influence in the Kirsten family may have been less constructive than ideal.

The effect on Kirsten was to inhibit any natural game that he might have developed. He learned to avoid playing risky shots lest he should get himself out. His goal became one of accumulating runs. He considers this to be the wrong goal for a young player as it prevents him from developing a full range of strokes at the very time that the acquisition of such skills is the most easy.

This experience has taught Gary that when he brings up his own children, his goal will be to inculcate the determination and ambition for them to express themselves in all walks of life but not at the cost of limiting the way they do things. In his case, the paternal emphasis on scoring runs limited his full development as a young cricketer. He would personally specifically avoid placing any emphasis whatsoever on the need to score runs in schoolboy cricket.

Besides this pressure to score runs on the cricket field, Kirsten felt that he had also been over-pressurised to study hard at school. His reaction was to rebel by devoting his time to sport and not to academic endeavour. This, too, he felt was wrong as he considers it dangerous to force a child at the impressionable age of 16 when the child is learning to think for himself. At that age, the adolescent is fighting for freedom, in particular for an independence of thoughts and a freedom of expression. The parental goal at that age should be to give their children the freedom to develop their independence with discipline. In particular, the young adolescent must be taught the importance of personal discipline. He considers that the pressure to succeed especially in school sport is irrelevant as success at that level is of no consequence.

Kirsten was particularly incensed by his father's refusal to allow him to go on an overseas rugby tour in December, as this would cause him to miss playing in the Nuffield cricket week and hence prevent his selection to the Nuffield team. He soon learned that performance in school sport is not particularly important when, the year after captaining the South African schools team in 1985, he was batting at number 9 for the University of Cape Town.

11

A great honour, but not for me

Captaincy

People often asked me about the captaincy of the national team, and whether I was motivated by the prospect. I wasn't. It is undoubtedly a fantastic honour but there were a couple of other people who could have performed the role and fulfilled the duties as well as, if not better than I could. I knew I could have done the job well but we all thought Hansie would be around a lot longer than he was, and I seemed bound to finish my career before he did. The other candidates were also younger than me.

Apart from those practical issues, there were others that strongly dissuaded me from becoming a candidate, despite being vice-captain for a couple of years before resigning the position in 1998.

The captaincy system is wrong. There is far too much emphasis on the captain's off-field duties. Press conferences and interviews are never-ending in the build-up to every series and every match, let alone the semi-official duties like after-dinner talks and sponsors' functions. It is natural for people to want to talk to the national captain, but a system had developed – and Hansie was partly to blame for not off-loading more appointments – whereby the duties of the captain were so overwhelming that he simply could not, with the greatest will in the world, give his best to the team in the build-up to matches and while they were happening.

With responsibility comes power, and with power comes responsibility. Hansie, I believe, at one stage of his career, ended up with too much of both. He and Ali Bacher were making many of the important decisions between them, with the board members, but how the national captain was expected to focus on the main job was beyond me. Hansie was often a 'shadow' of himself. I presumed that his many media and sponsor duties were distracting him.

Not much changed in the years after Hansie. Shaun Pollock and Graeme Smith had just as much to deal with and I felt just the same. I am amazed by the stupidity of it. I never shunned the media, or preferred not to conduct interviews - far from it. I would have thoroughly enjoyed being part of a roster, if that is the right word. Not something 'fixed' but a flexible schedule of media appointments that would relieve the captain of the hundreds of interviews that crowd his professional diary and cramp what little remains of his private life.

Many interviews are pain-free and genuinely challenging, but there are so many that come from minor, nondescript, amateur organizations that are pure misery. 'Hi Gary, it's Fred's Personal FM here. Could you spare us two minutes?' The truth is, by the time they've called back an hour later, they are already running ten minutes behind schedule. The 'two minutes' they mentioned actually means 12 minutes and by then you've missed the dinner date with your colleagues and end up having another lonely night in with a room-service club sandwich. Senior players and the coach simply have to be involved in the equation, almost whether the captain likes it or not. Besides, variety is the spice of life.

My services as vice-captain weren't really required. My input at selection meetings was appreciated but I occasionally felt as if my most important role was to make the tea. It quickly came to pass that I didn't actually need to be a part of selection meetings and it seemed right to leave it to those who actually wielded the power. I have never been a power-seeker in my life, but a small, considered contribution to the process was fine. It wasn't often sought and didn't happen often, and that was why I resigned the post. As far as Hansie was concerned, the vice-captain was only there in the event that he wasn't – he had no desire or need to involve me or use me in the day-to-day running of the team. My view of the vice-captaincy however, never affected my respect for or appreciation of Hansie as captain. I became immune to the whole situation; it was a harmless irrelevance, so I gave it up.

Shaun was appointed and that seemed the natural progression. Hansie was captain for the foreseeable future but Shaun was the natural man to take over in an emergency. He was a brilliant performer on the field and had always been a prolific contributor at team meetings. His knowledge of the game was as good as anyone's in the team and, above all, he was respected.

One Test wonder

Before it ended, however, I had a single taste of what it was all about. Hansie finally succumbed to a knee operation he'd required for some time and I took over for the first Test against Pakistan at the Wanderers in February 1998.

The off-field workload came as quite a shock and even more reason, I believed, why Hansie should have delegated more. I hadn't had much experience of answering so many 'obvious' questions – 'Are you looking forward to captaining your country?' – or so many of them. It takes skill to answer a question like that a dozen times and still sound sincere, or even interested.

There seemed to be endless meetings, too. Meetings with the UCB, the match referee, team meetings, management meetings and meetings with sponsors.

Just as I thought I'd made it to match day, it was postponed for 24 hours. Two of the Pakistan team had been assaulted in Jo'burg city centre the night before and obviously the tourists weren't happy about it.

As captain I sat in the meetings with the tourists' management as they called for time to consider their position. They were very unhappy. I had the impression they would

A great honour, but not for me

have liked a longer delay. In fact, I had the feeling they weren't interested in playing the Test at all. At one point I had the distinct impression they were pushing for a victory by default.

By midday details of this 'assault' starting emerging and the press and media were all over it like dogs with a bone. It had taken place in an establishment with an adult theme and, apparently, there was some confusion over the bill and exactly what was included and what wasn't. And what the service charge was for. I began dreading the media questions that would follow. What was my opinion? What did I think? For goodness' sake…

When play finally got under way we were saved from disaster by a world record ninth- wicket stand of 195 between Symmo and Mark Boucher and, later, by the rain. I was hit on the head by a Shoaib Akhtar bouncer, the second of three occasions in my career, but not the most serious. That was to come six years later in Pakistan.

On the fourth day it rained heavily from early in the morning and by lunchtime it was clear we weren't going to get on the field. By mid-afternoon we returned to the Sandton Sun and dispersed to the gym, the swimming pool or just the comfort of our rooms.

Ernie Els arrived at the hotel a little later than evening and, with no chance of a result in the Test and a weather forecast that suggested it would carry on raining for the whole of the fifth day, a small group of us settled in at the Villamoura bar with Ernie and, given the circumstances, decided to break the normal mid-Test routine by having a beer.

I woke on the fifth morning not feeling as strong as I would have preferred. I opened the curtains to see the kind of bright blue, summer sky that Jo'burg specializes in. Oh dear.

Pakistan declared immediately and we started batting straight away. I had recovered all my strength and senses after a good workout and warm-up session but I still wasn't quick enough to avoid the Shoaib bouncer in the second over that clanged into the side of my head.

Fortunately Adam Bacher and I batted very well and survived the session. Clearly the Test was saved. Pakistan would had needed to take seven or eight wickets in the morning session to have had a chance of forcing victory and everybody accepted that the match was a draw.

Ernie

It was fantastic to meet up with Ernie again. We had first met at 'nets' a few years earlier. I was near the completion of a 60-hour batting marathon at Cape Town's Waterfront in aid of the Red Cross Children's Hospital when Ernie and Joel Stransky pitched up to bowl a few deliveries. I can't recall what the prize was for getting me out, but there was no way either of them was getting it. Ernie bowls very decent off-breaks. From a height of about nine feet they're always coming at you from way above eye-level, but I was able to handle them, despite the laughter. Afterwards we chatted away about sport for hours and it was amazing to hear how much he followed our game and supported us, no matter where in the world he was playing. Getting hold of

Test match results in Hawaii, Miami or Hong Kong isn't the easiest, but Ernie reckons he always manages it somehow. The cricketers all follow the golf Majors religiously and cheer on Ernie and Retief Goosen every day. He's a genuine legend of South African sport; it was difficult to believe that he thought the same of us.

Ernie plays four Majors a year and if he has one bad day the whole country gets down in the dumps and criticizes. If I had one bad day then I had the chance to put it right two days later, and we played 15 Tests and 30 one-dayers in a year. It was difficult not to feel inspired by him, and even more so because he has stayed so true to his personality – a genuine and sincere 'oke' who enjoys a chat and has no pretensions, despite his incredible success and resultant wealth.

During the Test Symmo was being bounced constantly by Shoaib and Waqar. They felt, probably because of his extreme age, that he was susceptible to the short ball and, to be fair, Symmo wasn't looking terribly comfortable. His answer was to hurl a mountain of verbal abuse back at them, yelling at them to pitch the ball up: 'What's wrong with you? You're scared of being driven!' he shouted loud enough to be heard in the pavilion.

Eventually the bowlers would fall into the trap and every time they pitched it up Symmo smashed it back over their heads for four to roars of approval from the dressing room balcony. He could really bat a bit, Symmo. I think he became just the third man to score a century batting at number 10. It was a fabulous effort.

I pondered for the first time during the rest of that series the possibility of 'standardising' Test pitches. It seemed far too bizarre that a team of individuals as talented as the Pakistanis could struggle so much in our conditions. They were brilliant but almost routinely hopeless against fast bowling on fast, bouncy pitches, and the same applied to us for many of our tours to the subcontinent in regard to spin bowling. It seemed wrong that conditions should play such a role. After a period of rationalizing, and talking to my team mates, it was obvious that I was backing a loser. Different conditions, however extreme, were what made champions. Nevertheless it amazed me for the next five or six years that, every time a team from the subcontinent came to South Africa, they struggled and never did themselves justice although the frequency of tours these days means that will change – surely.

Hansie made a rapid recovery from his knee operation and returned straight to the side for the second Test of the series at Kingsmead. He was desperate to take charge again. It hadn't been much fun for him watching me at the Wanderers although, to be fair, he didn't interfere. He watched from the dressing room balcony on the first day but otherwise he left me to get on with it.

As things turned out I was lucky Hansie did rush himself back. At Kingsmead we left Symmo out of the team and proceeded to be ransacked by Mushtaq Ahmed on a pitch that was turning square by the third day. Things might have been very different if Azhar Mahmood hadn't scored his third hundred against us in the space of about a month. From 153-8 on the first afternoon Azhar made another 130 and then Shoaib took 5-43 to earn them what had seemed a highly unlikely lead. Mushtaq took six wickets in the second innings to win the match for them and finish with nine.

Lecture

The day after the match Ali Bacher came into the dressing room and delivered a half-hour lecture that left us in no doubt about what he thought of our performance. He wasn't afraid of using a few strong words and suggesting that we were letting the South African fans down and getting very well paid to do it. He said that if things didn't change on the field then they would certainly change off it. It was a 'full and frank exchange of views' session and the threats weren't particularly well veiled – if we didn't improve we had two choices, either expect pay cuts or, worse, expect to be dropped. There were plenty of young players waiting to take our places, Bacher said. It was the first time I'd heard Ali come 'hard' at the players in all the years I'd been involved. It made me realize that one wasn't just part of a little team and that we were representing South Africa and were responsible to our supporters. Poor performances simply weren't going to be tolerated and he made no secret of the fact that he felt we were just bumbling along without the required passion and determination.

Generally Ali was an inspiration to me and I had an unqualified respect for him as an administrator. I know he was criticized for being a one-man show and sometimes autocratic but he also kept things together within the team on a couple of occasions when they could have fallen apart. He never failed to send a fax or a phone message when a player had done well and we appreciated that. He made me believe I was important to South African cricket, and no employee can ask more from his employer than that.

But this was the wake-up call I needed. I hadn't scored any runs and I was feeling miserable and determined in equal measure.

It had the desired effect. In the following Test we improved hugely, easily winning a rain-affected match in three days with Fanie de Villiers, in what turned out to be his last Test, taking six wickets in the first innings and eight in the match. I made 38 and 44 and it was one of the only occasions in my career when I sat in the changing room and cried. I was so determined to make a difference in the Test and yet I'd got out after making a 'start'. It felt horrible. But from a team perspective, we'd turned a major corner.

It was the umpteenth example of how quickly your fortunes rise and fall in the world of professional sport. I understand how it can happen. I watch television and find myself criticizing a golfer, for example, without having a clue about what he did the week before or anything about his season. As spectators and supporters we make snap judgements on the sportsmen we pay to watch but let me quickly say, from the other side of the boundary, it doesn't make it any easier to cope with. Right at the end of my career Graeme Smith was captain of a team that chased down 300 runs to win an exceptional one-day series against the West Indies and yet, a couple of weeks later on a different continent on the other side of the world, he was in charge of a demoralised team that had just been hammered by New Zealand.

A few weeks after that he stood on the brink of complete disaster as we entered the final Test one-nil down in the series and facing a second, unprecedented series defeat. There were mutterings about Graeme's captaincy and knives were being sharpened.

Three hours into the fifth day, Graeme had scored a century to win the game and we returned home to, if not quite a heroes' welcome, then certainly a warm one.

It was another very good example of why we 'mortals' should leave captaincy to those who were born to it – like Graeme – or those who desperately want it.

Bob Woolmer (South African coach): *I called him 'Mr Dependable' but he was so much more than that! He would do anything for anyone, was always willing to learn and was never afraid of criticism or analysis. I don't think he ever had a bad word for anyone and I'm absolutely certain I never heard anyone say a bad word about him.*

I'll never forget his maiden Test century and the profound feeling of achievement it gave him. He didn't charge around celebrating and tried to stay low-key about it, but I knew he wanted to scream his delight from the rooftops.

As a coach I'm afraid I have to be honest about one thing - he couldn't bowl. He was useless. I don't know how he came to be known as an off-spinner. Mind you, he was too good for Mark Taylor – that's not a bad wicket to have as one of your two Test victims!

From a technical point of view I was particularly indebted to Gary because he was one of the first 'right-handed left-handers' that I really worked closely with and he made me question and re-look at a number of principles I had always taken for granted. He did everything else right-handed – bowled, threw, wrote – but batted left-handed. It meant he could actually play the reverse sweep more powerfully than the orthodox sweep.

He had one of those 'naughty' streaks that were so innocent and benign it was impossible ever to get angry with him, or even cross. I'll never forget him sitting in the corner of the manager's room after a team fines meeting in New Zealand. There was always a corner of the room that became known as 'Amen corner' because the same players kept being fined over and over and were forced to down lots of beer very quickly.

Gary peered at me from behind a large pot plant and uttered this immortal line: 'You can hide but you can't run.' Actually, I don't think he could move at all.

Then there was the time he was celebrating the tournament win in Kenya in 1996, sitting on the window ledge of his sixth floor hotel room with a large cigar in one hand and a beer in the other. He leaned back to take a swig of his Castle and began to overbalance. I thought he was gone – I was already thinking how I was going to explain that in my end-of-tour report. But someone grabbed him and pulled him back in.

Gazza. What a beauty.

12

The ultimate disappointment

'99 World Cup

Of the three World Cups I was involved in, this was our best chance. We had been contenders three and a half years earlier but now we were experienced, hardened to the demands of the tournament and even wiser about one-day cricket. We had three of the best all-rounders in the world in Kallis, Pollock and, of course, Lance Klusener, who was playing some spectacular cricket. We should have won it and we have only ourselves to blame for the spectacularly bad way it finished.

From a personal perspective I was my own worst enemy, having allowed myself to believe all the pre-tournament talk about seaming pitches and 'impossible' conditions for openers in May in England. 'Negative' thinking is probably too strong a description but I was certainly too cautious and I suffered. I had a very average tournament. In fact, I averaged 26.

Fortunately the middle and lower order, particularly Lance, made up for the lack of runs being scored up front and we managed to scrape through the pool matches without any major harm being inflicted on the campaign. Lance continued his incredible form in the Super Six stage and we were within a nano-second of qualifying first for the semi-finals and eliminating Australia at the same time.

We had travelled to Headingley in the clear knowledge that victory meant a semi-final against Zimbabwe while a loss would have meant a semi-final against the Aussies, again. We were fiercely determined to overcome, once and for all, the psychological edge they had over us and we could hardly have performed much better. Like so many games we'd played against Australia in the past, it was pretty much decided by a single delivery. That's how close the teams were.

Herschelle Gibbs had scored his best one-day century and we had a match-winning score of 271 on the board at a ground where it was infamously difficult to post large scores, let alone chase them. Australia were in early trouble at 48-3 but Steve Waugh was fighting like crazy to keep them alive. He had just reached 50. Moments later we saw the ball flying to Herschelle at mid-wicket. He caught it. We were going to win. I started to feel the thrill of victory. He had dropped it. What the hell was going on?

It was the strangest catch, or drop, I've ever seen. It was too bizarre for words. I still shudder when I think back to the moment. Hersch actually caught the ball but lost it in the act of throwing it up in the air to celebrate. Instead of coming to terms with it as the years have passed I find it harder and harder to believe. The law is clear – control must be maintained throughout the act of catching the ball and disposing of it. There was no controversy, just a great deal of disbelief and frustration.

Waugh went on to play one of the best one-day innings I ever saw, perhaps the best. By the time he'd reached the 80s he was slog-sweeping fast bowlers and hitting the ball wherever he wanted. Steve always had a great sense of fate and destiny and when his moment of good fortune came along he became a different player, a man on a mission with complete and total belief that he was going to win the game. They needed more than eight an over and he was picking which ball to hit for four before it was even bowled and then picking a couple of ones and twos. It was brilliant, if painful.

I stood on the boundary with an increasing feeling that our destiny was beyond our control. I genuinely had the feeling that fate had played its hand and that, unlikely as it seemed, Waugh was going to score the runs. His day had come. The crowd were going crazy behind me, screaming their appreciation of the onslaught. A neutral crowd always supports the underdog, and Australia – even Australia – had looked well beaten just an hour earlier. I felt desperate and absolutely helpless. I knew we had to get him out quickly but I just couldn't see it happening. It was going to take something truly spectacular, an amazing catch or a brilliant Jonty run-out.

Neither of these happened. Waugh scored 120 not out. Australia won by five wickets.

Immediately after the game there was an undeniable feeling that we had made life extremely, extremely difficult for ourselves. On the face of it we were playing pressure-free cricket because we had already qualified for the semi-finals and Australia were facing elimination if they'd lost. But we were very aware of the permutations and we knew we would be facing them again in the semi-finals if we lost. For me this was the game we had to win to have our best chance of winning the World Cup. Afterwards, there was a general feeling that it was going to require a massive effort to pick ourselves up and recover in time for the semi-final at Edgbaston.

Semi final

The semi-final was equally bizarre but far, far more painful. The truth about that final over with Lance and Allan at the crease is that it was irrelevant, at least it was to the majority of the players in the team. If you ever win a match with number 11 at the crease you have to regard it as a very big bonus indeed. In fact, if any match comes down to the last ball or two then you know you haven't played it well. Lance and Allan may have got it wrong with four balls to go, but we panicked as a team well before that. Actually, both teams panicked. Australia bowled no-balls, had fielders out of position and even dropped catches when the pressure was at its greatest, but we panicked more.

We'd made a reasonable start but Warne changed everything by bowling Herschelle with a classic, not unlike the famous ball that bowled Mike Gatting at the beginning of the 1993 Ashes that set up his entire career. It drifted in towards Hersch's pads before clipping the top of off stump.

Deliveries like that cause batsmen to do strange things and I made a bad judgement call which resulted in my dismissal soon after. Perhaps I was slightly panicked by the delivery but I decided to try and take him on, to attack him to prevent him from dominating. Instead of working the ball around and being patient – we were only chasing 213, remember – I tried to hit out, but got out instead.

It doesn't matter why Allan ran when he did, or why he didn't stop, or why Lance didn't call. In situations like that match each individual in the team must look at himself and ask what he could have done better and where he went wrong. The team wins and loses and the team accepts responsibility.

I have never seen a more devastated and desperate dressing room in my whole life, and I hope I never do. The Australians were deeply affected by the pressure, too. All that remains at the end of a match, particularly in the semi-final of a World Cup, is the result. Most of the detail is forgotten and, rightly so. It's irrelevant. Both teams had made mistakes but the Aussies were in the World Cup final and we weren't, and that's all that mattered. We had to take it on the chin. There was no point doing anything else. The pressure had got to everyone but they had dealt with it better than we had.

Steve Waugh came into our dressing room after an appropriate period of time. I have no idea how long it was; time seemed to stand still after the match. There was absolute silence. He walked up to every single member of the team and said 'Hard luck, mate, you didn't deserve that.' And he meant it, too. He really meant it. Even at the time I appreciated what he was doing and knew I'd remember it for a long time. It would have been far easier to celebrate with his team and leave us to suffer. And it must have taken a bit of courage to 'intrude' into our grief, but courage was never something he lacked throughout an amazing career. My respect for him, which I thought was complete, increased even more.

Many hours after the game we finally made it back to the hotel. For some strange reason, call it irony or whatever, I went with Allan and a couple of other guys to a well-known Australian bar in the centre of Birmingham that night. I think it was called 'The Outback'. The place was ablaze with celebration and, invariably, there is no shortage of Aussies whenever one of their sports teams is successful. There was an understandable look of shock on a few faces as we walked in, as though we had come straight from a family funeral to join the party. Warney was there and treated us with great respect – he was happy to see us.

It had been such a monumental match that nobody felt the need to gloat or stick the knife in. We found a good few of the team there and discussed the match in a pretty civilized way over a couple of beers. But a lot of people kept talking about the 'loss' and the 'victory'. Nobody had won or lost, of course. It was a tie. Australia went through because they beat us at Headingley.

The following morning we had to deal with the realities of the situation and the sense of disbelief was widespread, inside and outside the team. It was a strange way for it all to end. For six or seven weeks we'd lived in each other's pockets, eating, drinking, thinking, talking and living the World Cup. Team meetings every day, sometimes twice a day, planning every aspect of the tournament and always having a specific goal to focus on. Then, nothing.

It was bizarre, almost surreal. Everyone just left and went their own way. A few guys said goodbye at breakfast but otherwise there was nothing. I'm not sure we wanted to dwell on what had happened but it was a very sudden and cold ending. Most of the guys were offered tickets to the final but declined them. I don't think anybody could have watched it on television, let alone live, in the knowledge and belief that we should have been there. It was simply a case of 'See you in a couple of months…' Debs and I fulfilled a long-held dream and went to Paris for three or four days. It was fantastic, everything we'd imagined.

Less than 48 hours after the most miserable day of my sports career, I was standing on top of the Eiffel Tower, gazing across one of world's most romantic cities, arm in arm with my wife. Nothing could better illustrate the range of highs and lows experienced by professional sportsmen. Having just spent three weeks watching me play cricket nothing gave Debs more pleasure than hauling me around every art gallery in town. Being in the Louvres was a special moment for Debs, and an equally special moment for me seeing her there.

Marty in the bath

The tournament had started with a tense but excellent match against India at Hove. We paced a run chase of 254 perfectly with Jacques and Jonty both playing superb innings. Our confidence was high before the match, we had faced a genuinely stiff test and we'd come through it well. It was confirmation that our confidence was not misplaced.

Debs had arranged for two cousins to travel from London for the match and I had secured a couple of tickets for them from the players' allocation. Rather than travel back straight after the match and not be able to share in the celebrations, I suggested that we spent the evening together and enjoyed a couple of beers. No point travelling all that way if you couldn't celebrate at the scene of the victory.

The longest nights are never planned. I can't recall ever going out and saying: 'OK, let's stay out for as long as possible.' But this was one of those nights that never seemed to end. Every ten minutes another hour passed. Eventually we all crashed back in my hotel room. Gareth Evans shared what was, fortunately, a very large double bed while Marty Springer, in one of those clear-thinking moments that we all specialize in at two o'clock in the morning, decided to sleep in the bath. I wasn't worried. The team bus wasn't leaving until 10 am, which was as luxurious a lie-in as we ever get on tour. Besides, late as the night had been, I'd been careful not to drink too many beers. Mineral water had been a constant companion.

The following morning was not a smooth operation. The red numbers on the radio-alarm (which I had failed to set) by the side of the bed were blinking at me. 9.48 am. I was not feeling strong. I had not packed. Gareth had migrated to my side of the bed and Marty was snoring, loudly. I went for a pee and saw he was still in the bath, lying in the most uncomfortable sleeping position I had ever seen. I thought he might have broken his neck. I had clothes all over the room. It was mission impossible. I had 12 minutes to get on the bus.

I grabbed whatever clothes I could see, woke both of them and told them to pack whatever I had left behind and settle the bill. A few splashes of cold water, clean teeth and a juice from the minibar and I was off. I made it with about 30 seconds to spare.

Punctuality was critical to the squad throughout my career and large fines were handed out to anybody and everybody who was late for anything that involved the squad. Lateness was regarded as a clear lack of respect for your team mates and frowned upon far more than other, more conventionally serious offences.

In ten years I missed only one bus and it was just a few hours after arriving in Bombay. Everybody was so jet-lagged that we were given the chance to sleep for a couple of hours before an afternoon practice. I slept straight through the wake-up call and ended up catching a taxi to a ground I'd never seen or heard of before. But I had a highly entertaining drive which included some commentary on the sights of the city and I actually arrived before the team bus. The looks on the faces of my team mates as they climbed down the stairs was priceless. But I was still fined, and rightly so.

I don't believe I would have been able to last as long as I did and achieve the results I did if I had overdone the partying. There were many, many more abstemious days of mineral water, pasta and 9.30 bedtime than there were of staying up late and throwing caution to the wind, but it was important to let off steam and release tension from time to time. The secret, as always, was knowing when the time was right. The night after a match with a scheduled day off to follow was clearly a time to unwind, and there were a few of us with some unwinding to do, having spent the best part of a year building up to the World Cup.

Zim shock

The defeat by Zimbabwe later in the tournament was a surreal experience. We had just arrived back in England from Amsterdam, where we had played Kenya. It was a strange and slightly distracting experience travelling to one of Europe's most interesting cities in the middle of a tournament that meant so much to us. When we arrived back it was straight back to action and we probably hadn't refocussed. We certainly hadn't.

It's not an uncommon occurrence in Cape Town, to be fair, where visiting teams can be distracted by the choice and variety of things to do away from training. We really played poorly against Kenya, too, but instead of that performance serving as a wake-up call we just put it down to a bad day at the office and moved on. We were, however, dreadful against Zimbabwe.

The strange thing about the format of the tournament was that we had qualified for the next stage of the tournament some time before and I believe most of us knew we'd been coasting a little bit and hadn't really clicked as a team. So nobody was devastated when we lost that game to Zimbabwe, and it was partly superstitious. We'd won everything before the quarter-final in Pakistan four years earlier and then gone home early, so, if we were going to lose a game this time, we preferred it to happen in the first round rather than the semi-final. As it transpired, of course, we didn't lose in the semi final and still went home early.

I was dismissed first ball by Neil Johnson and the rot set in thick and fast. We were 40-6 before we knew what had happened. Everyone kept nicking it. Zimbabwe were a talented team back then with a couple of genuine match-winners such as Johnson, Heath Streak, Henry Olonga and the Flower brothers, not to mention Murray Goodwin and Alistair Campbell. Upsets happen in one-day cricket: why did Kenya beat the West Indies in '96, why did Bangladesh beat Pakistan (admittedly the strangest match and result I ever saw) in 1999?

Wasim and Shoaib

The Super Six match against Pakistan at Trent Bridge was another fantastic game of cricket. If I had ever had a doubt about the ability of Wasim Akram – which I did not! – it would have disappeared that day, and not just because of my own dismissal. It was particularly interesting facing Wasim at one end while Shoaib was bowling at 155 kilometres at the other. Wasim bowled me three successive away swingers that left me late. They were dangerous deliveries, easily full enough to drive and tempting, but the late movement could only bring disaster, particularly early in the innings. I was pleased with myself for not falling into his trap and resolved to leave them all alone, even if it meant playing out a couple of maidens. So I resolutely shouldered arms to the next one, too, and watched it swing back sharply before hitting my front pad, at shin height, in front of middle and off stumps. I've been 'done' a few times in my life, but rarely as comprehensively as that.

The opening spell from Wasim and Shoaib was the most aggressive two-pronged new-ball spell I ever faced. There was one delivery in particular, from Shoaib, that stunned me. It was short and wide of off stump and I picked it early, got into position and was confident of hitting it hard for four. But I hadn't picked it early at all. I was barely halfway through the shot when the ball flew off a thick top edge and cleared the slips by about five metres. It might well have cleared them if they'd been standing on the boundary.

You need the adrenalin to be flowing in order to be sharp enough to survive in circumstances like that, but you also need to be calm. The crowd is screaming, Shoaib is sprinting in and the ball arrives so quickly it is barely possible to flinch. A batsman's mind is always his most important weapon but in circumstances like that you need it to keep you alive as much as to score runs. The atmosphere was electric. It was the only time in my career when I genuinely contemplated changing my game – not just my game 'plan', but my whole game.

I was thinking: 'Gazza, you just don't have enough time. You're not seeing it quickly enough to play a shot...' For a moment I actually contemplated my options. Pick the bat up less? Try to 'nominate' what he was going to bowl and start playing the shot early?

They were crazy thoughts and, fortunately I settled in after a couple of overs, but it gives you an indication of how fast he was bowling. What I was contemplating was

The ultimate disappointment

the equivalent of a golfer remodelling his swing halfway through The Open.

Another abiding memory, unfortunately, was of a tournament taking place in spite of England rather than inside it. The host nation's early exit seemed to kill off what little interest had been generated in the months and weeks before the tournament and the newspapers treated the Super Six stages as an irritation that could not be ignored. In one tabloid the cricket appeared on the 11th, and final page of sport, just before a woman's gossip and agony page.

The SA-Australia semi-final was one of the best one-day internationals ever played, however, and suddenly the country was interested – with less than a week of the tournament to go. But by then we had packed our bags.

Steve Waugh: *I can still remember standing outside the South African dressing room (after the 2003 World Cup semi-final tie) and wondering whether I should go in. I felt apprehensive. But all my career I had a belief that the teams should shake hands, win lose or draw, and that prompted me to go in.*

The first thing that struck me was the deathly silence. I had spoken to Hansie Cronje upstairs and I knew he was devastated. When I saw the rest of his team I knew they were as well. I can still see Gary sitting there. It's just so hard when you go so close to fulfilling your dreams and suddenly they are shattered. I didn't linger. It's hard to know what to say so I just said 'Well played, bad luck, someone had to lose,' and I got out of there quickly.'

The Australian team really admired Gary because he reminded us of ourselves and how we like to play the game. I remember when his half-brother Peter toured Australia he had all the big wraps on him and Gary had next to none, yet when he arrived it struck us that he was an equally good player.

We always felt he was a much better player than he was ever given credit for. He will be very hard to replace. South Africa will miss him.

We considered him their glue. If you got him out it always felt like a major breakthrough. Even the way he talked to his batting partners was important because you could see it lifted them.

We put a lot of thought into trying to get him out and basically we had two ways. We tried to get him caught in the gully because we felt he did not move his feet a lot and tended to play wide of his body.

Sometimes it worked but it was a dangerous plan because by giving him width he often punished you through the covers. Once he got set he would do this well so it was a fine line because what we saw as a weakness could also be his strength.

We also tried the short ball at the body. The thing that impressed us about him was he never flinched when he was hit. He was very tough. You rarely saw him show any sign of pain. You have to respect that.'

We felt was that he was a particularly nice bloke off the field. No matter what happened on the field he just got on with life. Everyone liked that about him.

Left: Kirsten and Adam Bacher walking out at Lord's. The only time my mother watched a live test.

Below: Slip catching practise in Pakistan. I was never shy to join the cordon but there were always two many bowlers - Pollock and Kallis - wanting a rest in the slips so this became my job. And fielding at mid on. I wasn't any good there anyway.

Above: I loved the subcontinent, both on and off the field. Opening batsmen often enjoyed the best of the conditions while the ball skidded straight onto the bat and before the spinners came on.

Below: Man of the match awards or not, it was back to nets the following day. I never dreaded or resented a practise in 17 years. Nets and training are as much of what professionals do as playing matches and winning trophies. Despite the look on my face I really did enjoy training.

13

Last throw of the dice

England in SA, 1999-2000

It was the penultimate series we played before the match-fixing scandal blew up in everyone's faces and I genuinely thought it would be the end of my career, but for different reasons, I hasten to add. I hadn't scored runs in the first Test and only a handful in the second. I was literally down to my last roulette chip, the last roll of the dice. It hadn't been spelled out to me but I knew. It was my last Test unless I produced. And if I didn't, that would be it. If I was dropped I wouldn't get back at the age of 32.

I scored 11 in the first innings at Kingsmead and set the tone for a shocking batting display in reply to England's 366. We followed on. Now I was down to one innings to save my career and we were staring defeat in the face. How had it come to this?

We had four or five overs to survive on the third evening followed by the prospect of two more days' batting. My confidence was shot to pieces and I walked out expecting to be dismissed well before the close of play. Would we use a nightwatchman? I didn't expect to survive the first over, let alone make it to the following morning. In fact, I still don't know how I did survive. Sometimes you need a bit of luck.

I played at and missed virtually everything for a couple of overs and I was swamped with negative thought. I was convinced that it was all over. I was miserable, dejected and angry that it was going to end like this. When I got back to the change room I felt useless. I'd survived half an hour but I hadn't convinced anyone.

Debs was with me - it was the Christmas Test and families always joined us for the match. I wasn't much fun when I finally returned to the hotel room.

We talked pretty late into the night. Debs spoke about destiny and suggested that, if it was time to go, to finish with cricket, then perhaps I should accept it, embrace it and move on to the next phase of my life. Together we tried to make sense of the situation and see the way forward. Debs also said that perhaps it wasn't time to go, perhaps I would turn it all around the following day. Either way, she said, I wasn't helping the situation by becoming so tense and miserable.

From the moment I woke up the following day I felt a calmness I hadn't felt for years. Breakfast, the short trip to the ground, warm-ups and a brief net, they were all peaceful.

I didn't know what was going to happen but I was going to try my hardest and accept the consequences, my fate.

I walked to the crease in a very controlled and calm way. I wouldn't say I was feeling confident because I was still in a terrible run of form, but I was relaxed. I received a couple of loose balls up front and hit them for four. I looked at my bat to confirm it really did have a middle.

I was still there at lunch but there was so far to go that nobody was thinking beyond the end of the fourth day. By tea I was really feeling good. Once you hit 50 or 60 you can lock into a zone of concentration that is a comfortable and secure place to be. I remember saying to myself 'You've had a torrid time, the press have been on your back, you're down to your last innings…if you get a chance, don't let it go. Whatever you do, don't give it away. If they get you out, fine, but don't give it away.'

Towards the end of the fourth day I knew, without a doubt, that I could go all the way. Once again there was such a calmness about my attitude there didn't seem room for doubt. I knew I could save the game. I was in the most powerful concentration bubble of my life.

From then I have almost complete memory loss. I just batted and batted and batted without seeming to give the innings much thought. I remained completely focused on every ball but I thought nothing between deliveries, my brain was an empty space. I couldn't tell you if the England players were chirping me or what any of the bowling changes were. I couldn't tell anybody anything about the final day, except that we saved the Test match. But while I may have had no specific thoughts, I was aware of the intense thrill and excitement of being in unknown territory. It was as much fun as I'd ever had, exploring new dimensions of the game and being so determined to push the boundaries even further.

Mark Boucher batted beautifully during that innings, absolutely superbly. He was so positive from the moment he came to the crease despite our still being in a position to lose the Test. Bouchy hit the ball hard whenever he had the chance and the punches he struck early on quickly caused English heads to drop.

I've always enjoyed batting with Bouch, although it didn't happen very often, but when it did there was inevitably a positive, energetic vibe in the air. Although I'd been batting a long time when he walked to the crease I felt it was a fresh start when he arrived. He stamped an instant authority on proceedings and allowed me to take a back seat. He never said anything to this effect, and perhaps it was purely subconscious, but I felt he was taking as much of the sting out of the situation as he could. I was literally just pushing singles and trying to relax a little at the other end.

At one point he did say: 'Listen, I'm going to take Caddick on here. Don't worry.' Andrew Caddick had been bowling extremely well and he was the major threat. I didn't say a word. Eventually Bouch started pulling the short ball to great effect and the counterattacking tactics worked superbly. Caddick was removed from the attack and the pressure instantly eased.

When Bouch first came into the team as a teenager in Pakistan three years earlier I was sceptical. I was biased, too, of course, because I wanted to see my brother, Porks, in the team, but the selectors said they wanted to invest in a youngster for the future and they believed his batting was good enough to make a huge impact in the years to come. And they were absolutely right.

We became great friends over the years and it was based on mutual respect. I recognized his rare ability to play his best under extreme pressure and he enjoyed my determination to fight all the way through an innings without giving anything away. Right at the end of my career we motivated each other by identifying the critical moments of a match, sometimes in advance, and psyching ourselves up to be the person with the privilege of seizing those moments. We called it 'stepping up to the plate.'

The 275 is obviously a career highlight but not for the innings itself which can only be described as long! But the crisis I was facing in my personal career, and the fact that the team faced the prospect of batting so long to save a Test, makes the achievement feel very special. Not many teams have saved a match from such a position. I suppose I should feel proud of my fitness, too, but I would have been disgusted with myself if I hadn't been up to the job physically. That's always been a vital part of my game.

Having never been a dashing stroke maker or 'entertainer', I knew from my earliest days that I needed to maximize the assets I did have and I trained for endurance and distance from as far back as I can remember. Not just physical endurance, but mental strength, too. One is useless without the other.

Winter training sometimes lasted the whole day, starting with a bat in the nets against anybody prepared to bowl or throw balls at me for at least three hours. With recovery breaks, a gym session, some weights and a road run, I would sometimes be there all day. Not every day, I wasn't mad. But I was never afraid of hard work, either. I never batted against a bowling machine because I found it very unnatural, but if I had I would probably have batted for six or seven hours. Often I would stop only because there was nobody left to bowl or throw the ball to me. If I wanted to bat for a whole day during a match, clearly I had to bat for most of the day in the nets. It was an obvious equation to me. A three-hour training session is often described by players as 'long' but it's only half a match day.

I was a firm believer in aerobic endurance training, too. Long runs in the rare off-seasons were common and they were followed by gym sessions, perhaps squash, and whatever other physical activities were available or convenient. Sometimes, at the end of a long training day when the muscles were tired, I would persuade another batsman to come and have throw-downs with me. I thought of that as 'mental training'. If you could make yourself function and perform when you were tired on a rest day, it would surely make it easier on a Test day.

The Kingsmead innings justified all those hours and days of endurance training. Having watched Michael Atherton bat for 10 hours to save the Wanderers Test five years earlier, I believed I would get my chance to do something like that. I also knew that, when my chance came, it would probably be a once-in-a-lifetime opportunity. I had to be ready for it.

When I walked off Kingsmead I knew my one chance had come, and I knew I'd taken it. All fourteen and a half hours of it.

c. Kirsten b. Donald

As it turned out, the innings almost certainly contributed to our winning the next Test and the series, not just keeping us alive by saving the third Test. By the time we arrived in Cape Town for the fourth Test, just two days later, the England bowlers were still exhausted. December in Durban serves up some of the country's most debilitating weather and they had been standing in it for three days. It had been brutally hot and humid and a constant battle to stay hydrated.

We were able to pounce on their weakness at Newlands and post a big total that secured the series win, two-nil with a Test to play. I would have loved another hundred in that game, especially at home. When I reached 80 by the close of the second day I knew I'd played as well as I ever had, at any time in my career. I was seeing the ball well, choosing my shots well and hitting the ball well. And just a few days earlier I was hopeless. But I was out immediately when the third day started and that was that.

The consolation prize had come on the first day though, and it was outstanding. My very first Test match catch had read: 'MJ Slater c. Kirsten b. Donald 32'. It had been a special moment. Now during England's first innings it happened four times, equalling the record for catches off the same bowler in a Test innings. Statistics like that don't usually turn me on but for most of my career Allan was our one and only true superstar and when you contributed to one of his wickets it felt particularly rewarding. I finished with 18 catches off AD – three behind the 'c. Kallis b. Pollock' combination (but a long way off the world record of 51 held by Mark Taylor and Shane Warne).

The final Test, at Centurion Park, will always be remembered for our captain taking money from a bookmaker. And that is all it should be remembered for. I don't care about the result, although I've always hated losing a Test match, but I still don't believe that match deserved Test status. Test cricket should be above and better than that.

Hansie accepted the money – R50,000 – from a South African bookmaker.

His 'job', in exchange for the money and a leather jacket, was to negotiate a deal with Nasser Hussain to 'make a game' of the Test on the final day when the middle three days had been completely washed out. It involved declaring our first innings and forfeiting our second. England would then forfeit their first innings and chase our score. It was basically a one-day match played to Test match rules.

On this occasion I have no need for hindsight. I hated it and the rest of the team hated it. We thought it was absolutely crazy to even consider trying to force a result from a Test match. Unlike in English county cricket there has never been a culture of result manipulation via cheap runs and forced declarations in South African cricket, and we were appalled. The England team were surprised at the offer, I believe, but they were at least familiar with the concept of 'forcing' a result after bad weather and they had nothing to lose. Even so, they initially declined Hansie's invitation until he made such a generous offer they would have been mad to refuse. They started as strong favourites.

Most of us were extremely angry when we lost the match. We'd won the series but we'd given them a Test when we should have won two-nil. Before the 'match' was made, Hansie asked the team what we thought of his proposal and there was no question that the majority of us were very firmly against it. It felt badly wrong and we felt it cheapened Test cricket and showed a disrespect for the history of the game. But he went through with it anyway, and now we know why.

A few weeks later we travelled to India. I, for one, tried hard to wipe out the memory of the Centurion debacle.

Angus Fraser (England bowler): *My worst memory of Gary was bowling at him for about three days while he made a double century at Old Trafford in 1998. It was like bowling a tennis ball at a brick wall. But that wasn't the best innings I saw him play, a long way from it.*

I'd moved to the commentary box by the time he came back for the next tour of England and his hundred at Headingley in 2003 must, surely, be one of his defining moments. On a difficult wicket and terrible conditions, with the team all but dead and buried, he scored a hundred in the company of the tail-enders and won the game. Brilliant.

He wasn't pretty and he had limitations, but he knew that and that's what made him so effective. You always knew he wasn't going to give his wicket away when you were bowling at him but, on the other hand, if you were feeling under a bit of pressure then you could always bowl maidens at him. The trouble is, that meant he was still there at the end of the day.

If I had been a bowler in the South African side I would have loved having Gary at the top of the order because it meant that, more often than not, you'd be guaranteed the chance to put your feet up for a day and a half – and you still wouldn't be in a position to declare.

14

Match fixing – the bad days ahead

India 2000

This is the only chance I'll get to talk about the cricket on this tour, so please bear with me. I'm pretty certain most people have forgotten that we played some fantastic cricket and won a Test series. The achievement ranks amongst the best during my career yet the tour will be remembered for all the wrong reasons.

Although the series was cut to two Tests because of time constraints and the fact that the BCCI wanted to stage five one-dayers, the result still felt fantastic. We won a low-scoring first match in Mumbai after conceding a first-innings lead of 50 and then made it two-nil in Bangalore after building a first-innings lead of over 300. Mohammad Azharuddin smashed a century with India batting a second time but then immediately hit the ball down my throat at deep square leg.

Everybody chipped in during the Bangalore Test although Nicky Boje's 85 as nightwatchman was especially impressive and important. Mark Boucher's aggressive and fearless sweeping of Anil Kumble in the second innings of the first Test, when we were still 50 runs short and six wickets down, was just as impressive. Lance and Jacques both missed out on hundreds by a couple of runs each in Bangalore but, frustrating as that can be, the series win was a heck of a consolation.

But it was Hansie's recorded conversations with a bookmaker and his match-fixing offers to Herschelle Gibbs and Henry Williams that created the biggest cricketing scandal since 'bodyline', possibly of all time.

It was a very different environment to the previous tour when Hansie had made the infamous 'Benefit Match' offer to the team. By now everybody had heard of match-fixing and there wasn't the same naïvety that characterized the '96 tour.

I was suspicious. Something wasn't right. There was just a bit too much banter around the subject within the team. It was normal to make a few sarcastic comments and the odd tease – that had been going on for a year or two – but there was too much.

It's easy to be wise after the event but I did nothing at the time. I'd basically forgotten about the '96 offer as soon as I walked out of Hansie's hotel room because it was too big for me to contemplate. But now the captain of six years' standing was talking about match-fixing a lot and joking to his players about becoming involved. It really wasn't possible to know whether he was being serious or not. All his life he'd been a practical joker and it was perfectly possible to believe he was messing around again. I just ignored his banter about match-fixing, although he never spoke to me directly.

One of the games under suspicion was the one-dayer in Cochin. If it was fixed in any way, I must say it would have taken the concentration of a genius and the strength of Atlas. It was the hottest day I've ever experienced on a cricket field. The stadium is an enormous concrete bowl, almost the perfect heat trap. After 10 overs I told Herschelle that we should stop running hard when we played the ball to third man or fine leg, as we had always done previously. It was the one and only time in my career that I ever held back on a run. It was just too hot. We called for water every five overs and Nantie Hayward was placed on a rehydration drip after the match.

Hersch and I both scored centuries and I'm still proud, to this day, that I outlasted my younger partner. He cramped up terribly and was dismissed soon after, but I carried on a bit longer. When I was out I genuinely had doubts about my ability to make it off the field and when I walked into the dressing room my legs buckled and I collapsed on the floor in a heap. I couldn't move for ten minutes while ice and towels were packed on to my neck. When I did move it was to crawl; I couldn't walk. I lost five kilograms during the innings.

It was hard work staying alive that day, let alone playing cricket. I cannot imagine thinking about anything else. We scored over 300 and lost, which doesn't happen very often. It's desperately disappointing to lose a match after scoring a hundred and posting a total like that but the conditions were incredible. Most other sports would probably have suspended play.

Hansie's little chirps and jokes about match-fixing continued, though. Virtually all my evaluation of the situation has been done in hindsight. At the time I laughed it off and didn't take it seriously, largely because, as far as I knew, nobody had been 'caught' and the whole subject could still be fictional as far as I knew. Perhaps Hansie was hoping that some players might ask, privately, whether he was serious. Then he would know who was interested.

Hindsight tells me clearly, now, that something was badly wrong. My overwhelming emotion has always been sadness. His positive traits and influences were enormous, and he had an especially important influence on my career in the game. I certainly wasn't alone in looking up to him as a cricketer and leader and would never have believed him capable of corruption, other than cheating at a game of cards with the intention of getting caught. But the power of wealth and the greed for money were his weaknesses and he was more heavily addicted than any of us knew.

He had obviously reached the stage where enormous pressure was being applied by the people he was working for and, in desperation, he had to widen his net. Hooking in younger players, I felt, was particularly unfair although that wasn't his starting point. Having been rejected by three senior players, Lance Klusener, Mark Boucher and Jacques Kallis, I think he was searching around for anybody he could get.

Barring the final match in Nagpur, which remains a doubt, I don't believe Hansie

Match fixing – the bad days ahead

Cronje ever tried to 'throw' a match while playing for South Africa. Apart from the Nagpur game, I cannot think of a single game that caused me to be suspicious. We certainly won a few we had no right to, but I never questioned the genuineness of any defeat.

I'm prepared to admit that I wasn't always the most switched on guy in the dressing room and I'm also prepared to accept that throughout my career I was probably one of the more naïve players, certainly as far as anything corrupt or dishonest was concerned. When we needed a cold beer and a box of Cuban cigars to celebrate a win, I was the right man to turn to. But if you wanted a man to throw his wicket or drop a catch, I clearly wasn't a good choice and, presumably, Hansie knew that. I would never, ever have contemplated it, under any circumstances. Apart from the team meeting in 1996, he never approached me, directly or indirectly. I'll always be relieved that he spared me making that decision.

Nagpur was a strange match...but once again I speak purely with the benefit of hindsight.

I was run out for a single by a direct hit from Sachin Tendulkar at mid-off and I sat back to watch Herschelle play a ridiculous innings. It was the match in which he'd agreed, in principle, to score less than 20 in return for a payment of $15,000. As we all know, he never did receive the money.

In the second over he slogged a good length ball from outside off stump over deep midwicket for six. Such is his talent, there is no shot he can't play, but I'd never seen anything like it before in 12 years of playing with him. If he was going to 'slog' it, he would have hit it over extra cover. He played a couple more absurd shots before he got to 20 and then finished with a blazing 70 from 50 or so deliveries.

Perhaps that game was a chance for Hansie to take the heat off himself by losing the series and giving the bookmakers (or gamblers, I'm not sure which) the result they wanted.

A couple of his approaches to team mates have been recorded but it was a subject that never really went away during the one-day series. Anybody could conceivably have said they were 'approached', depending on your interpretation of snippets of conversation and chirps. In retrospect he appeared to be handing out invitations all the time in the form of silly little comments like 'If you make nought today somebody will get very rich' and 'It looks like a belter, someone could go for 60 today and the bookies will cash in.' If anyone was interested they could easily have approached him privately.

Jacques Kallis and Mark Boucher were room mates on that tour and they spoke at the King Commission of the approach Hansie made before the Test series began. Once again it was shrouded in jest and easy to laugh off, which they both did. I'm pretty sure they felt very uncomfortable about it, but it was easier to try to forget it ever happened than to dwell on it and contemplate taking action. Hansie wasn't just above the law, he *was* the law in the eyes of most South Africans.

The approach to Lance Klusener was also disguised as a joke but I understand Hansie was more forthright with Pieter Strydom, Henry Williams and Herschelle. Having dangled the 'carrot' in the form of $15,000 (according to King Commission testimony), he had no difficulty in reeling in Henry and Hersch. That was extremely sad.

Perhaps, as a senior player I should have acted, but hindsight is a perfect science and life isn't. The knowledge we have now is infinitely greater than we had back then and nobody wanted to start rocking a boat that seemed pretty stable.

Initially I asked myself whether I could have changed things at the time, whether I should have been able to interpret the clues. I think several players asked themselves that question. But it wasn't as if I was tossing and turning at night wrestling with a moral decision – it just wasn't that obvious. I probably considered whether the situation was serious about twice on the whole tour. The subject was more a pest to me than something serious. Like almost everyone else I just believed the best thing to do was keep my head down and play as hard as I could.

MBL

At about the same time Hansie had started studying for a Master of Business Leadership (MBL) through Unisa, and it required many, many hours of hard work in his room. However you look at it, the time he devoted to the course was extremely impressive. I was aware that he was motivated by a desire to manage his own growing portfolio of interests. He often spoke with enthusiasm about entering the business world after cricket.

I had felt concerned for a couple of years about the obvious liking he had for money, a liking that I thought had become an obsession. It seemed that it was the 'making' of money that drove him rather than merely 'having' it, and he certainly wasn't too interested in spending it. The subject was never far from his lips and he always seemed to have some deal or other that he was working on, whether it was for free clothing or speaking to an executive box after a day's play in return for an envelope of cash.

We travelled directly to Dubai from India where our wives and partners joined us. (Debs was most disappointed to have missed out on India but it had been a seriously congested schedule there.)

Whenever Debs joined me, anywhere in the world, I made a special effort to find the best restaurant in the city in order to take her out for dinner on the first night. Quality time together with good food and a bottle of wine, there's nothing to beat it.

The following day I was chatting at nets and I asked Hansie what he and Bertha had done. He smiled and said they had gone to Burger King, or Pizza Hut. There are plenty of those 'westernised' options in Dubai and Sharjah.

I smiled back and shrugged my shoulders. He continued the conversation by asking why I wanted to waste money on an expensive restaurant when you could get perfectly adequate food for a quarter of the price in a cheap restaurant. And wine, of course, was very expensive in restaurants, he said.

It was a very small example and probably the not the best one to describe his approach to wealth, but it was the moment when I knew for sure that something had gone wrong and it disturbed me; I couldn't get the idea out of my head that he would rather eat a burger than have a really pleasant meal. He was very wealthy but also far too driven by it. I think our relationship changed a little that day. We were still friends, and stayed friends until the end, and I retained enormous respect for him as a cricketer and a captain, but I realized how different we actually were. But I accepted that difference and had no desire to judge him.

Like many other people, I thought first of Bertha when the match-fixing story broke. She had always had a fabulous relationship with Debs and she was always so easy to get along with and to chat to. Virtually every player that came into contact with Bertha developed a great affection for her and, above that, a great respect for the way she handled the demands of Hansie's job. Time and time again we would see Bertha forced to be alone, even when all the wives had joined us on tour, because Hansie had yet another captain's function, duty or responsibility to carry out. But Bertha never complained – in fact, she made it her duty to put a smile on the face of anyone else who was feeling a bit gloomy for whatever reason.

Bertha will remain an inspiration to many of us for the rest of our lives but particularly in times of adversity. The dignity with which she handled the initial match-fixing story and the subsequent scandal, followed by Hansie's tragic death, would have been beyond most of us.

Bertha remarried a couple of years after Hansie's death and I could not have been more happy for anyone on their wedding day. She will never forget her time with Hansie but if anyone ever deserved a second chance at happiness, it is Bertha.

Presumably Hansie was as deep in the match-fixing thing as he ever had been during the tournament. Once again it's easy to look back and recognise many telltale signs that all was not well but, unless you are looking for them at the time it's equally easy to shrug your shoulders and not think too much about it. Whilst I was always available to talk to anybody about any issue or any problem they had, I preferred not to become involved unless I was asked. I didn't like to interfere.

There was a 'rogue' cell phone within the squad that made me particularly uncomfortable. Several guys used it to call home and spent long periods of time chatting to family and friends without thinking of the cost. Hansie encouraged them and said the cost didn't matter because the phone belonged to a friend of his. It didn't make sense to me; it didn't add up. But Hansie was a law unto himself and if he'd persuaded some rich businessman to give him a free cell phone then that was his business. I didn't make any calls on it, however.

I thoroughly enjoyed Sharjah and Dubai; it was a fabulous tour. Apart from the obvious attractions like the magnificent hotels and the famous 'souks' and markets, the chance to play international cricket in a virtually pressure-free environment didn't come along very often. Any chance we had to live a 'normal' life with our wives was gratefully received by me and the short tours to Singapore and Morocco stand out as particular highlights of my career.

The irony and sadness of those 'exhibition' events is that they should produce exciting, highly entertaining cricket matches, and, without the pressure of a World Cup or other high-profile events, the best team should win more often than not. But I understand now that international cricketers in those situations are soft and obvious targets for corruption. It never occurred to me at the time but I can see how tight security must be to make them work.

If the low-key, more 'exotic' events were thrown out of the game then I would feel that gamblers and bookmakers had won some kind of immoral victory. The chance to travel and experience different cultures around the world was an abiding motivation for me during my career. We need as much opportunity to go off the beaten track as possible – there are only nine other Test-playing countries, after all.

Shot

This was our second tour to Sharjah after first visiting in 1996 when I scored a couple of hundreds and was named man of the series, so I arrived with very fond memories and was looking forward to it despite coming at the end of a long tour to India.

Things didn't go according to plan and we started the final qualifying match against Pakistan, which was a dress rehearsal for the final three days later. As I walked out to bat chasing 168 for victory, I felt a twinge in my back that I hadn't experienced before. I assumed it would pass once we were under way and the adrenalin was flowing.

A few overs into the innings, however, Herschelle and I sprinted a run and turned for the second when it felt as if I had been shot in the back. I collapsed to the ground and tried to crawl for the safety of the crease. It must have looked quite humorous from the dressing room and, although it was agony, I immediately realized it was a spasm and waited for it to unlock itself. But it didn't happen. I lay on the ground writhing in agony but the relief didn't come and I couldn't carry on. In fact, never mind batting – I literally couldn't move.

Physiotherapist Craig Smith supervised me being carried off the field and when I was still suffering excruciating pain in the dressing room he suggested he organize an ambulance to get me back to the hotel, which he did, to my great embarrassment. When an ambulance pulls up outside a five-star hotel it attracts an audience like a candle attracts moths. So I was stretchered through the marble-floored lobby of the hotel and up to Craig's treatment room in the lift, with guests and staff staring at me every step of the way. I was extremely grateful to have Debs with me although it wasn't quite how we'd planned to spend our last few days in town.

I spent the 24 hours on my back without moving before the spasm finally started to ease. I could walk again by the following evening but a lot of damage had been caused and my tournament was over.

I watched the final, also against Pakistan, on television. It was a good match to miss. We were well placed batting second, under lights, but were then bowled out very quickly and cheaply. Lance told me it was the only time in his life he had literally not seen the ball, but he certainly isn't the only batsman to have experienced that fate against Shoaib Akhtar.

I know there was speculation that the match might have been fixed. The truth is, I wasn't interested, so I didn't listen. I didn't look and I didn't care. I preferred to care about the cricket and playing the game as well as I could.

15

Aussies arrive to crisis

Hansie's nightmare

A few days after our returning home the Australians arrived for a series of three one-dayers, organized by Ali Bacher and his Australian counterpart, Malcolm Speed, in the immediate aftermath of our dramatic World Cup semi-final the year before. Both men decided it was ludicrous for cricket fans to have to wait another three years before the world's two top-ranked teams played each other again.

The Aussies had just arrived. It was a Monday. The story had broken over the weekend and the newspapers were absolutely full of it. Indian police were charging Hansie with match-fixing and three others were implicated, including Nicky Boje and Herschelle Gibbs. Mostly the coverage expressed strong doubt that it could be true and we were aware of the total disbelief coming from the public. It simply couldn't, *could not*, be true – that was the overwhelming emotion. Most of the players kept very quiet. I probably knew less than anyone but even I, finally, had developed some doubts. Other players, obviously, had much more of an idea of what might have happened.

Hansie had been avoiding and evading the team all weekend. He had held a press conference on Sunday evening where he denied it on camera. He even said he hadn't read the transcript of his alleged phone conversations, even though they'd been in every newspaper. We had all arrived in Durban on Monday morning for a practice match in preparation for the series.

During the practice match he batted and made a very good 50 before retiring. He bowled, too, and captained in the usual way. Just for a moment everything felt vaguely normal, but we knew it wouldn't last long. The atmosphere was pregnant with tension. The players knew something was wrong; we just didn't know how badly wrong. We felt there might be more coming. It felt like something was 'brewing'.

I believe the team meeting that Monday evening played a big part in his decision to go public with an admission of his guilt. I think he struggled enormously with the concept of lying to his team mates, his family for the last eight years. We asked him whether he had done it and he said 'No'. Every one of us then said we'd stick by him and back him 100 percent, come what may – even if it jeopardised our own jobs. But he was extremely unhappy with the situation and he wanted to put that right.

The following morning I had a phone call from Shaun Pollock to say that Hansie had done it. Overnight he had admitted to being involved in match-fixing in 'one form or another', Shaun said. It was a good thing I was still in bed. I could not have stood at that moment; my legs would have buckled from under me. I was suddenly short of breath. Hansie had called team manager Goolam Raja into his room at three o'clock in the morning and confessed to his involvement. He asked what the procedure was from there.

Disbelief

The news came as an enormous blow to me as a person. I was devastated. Having played so long with Hansie, and become a very close friend, I simply couldn't believe what was happening, and I mean that literally. Nothing in my career had prepared me for something like this and I struggled with the disbelief for what seemed like an eternity before moving on to the many other emotions I was to feel.

No matter how much money he'd taken or how many bookmakers he'd conspired with, I wouldn't have wished the resultant shame and condemnation on anyone. I felt deeply for Bertha, too.

I started remembering all the good times we'd had, the runs around Sydney Opera House, the bad birthday cakes, the practical jokes. I was sitting on my bed feeling as though I was in trance, a nightmare. I couldn't snap out of it for what felt like hours. I was trying hard to believe it couldn't be true and I was still hoping there had been a mistake but I knew that wasn't possible.

I was also struck instantly by the devastating effect this would have on South African cricket. As time has moved on so the healing has begun, but at the time it felt too big and too serious even to contemplate healing and recovery. When people said: 'This will kill the game in South Africa,' it was hard to disagree. It was suddenly impossible to imagine a 'normal' life again.

Literally every radio and television broadcast was filled with the subject and the newspapers just didn't have enough space. When I thought of Hansie I was filled with thoughts of escape – he had to get away from this. Whatever he had done, he had to get away, at least for a while. It was difficult to imagine the shame he would be feeling. Debs and I had been to America and experienced the anonymity that cricket and cricketers experience there. He had to get away. I genuinely wondered whether he should leave the country and 'lose' himself amongst the millions of people for whom cricket meant nothing. Just run and escape.

I wandered over to Mark Boucher's room to have a chat and then spoke to a few other players. Everyone was very emotional. Although it was the captain who had been implicated, other players had been mentioned on the alleged tapes that no one has ever seen or heard and there was a strong feeling that, effectively, we were all implicated. South African cricket was implicated.

There was talk of delaying the game against Australia by 24 hours while the pandemonium was at its height, but it was such a short tour there simply wasn't time.

Aussies arrive to crisis

The game went ahead on Wednesday and I still regard the team's performance that day as one of the best I ever saw, or was part of.

The circumstances surrounding the game were more intense than any others we played in. There had never been a greater passion for the flag and the badge than on that day. I personally felt I was playing for the future of the game. I genuinely did believe I was trying to show the country what we could do, to try to offer some perspective to their disillusionment and disappointment. I managed to score 98 and we won the game, against all odds, but the celebrations were short-lived. In fact, there weren't any.

Nobody went out that night. We didn't even shower and change in the dressing room. The bus went straight back to the hotel after the game. We all headed straight for our rooms. I had a shower and just sat on my bed, thinking of the days ahead and what we could be in for.

Comedians

We lost the second game in Cape Town but won the decider in a thrilling match at the Wanderers. Although most of the world's media attention was still focused on Hansie and his disappearing career, it was a stunning victory for the team. Personally, I knew after that result – given all the dreadful circumstances – that the team, and even South African cricket, could survive. Would survive. And yes, there had been moments when I'd questioned what would become of the game in our country.

After the match, as had become tradition between the teams whatever the result and implications of the occasion, we grabbed a couple of beers and went into the Aussie change room. I remember watching Andrew Symonds perform some amazing impersonations of every single member of our team. I was sitting next to Warney, chatting about the game and cricket in general, waiting for my turn to come. Symonds was amazing – he had identified the tiniest little quirks and characteristics that some of our players didn't even know they had. The laughter that night was always spontaneous and, occasionally, hysterical.

Every team has their comedians and it would be remiss of me not to mention Allan Donald and his repertoire of accents. For the one night of laughter provided by the highly amusing Symonds, there would have been a hundred provided by Allan. Whether it was an opposition sledge, a mayor's welcome speech, a match umpire's reprimand or a chirp from the crowd, when AD repeated it – in perfect mimicry – we collapsed in laughter. To hear Al say: 'My granmoother could have played it better,' in Geoffrey Boycott's accent, or to hear him repeat anything Imran Khan has said was inevitably a tour highlight. Great cricketer, one of the greatest fast bowlers of all time…and just as good a comedian.

But it was impossible not to dwell on the brutal realities of Hansie's situation that evening. He had the world at his feet in so many aspects of life and yet the lure of money commanded him to take the extra step, to try and go the extra yard, whatever the consequences, and the extra yard was the illegal route.

It was a powerful lesson to all of us, and if it remains a lesson that cricketers learn, and Hansie isn't forgotten, then a great deal of good will have come from the tragedy of his life. Greed can be a killer as surely as any drug you care to mention. It was the hardest lesson we, his team mates, ever learnt.

I have always maintained that the great game of cricket is bigger than any individual. I'm not a historian of the game but I would like to believe that has always been true – whether you're talking WG Grace, Graeme Pollock or Ian Botham. It doesn't matter.

So when people asked me repeatedly how the South African game was going to cope without Hansie, and cope with the trauma that his vacuum had created, I always replied that we would overcome the crisis because of the strength of the game and the resolve and character of virtually everyone who played it. Cricket is not a game you can take advantage of. There are far too many unpredictable elements to it and, for almost two centuries, it has gained a reputation for kicking its players in the teeth as soon as they start thinking it's easy.

The team did well in the early days of the post-Cronje era. We received plenty of taunts and abuse from the crowd, and our opposition, about match-fixing and some of it certainly hurt. If it hadn't there would have been a problem.

16

A shock to the system

King Commission, USA and Sri Lanka - 2000

During the King Commission I felt my life and career being pulled in one direction after another, on a daily basis. It wasn't possible to avoid it on radio and in the newspapers, but I couldn't watch it on television. It was just too depressing and I didn't feel up to it. Hansie had been a great friend of mine and a great captain who helped me hugely during my career, both technically and mentally, and he was similarly instrumental in many other players' lives, not just in South Africa. He also had a serious weakness in one aspect of his life and it led to a dreadful conclusion. But we all have weaknesses, some that aren't ever exposed let alone to the extent his was. I'm loath to be judgmental about anybody because it's more important to look at yourself and try to be the best you can without criticizing others.

My attitude has been misinterpreted as condoning his behaviour, which I would never do. What he did was completely and totally wrong, unacceptable, particularly when it came to influencing other players and tempting them to become involved, and he would have been the first to admit that.

Perhaps some people turn their backs on friends when they have made colossal mistakes, but I have never done that to anyone and I certainly wasn't going to start now. We didn't actually speak much, but I didn't speak out against him and I would always have been available to talk, if he'd wanted to. And Hansie would have known that.

The Commission had barely started when I received an invitation so welcome it might have come straight from heaven. It actually came from former Western Province chairman Clem Druker, who had a long association with the Philadelphia Cricket Festival – yes, in Philadelphia. America.

Debs and I needed less than a minute to think about it. We had often talked about visiting the States and how difficult it might to find the time to complete the kind of tour we wanted to do. Debs' sister, Cathy, and her husband Jonathan, also lived in the country, so the opportunity was too good to miss. And the chance to escape what was happening at home was greatly appreciated.

I was invited to be the guest speaker at the end of the festival but I became so intrigued

Above: Long standing victory tradition was the smoking of a large, preferably good quality cigar. After some interesting experiences with local cigars around the world I took to carrying a couple of Cuba's finest in my coffin. This was a good one.

Above: Not interested in a media career but taking an active interest in life around me. After the usual period of suspicion caused by lack of knowledge, I hope I became closer and closer to the media as my career progressed.

Left: The best day of my life. Deborah Cassidy becomes Deborah Kirsten and we celebrate with 280 guests followed by a honeymoon split between Lake Kariba and Mozambique. Still almost too good to be true, everything.

Top left(opposite page): A fun evening in Cape Town although ending in unfortunate circumstances with Bob Skinstad injuring his knee in a car accident

Top right(opposite page): One of SA cricketers greatest supporters as you can see by the clothes. 'Dad' Michael Cassidy pops round to see Joshua.

Below right: Escaping into the hills of New Zealand, one of our favourite countries to tour and one we'd love to return to as a family one day.

Above: Second best day of my life. Joshua makes it into the world and is instantly blessed with my hairline. Hours and hours of fun and the perspective on life I didn't have for many years!

Above: The first meeting with Madiba - unquestionably one of the proudest moments of my career. As South Africans abroad he gave us all reason to feel proud, appreciated and protected. His 'presence' is like no other I have experienced.

Above: Man of the series in Singapore. I loved the smaller, more exotic locations and felt so lucky to be able to travel and see the world. In an ideal world Sharjah, Morocco and Singapore would stage annual tournaments.

and absorbed in my research for the speech that I asked if I could play, too. I didn't miss a day. Actually, I was so intimidated by the last two speakers at the festival – Sir Gary Sobers and Sir Richard Hadlee – that I asked to play just so I had some runs to offer in case my talk was a flop.

There are over 160 leagues in the States and although most players are of Asian or Caribbean decent, I became convinced there was enough interest to build an international cricket culture.

I also had the privilege of playing golf at the Merion Golf Club which, I was told, hosted the US Open which Gary Player won in 1965. If that piece of information was designed to persuade me to play, it wasn't necessary. I would have paid the full green fee happily. It was absolutely spectacular. Anyway, I later learned that Player won at Bellerive in 1965 although the Merion has hosted three US Opens.

From Philadelphia we travelled to Florida where we stayed in a classic beach house and then moved on to Southern California where, once again, I saw more signs of cricket than I could ever have imagined. Underprivileged kids in downtown Los Angeles playing cricket. Amazing.

Baseball

It would have been rude not to attend at least one Major League baseball match and we were lucky enough to see two. A couple of people had heard of cricket and we started down the old road of how long the game takes compared to baseball. In my case, however, I spared my new friends the incredibility of Test matches. I don't think they would have been able to cope with the idea of a match lasting five days – with the prospect of a draw. It was hard enough persuading them that even a one-day international match lasted seven hours and there was only one break to buy hotdogs and go to the bathroom.

The importance of fielding positions intrigued me. There appeared to be little or no flexibility. If you were 'centre field' or 'short stop', that was it – that's where you fielded. No taking a breather for a couple of overs at third man. I couldn't help imagining cricket with a similar emphasis. At the end of my career there would have been no moving down the batting order in deference to my age. Instead the headlines would presumably have been: 'Kirsten moves from gully to mid-on.'

During this fascinating and fabulous holiday, the King Commission had been doing its work, resulting in a six-month ban for Herschelle and Henry. I missed almost all of it and I will probably never know everything that was said and done. The prospect of involving myself was just too unpleasant. A few weeks later we set off for Sri Lanka. Amazingly, it was the first time I'd been there.

Sri Lanka was vastly different from the other subcontinental countries. Much, much smaller and therefore far more intimate and able to provide you with a feeling of being 'at home' after just two or three days.

It was also extremely hot. India and Pakistan had their moments, as did Adelaide and Perth, and Durban is always hot, but Sri Lanka seemed to me to be the most consistently hot and humid place of all. Strangely, however, it was only uncomfortable on the field where the sea breeze was blocked by the buildings and stands around the ground. Living in and travelling around Colombo on non-match days was a great pleasure.

But training and practice, and the matches, were hard work. Humidity was the greatest battle and it was difficult to fill your lungs up when you needed to. Herschelle Gibbs produced one of his most famous comments on a training run along the beachfront outside the team hotel one morning on a different tour when the pace was fast enough to really hurt. With the Indian Ocean lapping at his feet, Hersch puffed: 'Jeepers, this is hard; what altitude are we at?'

It was possible to orientate yourself easily, to find some excellent restaurants and sandwich shops and not to feel so clueless about where to buy anything you needed. But it wasn't without its challenges, particularly on the field. The one aspect of playing conditions that was very subcontinental was the advantage that existed for opening batsmen. There was virtually no sideways movement with the new ball so, if you played decently, you could have 30 on the board by the time the spinners came on and the 'real' game started.

Tantrum

The one and only Murali (Muttiah Muralitharan) is a bowling attack on his own and extremely difficult to face in his home conditions. The first Test in Galle was a disaster but the kind of disaster that makes you laugh in retrospect. Sri Lanka had made thousands in their first innings with Jayasuriya thrashing 96 before lunch. Murali bowled us out for nothing and we were following on by the third evening.

Jacques and I had a couple of overs to go before the close of play and we were fighting for our lives. Two days to go against Murali and he was getting turn and bounce that was already unplayable. Still, we could reassess the following morning. Maybe there was rain around. I had just reached 50 and Jacques had a few, too. A partnership was building nicely. We reached the final over of the day. Three balls to go. I started to think the impossible. Maybe we could save the game.

I hit one to cover point and there was nobody there. Two men started chasing but they had a way to go. I was convinced there were two runs in it, so I pushed hard from the outset to come back for the second run. When I was halfway back Jacques decided it wasn't a good idea and sent me back. Run out with two balls of the day remaining. It was the most angry I've ever been on a cricket field.

As I approached the boundary on the way back to the changing room I took off my cap and threw it on the ground as hard as I could in abject disgust with what had happened. I was absolutely spitting mad.

In such cases it is prudent to vacate the changing room for a sufficient period of time so as to avoid injury, although this is not especially convenient with two balls of the day remaining. When I walked in there wasn't a soul there. I think they were all huddled outside somewhere. So as tradition demands, I went through the process of throwing my kit around the place and bouncing things off the wall to vent my frustration and eventually, when the noise had subsided and the danger had passed (about 15 minutes later), Jacques was the first to come in.

He shuffled over and mumbled an apology and I growled back at him. Sooner or later someone fails in this charade and giggles at the tantrum and the person who is throwing it. And sure enough, one giggle instantly sets off another and, depending on how quickly the source of the temper calms down, the mood invariably turns from blue murder to black humour.

Someone else stood up and imitated me throwing my cap onto the ground and soon enough I was forced to join them and started laughing at my own behaviour. There can be nothing funnier than watching a batsman lose his temper but, no matter how many times you've laughed at someone else, it still never occurs to you that people are laughing at you when it's your turn to hammer your bat against a wall.

I'm a huge believer in the privacy, almost sanctity of the change room. So much of the game, on and off the field, requires you to keep your emotions in check and bottle up your feelings, but if you do that all the time you would end up in therapy. You're not allowed to show your displeasure at a bad decision when it is made and you're not allowed to talk about it afterwards; if you can't let your hair down sometime in between you'll definitely go mad.

However, there's nothing wrong with sharing a few of the funnier moments of dressing room behaviour a few years later, and I've seen a few – beginning in 1994.

During a one-day international in Birmingham I had played particularly well and was feeling good – well set for something significant, I thought. But having reached 30 I was out, hooking, of all things. I was especially angry as I walked back towards the pavilion and my temper was just getting worse as I entered the change room. I hurled my bat as hard as I could towards my changing area without paying any attention to the very solid lockers that occupy all the central area of the Edgbaston change rooms and form reasonably narrow 'corridors' around the room in which players change.

Instead of landing flat on the floor my bat bounced off the toe and started cartwheeling down one of these corridors heading towards the far side of the room where a few of the guys were quietly minding their own business and trying to stay out of the way. Unfortunately for Richard Snell he was very much in the way and my bat's trip came to a shuddering halt on the side of his right knee. Snelly's attempt to get out of the way and the noise he made at the moment of impact caused a great deal of hilarity and my tantrum was prematurely over. I spent the next 15 minutes apologizing to Snelly while the physio, Craig Smith, applied ice to the bruise and tried to stop the swelling. It would be nice to say I learned my lesson but no batsman can honestly say that. When the 'red mist' descends following a dismissal it's just better to get out of the way of your team mates and wait for it to lift naturally.

Another hilarious 'red mist' moment occurred over a couple of hours at Headingley on the 1998 tour of England. Once again, it was during a desperately disappointing defeat. Somehow, the severity and importance of the situation determines just how humorous the explosions of temper can be. Much later, of course.

We were being shot out at a rapid rate of knots by umpire Javed Akhtar and there simply wasn't enough time for everyone to have their moment of madness before the next guy came in, also wanting to throw his bat and let off some steam. It's difficult to join a queue to have a fit.

The chaos started with me barely recovered following my dismissal when Kallis arrived back in the change room, also convinced he'd got a shocker from Akhtar. Perhaps he was trying to avoid me at the last second, but as he lined his bat up for a long-distance flight to the far end of the room, he twisted in his delivery stride and both feet slipped out from underneath him and flew into the air, spikes first. He landed heavily on his backside to a silence that was momentarily deafening. Not many of us had seen anything much funnier and it was extremely difficult to stay restrained. We managed it for about three or four seconds before the laughter began and I'm sure it would have carried on for several hours had the match not carried on slipping away from us and the string of interesting decisions from Akhtar not continued.

Muttiah Muralitharan (Record-breaking Sri Lankan spin bowler): *Gary was an extremely gutsy cricketer and a great performer. Off the field, he was always friendly. We had plenty of battles over the years and I always found him a tricky customer. He never gave away his wicket cheaply and he usually batted really well against my bowling.*

I had a lot of respect for him because he was clearly a man who loved the game deeply and was totally committed to his team, giving 200% every time he walked onto the field. His record speaks for itself with a century against each of the Test-playing nations. He has done South Africa proud over the years and will be sorely missed.

17

Wake-up time.
Long, long way to go

Australia 2001-02

There was spectacular hype ahead of the series. The world's best two teams going head-to-head in a bid to retain, or gain for the first time, the title of 'best in the world', and it wasn't just in Australia and South Africa that people were excited. Like many underdogs, we had attracted plenty of support from people who thought Australia needed to be dethroned for a while.

By the time we arrived in Adelaide for the first Test, the excitement was extremely obvious. Even at nets we could feel the tension, not amongst ourselves but amongst the hundreds of people who came to watch.

We had an experienced squad, we had a couple of the best all-rounders in the world and all but one of the key players in the team had been to Australia before. We had discussed the traditional distractions that Australia routinely served up and we felt prepared. Actually, we felt good. We were extremely highly motivated for the challenge.

We lined up and sang the national anthems on the morning of the match and the blood was pumping furiously. It was a joyous occasion, not tense, or hyped as it might be before a rugby international. There was a shared sense of achievement and celebration between both teams that morning. You can't allow yourself to be psyched up before a match that lasts five days – and if you do, you'd better learn to let it go. Those moments of intense passion and determination must be saved for appropriate moments in the contest to come.

I walked off the field with Justin Langer afterwards and he had a huge grin on his face. 'Isn't this just a magnificent place to play cricket?' he asked. 'Look at this, just look at this,' he said, pointing to the huge crowds and the Cathedral view of the city. He was bubbling with enthusiasm; he just couldn't contain himself. He was like a schoolkid being teased with a bag of sweets. 'I just want to get going, I can't wait,' he kept saying.

It was another important lesson to remember about the Australians and the success they have enjoyed for over a decade. You can be as fit and as well trained as you like, you can have all the benefits that science can offer and all the psychology gurus in the world, but you also need enthusiasm and, above all, you need to enjoy what you're doing. If an individual is not enjoying his cricket then he should immediately evaluate the reasons why and try to remedy them. It's an old saying but it's true: A happy team is a successful one.

They attacked us immediately. The idea of two heavyweights 'feeling each other out' obviously wasn't part of their strategy. We had planned almost exclusively around our pace attack, with Allan Donald and Shaun Pollock forming the spearhead and guys like Makhaya and Nantie Hayward in support.

The crowd also tore into the fast bowlers from the first day and stayed on their case throughout the series. Nantie was routinely called 'Nancy' and even the experienced guys began to feel the heat, particularly after Matthew Hayden had slapped their opening overs all over the ground. In many ways it was a high-risk strategy and approach, but perhaps that was a compliment. Perhaps they felt high-risk cricket was required to beat us.

I have little doubt that we were affected. The Australians' approach was so aggressive it was like being punched in the stomach and not being able to breath properly. The abuse from the public may have had an impact on some individuals, particularly those fielding on the boundary, but as professionals most of us had learned to deal with that. But some of the fast bowlers pulled back from the all-out strategy that we had decided upon and the cautious, defensive approach played directly into the Australians' hands.

A profound moment during the Test, however, was the performance of Makhaya. Makkie has admitted since that match that he believed his selection was politically motivated and that he was deeply hurt by it. He wasn't in great form, to be fair, and there had been a major push for Allan (who was also struggling for fitness) to play. But Makhaya was chosen.

He survived the ordeal but, possibly, others in similar situations haven't. One of the great dangers of fast-tracking selections is the damage it can do to the individuals concerned. Some have felt genuinely inclined to tell selectors that they aren't ready to play but the potential damage that could do to their careers is catastrophic. Could they become labelled as 'chokers' before they have even faced a ball? But then again, if they do play before they are mentally and physically prepared, do they suffer the same consequence anyway?

That day he bowled without confidence and duly suffered, but he batted with courage and determination well above his natural ability. Soon after coming in, he was hit on the head, hard, by Brett Lee. He was clearly out of his depth as a batsman and the innings created a flurry of media speculation afterwards, with Lee's approach and ethics being questioned, remarkably, by the local media, which we always felt worked exclusively to gain whatever advantage they could for the home team.

Makhaya showed amazing spirit and guts, getting into line and doing everything he could to keep Lee and the others at bay. He showed his team mates that he had the kind of determination needed to succeed at this level and he gained the respect of the Australians, who love nothing better than an opponent who stands up for a fight.

Unfortunately the same couldn't be said of Nantie, who came in to bat and immediately played his first ball from close to the square-leg umpire's feet. It was embarrassing, to be truthful. It summed up the mental strength of the two teams and showed how much of an edge they had.

The whole series was a terrible reality check. We had convinced ourselves we could match them man for man before we arrived but we had been deluding ourselves. We were horribly behind in every department of the game and never even managed to get a toehold on the series before it was lost.

Hayden and the other batsmen dominated from the first session of the first day and never relinquished the pressure. The same can be said for the bowlers, who simply never gave us respite. It was the best example of sustained pressure I'd seen, given that we were ranked the number two side in the world.

Things might have been different had we performed to our potential, particularly during the second Test at the MCG. A drawn series would have been a great result. But the batsmen were out of form and the bowlers, by and large, didn't stick to the plan. The dressing room became negative and defeatist and, when you lose a couple of games it's remarkable how quickly things spiral downwards. Bickering gives way to full-scale arguing and infighting and culminates in players wanting to go home and a general fragmentation of the squad. It's hard to play against anyone with that going on, but against Australia you are dead.

Ontong

We went to the third Test two-nil down and with spirits flagging badly. Just when things really couldn't get any worse, they got much worse.

Jacques Rudolph was selected to make his debut in the match but was replaced at the 11th hour by Justin Ontong after the personal intervention of United Cricket Board president Percy Sonn.

Results apart, it was one of the most upsetting times in cricket that I ever experienced, particularly at a time when the team was so vulnerable and in desperate need of positive input and support in whatever form we could get it. We were all looking for something good, something positive to give us a lead and yet by ten minutes past ten, as Shaun was completing the formalities at the toss, just 20 minutes before the start of play, we still weren't sure what the team was. It was miserable.

Apart from the complete disruption to the team and the ludicrous uncertainty in everyone's minds, I felt especially sorry for Justin and Jacques who were caught innocently in the middle of a controversy that neither had contributed to and neither deserved. Two young cricketers who had, ironically, been good friends for years and were actually rooming together in Sydney, and this is what they got for their troubles. Their selection and non-selection had been based on politics yet when they looked at each other they each saw only another cricketer. It was a desperate pity we hadn't been able to simply concentrate our energies on the cricket.

So we started the match with Justin in the XI, also on debut, and batted first. I was dismissed before Justin went to the crease and, to his great credit, he didn't allow the situation to overwhelm him despite what happened out there.

But when he returned to the dressing room he sat down, considered what he was about to say, and then said it: 'If that's Test cricket then I don't particularly want a part of it.'

He'd been absolutely roasted. One of the least offensive jibes was to call him 'Percy Sonn's love-child' but there was a non-stop barrage of abuse and 'clever' comments that only the Aussies could come up with. I have no problem with sledging but it has to be an even match otherwise it is nothing more than schoolground bullying.

I felt extremely sorry for Justin, though he handled it as maturely as anyone could have in the circumstances. He knew he hadn't been chosen by the selectors and that he probably wasn't ready, certainly not with a couple of hours' notice against the world's best team and one of the hottest cauldrons of sport anywhere in the world. The New Year Test at the SCG produces one of the loudest, hardest-chirping crowds in Australia, and therefore the world.

To Justin's further credit he batted extremely well in the second innings to make 36 as we passed 400 for the first time in the series on the back of 150 from the veteran left-handed opener.

The controversy of the situation and the shocking way it was handled set both players back in their careers and cost South Africa a couple of years of highly-talented potential. Jacques didn't actually make his debut until almost two years later and Justin suffered a stop-start international career for years. I hope he makes it, I really do, but he was thrown to the lions by administrators who had very little understanding of or sensitivity to the demands and effects of international cricket, either from an individual or a team perspective.

Fines

It was our third successive Test defeat and we had reached a crossroads of the tour. Either we went into a terminal sulk and allowed the tour to disintegrate completely or we threw off the sackcloth and ashes and had some fun. You can only take life and sport seriously for so long. So we stayed in the SCG dressing room for three or four hours after the match and had a fines meeting. Actually, we had the best and most memorable fines meeting of my 10 years in the national team.

For the uninitiated or uninformed, a fines meeting doesn't necessarily involve monetary fines, although it may do at the beginning of a tour when the squad fines committee is trying to raise money for a dinner at the end of the tour. More pertinently, it involves the forfeit of 'downing' a beer as punishment for some heinous crime like attempting to chat up a very mature lady in a bar. Tradition dictates that crimes must not be cricket-related to avoid causing conflict and to make sure we 'get away' from the business end of the tour for a while. Apart from the fines committee issuing punishments, each member of the squad is allowed to nominate a victim.

On this occasion the beers were flowing cold and fast and everybody seemed to be punished equally, which is unusual. Normally there are a couple of 'targets' who struggle to walk away in a straight line. We had also acquired a small juke box that day although I can't recall how. I appointed myself 'officer in charge' of the juke box and choosing an appropriate tune for every team member's fine. It led to a lot of laughter and, a couple of hours later, mass hilarity. By the end of the meeting the entire squad, including management, were dancing up a storm and singing like the fans that had watched their team triumph what felt like days before. It had been dark for so long by the time we wrapped it up that the entire stadium was deserted and our bus driver was the only man awake in the SCG – or so it seemed. It was the turning-point of the tour. That night and the following morning we decided there was nothing we could do about being given a hiding in the Test series, so there was no point brooding on it. We still had the one-day triangular series to come and we had a chance to redeem ourselves, to an extent.

We were especially pumped up ahead of the first game against Australia at the MCG. I was particularly pumped up, nothing like my usual 'quiet determination' before a match. I was almost fist-pumping…

The crowd, as usual, was a buzzing 70,000 and we had plenty of our own supporters in it including Wayne Ferreira and a couple of other South African tennis players who were competing in the Australian Open. It makes a genuine difference having support in the crowd on overseas trips. Even if you just catch sight of a flag in the crowd or hear a small group of people cheering whenever you hit a boundary, it's good to know there are other South Africans 'with you' for every ball. High-profile support from other people in the sports business, like Wayne and Ernie Els, produces a strong sense of camaraderie and inspiration. Wayne was sitting in the seats directly in front of the dressing room, so he was a constant reminder to everyone that there were many, many more South Africans hoping we'd restore a little pride to the team after the Tests.

I actually played very well and, hopefully, set the tone for the run chase, which is never easy at the MCG whatever you're chasing. We needed 199 and I made a flying start – way ahead of myself – before cutting prematurely at Andy Bichel and edging the ball behind. Once again I thought I could have made a significant difference, rather more than 22, so the disappointment was huge. Immediately offset, of course, by the victory.

Hobart Abuse

My determination had actually increased rather than declined by the time we reached Hobart for the second game against New Zealand and I produced one of the more fluent innings of my career. Things worked out perfectly from virtually the first ball and I made 97 before running myself out. At least, I think it was my fault.

One thing I do remember very clearly was the crowd abuse at the Bellerive Oval, some of which was extremely amusing. And some wasn't. Tasmanians. At one point Craig McMillan skied a catch to me at mid-on and I dropped it. At the end of the over I walked back down to third man where one particularly thirsty gentleman had positioned himself. He really, really didn't like me. He abused me solidly for the next two hours in a manner I can honestly say I've never heard before. I couldn't believe the people around him didn't say anything or move away. His language was abominable. I have to laugh about it now but at the time my only thought was how he must be ruining the day for the people around him. Or perhaps they thought he was part of the entertainment. I had to laugh out loud when he called me a *^#@! choker for not reaching my century. Run out for 97 in pursuit of quick runs in a total of 257 on a difficult, slow pitch. I wished I could have choked more often.

So we started the competition with two wins out of two and it was literally possible to see the confidence and self-belief come flooding back into the team. Body language, form, sense of humour, fitness…everything starts changing when you have some belief. If only we'd had a day like that somewhere near the start of the Test series, but then again, that's exactly why the Aussies hit us so hard. Unfortunately my own form started heading in the opposite direction and I lost my way a little bit as the tournament progressed.

At the 'Gabba in Brisbane Charl Langeveldt was finally given his long-awaited debut after what felt a lengthy time spent being an excellent tourist. He worked hard at nets, he was cheerful and positive, he never complained and he was genuinely good company to have around. So there was plenty of back-slapping from his team mates when he was capped and a power of goodwill behind him.

He didn't take the new ball, so he had a little time to soak up the atmosphere of yet another full house while he was fielding at fine leg in front of a particularly imposing section of the crowd. Cricket, as its players know, is an unforgiving game.

Bouncer, hook, top edge. Charl. Drop.

I was fielding at the other end of the ground, at mid-on, and I could clearly hear the things being screamed at him from 'his' section of the crowd. There was very little you could do except stare very hard at the ground around your feet and be grateful it wasn't you. It was like something out of a nature programme on television when the hyenas tear the rabbit to pieces. You can't stop it. All we could do was hope Charl survived.

But that's what international cricket can be all about, experiencing the heat of a packed stadium and reacting to those pressure moments that inevitably hit you when you are least prepared. Thankfully Langers bowled very creditably when he was brought on a few overs later and, despite operating at a time when the batsmen were looking to accelerate, emerged with his figures and pride reasonably intact.

By the end of the series Steve Waugh had effectively been sacked as one-day captain after Australia failed to reach the finals of the triangular. The reason they failed was because of the final game against us, at the WACA in Perth, when they needed to beat us with a bonus point to edge out New Zealand.

They played an extra batsman – Darren Lehmann – and the ploy seemed to pay dividends when they reached 283 after batting first. Although we always set out to win the game, when it became obvious that we were struggling, we adjusted our sights to the new target - 227 - that would see us deny the Australians their bonus point and qualify for the finals with the Kiwis. And thanks to a beautifully-judged century from Jacques Kallis, we completed the job with some comfort.

It was funny how nothing had been said about the new bonus points system before the tournament. And even funnier how much was said when it became so important to the eventual outcome. It was simple. We had a better chance against New Zealand in the finals and we simply played to the rules. We had played well against New Zealand over the years and it worked out that way once again. I'm not in favour of the bonus points system and probably never will be, but if it is imposed on teams then it becomes their duty to make it work for them. Rules are rules and I'm sure Steve Waugh felt exactly the same way, even though it cost him his job as one-day skipper and a chance to defend 'his' World Cup in 2003.

Smith in, Cullinan out

The return series in South Africa a couple of weeks later wasn't much better for SA cricket. In the first Test at the Wanderers we were absolutely useless but a couple of changes in personnel resulted in a new attitude and approach for the second Test at Newlands. One of those changes saw the debut of Graeme Craig Smith. He was feisty right from the start and I remember thinking: 'I hope he's good enough to back this up.' Little did I know then just how emphatically he was going to back it up in the next couple of years.

The Australians, with Glenn McGrath to the fore, tore into him, both physically and verbally, but Graeme didn't give an inch, let alone take a step backwards. He gave as good as he got and the heat from a couple of exchanges with McGrath could be felt from the change room balcony.

Another change resulted in the end of Daryll Cullinan's career when he withdrew from the team on the eve of the game after failing to reach agreement with administrators on a number of issues. It was a genuinely sad way for one of the country's greatest players to end his representative days. I would have relished the chance to continue our quest for centuries having been neck-and-neck for most of our careers.

We could have won the game after setting them 340 to win but our attack, determined and eager as it was, was desperately inexperienced, with two men on debut and both Pollock and Donald missing with injury.

A particularly quick delivery from Brett Lee delivery during the Test split my box in half and thereafter I wore two for the rest of my career. There are some things just not worth taking a chance on.

18

Sledging – we all do it

1994

South Africans are pre-programmed to associate Australians with sledging, and I don't think we're alone. Whilst it might be overplayed, there is obviously truth in the stories that have now become part of cricketing folklore.

South African teams have traditionally had plenty to say, too, and that was certainly the case during my career. No other teams have had as much to say as the Aussies and the South Africans although England and New Zealand have always had a couple of individuals keen on some banter. Nasser Hussain, Andy Caddick and Craig McMillan should certainly be mentioned in despatches. The West Indies, on the other hand, don't say a word but they are comfortably the best starers in the world. I imagine the West Indian glare would have been even more fearsome in the 1970s and 80s when there was more cricketing substance behind it, although today's players certainly haven't lost the art of saying: 'I'm going to kill you' without opening their mouths.

The subcontinental teams were generally quiet although Wasim and Waqar perfected the use of the verbal bouncer in English county cricket and used it effectively whenever the need arose – or when they were frustrated enough.

Frustration was most definitely what set Jacques Kallis off. When the ball was swinging and the batsmen were playing and missing, 'Jakes' didn't have a word to say. But when it was flat and there was nothing happening, he'd resort to bowling bouncers and then following them up with a few choice remarks, especially if the batsmen were hooking the short stuff and getting away with it. Kallis and Mark Boucher sledging in tandem almost required ear-plugs.

It was vital, however, to get the best men into sledging positions and not allow those who weren't qualified for the job to get involved. It would have been counterproductive, for example, for me to say something to a batsman. It would have sounded ridiculous.

The day before I made my international debut at the SCG on 14 December 1993, Kepler Wessels took me to one side for a chat. He told me that I would be sledged – fact – so I might as well get used to the idea straight away. He told me they would try to destroy me mentally, get inside my head and kill me off. He said they routinely targeted young players and players on debut, first and foremost, before turning their attention to the big guns, the 'key' players who often held the fortunes of the team in their hands.

There was little chance for me to experience this rare pleasure the following day because I made four and we were bowled out for 69. A couple of weeks later my Test debut was heavily affected by rain and the Aussies obviously felt that, with a draw heavily favoured from about day two, they would keep the full treatment for a time when I could really appreciate it.

It came during my second Test, also at the SCG. I'd been at the crease for some time during what became an innings of 67 out of a total of 169. I got the strongest, longest dose they could hand out in the 'surround sound' format that includes virtually everyone on the field.

Warney led the way and tore into me the most. He was still at a particularly talkative stage of his career. It's funny how most of us calm down and become a lot more controlled once we turn 30, and Warney was no exception. But I also had the impression, sometimes, that the rest of the team looked to Shane to take the lead when a member of the opposition needed a bit of a blast, and it has to be said I looked particularly dodgy during that innings. Warney could have had me three or four times. I even had the benefit of a couple of close lbw calls, so it really was my day.

Unlike the fast bowlers, Shane saved his best efforts for when you were standing next to him at the non-striker's end. It was a long time ago now but I do recall him telling me that I was wasting both my time and his – and that I didn't belong on the same field as him – and also that I might want to consider a career change if I wanted to make a living.

Craig McDermott gave me a good working over, too. I hit a couple of boundaries off him, which resulted in him shouting and screaming for quite some time. But there are many ways that sledging can affect a batsman. You can either listen to what is being shouted at you and become offended or you can be distracted by the 'performance'.

I didn't have a clue what McDermott was saying. I didn't even know if it was English, but his frothing at the mouth definitely distracted me. But where I felt McDermott was really smart was in his ability to get the next ball in exactly the right place to cause maximum discomfort. There's no point in disturbing a batsman's concentration if you bowl the next ball two feet outside off stump, but McDermott always made you play, and it was rarely anything predictable like a bouncer. In the second Test I was expecting a bouncer and standing on the back foot a little – he bowled me with a full-length delivery.

The experience did me good. It hardened me inside and taught me quickly what I had to deal with, and how I should deal with it.

Generally I'd have to say they were clever rather than just dirty although I was also the subject of plain, unimaginative, hardcore abuse. But when they try to work on your mind as well as just your emotions they become much more effective. The very best sledging has a technical edge to it, and when that is backed up by bowlers as good as Glenn McGrath and Shane Warne it really does affect you.

Ian Healy might shout for Warne to land a big leg-spinner in a certain area and then describe exactly how the ball was going to get you out. This was followed up by several snide remarks about your technique. When you see the next ball heading for exactly the right place there is bound to be a fleeting moment of doubt in your mind, and if that turns into hesitation then it could be fatal. The element of surprise is an important part of a bowler's armoury, but this was a form of reverse psychology. It was just as hard knowing exactly what you were going to get before the ball was bowled.

Tom Cruise

Humour, though, was always the best weapon and it was used against me mercilessly in the third Test of the 1994 series at Adelaide. To be fair, I had only myself to blame.

I was about 17 not out at the end of the second day's play and feeling good. That evening we'd all been invited out to the 'Trots', a form of horse racing that bemused us, to be honest. Why not let them run properly? Anyway...

Freshly showered and wearing one of my last ironed shirts, I joined the six or seven other guys in the hotel lobby bar for a quick beer while we waited for the taxis to take us to the track. As luck would have it, there were five beautiful- looking women in the bar, too. Being young, free and single, I naturally took it upon myself to start the introductions. I asked them what they were doing there and, would you believe it, they were waiting for a taxi to take them to the Trots. I assured them we'd take the trouble to find them there and returned to the group of boys feeling quite proud of myself.

When we arrived at the track we were shown to the hospitality box that had invited us and we met our generous host and placed a couple of bets – based, in our case, purely on the names of the horses. Things looked better and better about five minutes later when the same five ladies were also shown into the box. Naturally I was quick to offer our new friends a drink and to pick up where we had left off a little earlier. They even seemed to know a lot about cricket. In fact, they even knew who I was. Not even my neighbours at home knew who I was.

Another ten minutes passed before some more guests arrived. Five members of the Australian cricket team. They started walking in my direction. The reality of the situation was slow to dawn at first, but then the sinking feeling started. I had been chatting up their wives and girlfriends.

That night I had great difficulty sleeping. Great difficulty. The abuse I was sure to get on the field the next day chilled me to the bone. If only it had been something a little less embarrassing, like my trousers falling down in the middle of a crowded room. The prospect of the following day's play was gloomy, to say the least.

I walked out to bat expecting the worst. Nothing was said as I took guard. Nothing was said during the first over, or the second. In fact, not a word was said to me for the first hour. I even started forgetting about the incident for seconds at a time. Then Warne came on to bowl.

As usual, he takes a long time to bowl his first ball. He was meticulous about setting his field, discussing tactics with Mark Taylor, placing the bowling marker and giving his hat and sunglasses to the umpire. Finally he was ready to bowl.

The opening delivery was a loosener, which I left alone. Warney, though, added a dozen paces to his follow through and, when he was about five yards from me, shouted to Ian Healy – so everyone else could hear – 'So Heals, how we gonna get Tom Cruise out today?'

There followed a verbal roasting for the next 20 minutes, which never relented. I can't be sure of the details, but I'm pretty sure I didn't last much longer after that. Craig McDermott had me caught at slip for 43 but Warney had played his part in the wicket. He still calls me 'Tommy' to this day.

1998

It's not just sledging from the opposition players that can have an effect, of course. In 1998 I was named player of the one-day series despite our losing the finals – again – after winning the first match at Melbourne. The crown lampooned me and booed like crazy after my name was announced. It clearly wasn't the best decision they'd ever heard.

The prize was a fantastic motorbike, a Honda Goldwing that was bigger than some cars I've seen; it was a breathtaking machine. The guy presenting the prize asked if I'd like to take it for a spin around the boundary at the SCG. I had to laugh. Either he was very naïve or it was another example of Australian humour. I'd just spent three and a half hours copping a headful of never-ending abuse from the crowd, particularly virulent abuse I recall, and now the guy was inviting me to ride around in front of them well within throwing distance let alone verbal range. It would have been chaos – I immediately pictured the scene and couldn't get the image of a slave being fed to the lions in a Roman Colosseum out of my mind.

I declined the offer but the chap then became animated that I should do the lap. I presume he was keen on the publicity it would generate but I pointed out that it wouldn't look particularly flash if both I and the motorbike disappeared under a shower of chicken bones, pizza crusts, empty drinks containers, golf balls and marbles, the normal weapons of choice. So we agreed to take a few snaps with me sitting on the bike where it was.

Normally with a prize like that there is a cash equivalent option that players choose without even giving it much thought but it was a spectacular machine and I had visions of cruising along Chapman's Peak drive and through the heart of Cape Town with Debs on the back. I was very taken with the bike, so I faced a choice. In retrospect it would have been one of the stupidest decisions of my life if I'd taken the bike.

I'd never owned a motorbike in my life and had ridden one only a couple of times. Apart from those little practicalities, though, there was the transportation cost and taxation duties to consider, added to the fact that half the value of the motorbike had to go into the players' pool, money that I would have had to pay in myself. I would have ended up with very little for the sake of a ride through Cape Town on a massive motorbike – if I'd been able to ride it, that is.

I'd played well throughout the one-day series but it was extremely frustrating not to have contributed during the finals in Sydney. I was run out three times by direct hits against Australia and it was the same story in the third final.

The first match, which Allan Donald had won for us with a spectacular spell of death bowling, was even more memorable for another reason.

Warney and Daryll

The media had fired up the Warne-Cullinan saga until it was red hot – and that was before we'd even arrived in the country. There was a moment when Daryll could have ended all the hoodoos for ever, a critical moment when he could have changed history, but it didn't happen.

Once again there had been no love lost between the two of them from the outset. Warney had picked up quite a bit of weight since we'd last seen him and Daryll had certainly taken note. The first time they came up against each other Warney said: 'I've been waiting three and half years for you to come back,' to which Daryll replied: 'And it looks like you've spent the time eating.'

Daryll had decided he wasn't going to be the butt of Shane's verbals this time around and decided to deliver a few of his own. In one of the Test matches Warney came out to bat and Daryll had a field day. 'Come on boys, let's get rid of him and sent him back to the lunch buffet,' he chirped from second slip. 'Just put in the right area and he'll nick it, he's hungry.' So the banter continued. Once Warney had heard those words he declared open war. Nothing was to be held back.

Daryll's golden moment arrived when Hansie and Bob Woolmer asked him to open the batting in the first final. Bob had already inflamed the situation a few weeks earlier by admitting that Daryll was 'under a psychological cloud' when it came to Warne and it was perceived that Daryll was now being 'hidden' from Warne at the top of the order.

We walked out to bat at the MCG into a wall of noise so loud it was almost numbing. It was virtually impossible to have a conversation. The Cullinan 'thing' was at its greatest.

Steve Waugh, never one to miss a trick, brought Warne on to bowl the fourth or fifth over of the innings, much to the crowd's delight. The noise level doubled from 25 minutes earlier and the stage was set as dramatically as I'd ever seen.

Daryll attacked immediately and actually played him well, briefly, and took 10 or 12 off his first few deliveries. I'm not sure how he even made contact, let alone middled anything. The noise was so loud it was almost like a wind. I was breathing deeply and quickly at the non-striker's end, and I was just watching. Soon enough, however, the atmosphere probably got to Daryll and he charged down the wicket to the fifth delivery and was stumped. He was given the biggest send-off by Warne and the rest of the team I have even seen in international cricket.

The noise inside the stadium was now so loud all I could do was wonder how long it could last – and the answer was, every step that Daryll took until he was back in the change room. If he'd just played out three or four overs, perhaps stayed calm and waited for Waugh to take Warne out of the attack – he would certainly have saved him for later in the innings – then maybe the Cullinan-Warne battle would be remembered differently. Then again, cricket is full of 'what ifs'.

Another 'what if' that used to preoccupy me was the outcome of the 'Cullinan vs Australia' contest if Daryll had just backed his talent and allowed his bat and his runs

Gazza and Hudders. One of the kindest, most sincere men I ever played with and certainly one of the most humble. Here we leave Newlands in the New Year of '96 after an unbeaten stand of 70 which secured the Test and the series against England.

Inset: Fanie de Villiers was a keen supporter of the sponsors and did his best to keep up with me and Pat Symcox when it came to giving them as much exposure as possible.

Hansie and I take a breather on a river boat in Cochin in India. When he could truly relax, which wasn't often, there was nobody more pleasant and entertaining to be with. That's our bodyguards' boat behind. Just kidding...

Above: Eden Gardens, either the 'real' home of cricket or the 'other' home of cricket, depending who you talk to. Unimposing when empty but enough to make every hair on your body stand upright when it's full.

Above: Pat Symcox makes an emergency trip down from the commentary box to pass on a crucial message: "The seafood restaurant we went to last time is fully booked…"
"No way!"
"Yep, sorry. How about going back to the steak place?"

Top left: I was a good enough tennis player to be offered a scholarship in America as a schoolboy but the lure of cricket and rugby was too strong. I still enjoy playing, however.

Inset: Stepfather Adrian and half brother Matthew. I'm pleased to tell you that cricket is not Matthew's favourite sport.

Above: Golf - the passion most likely to compete for attention with my family in the years to come, though it will never win, at least, not until Joshua is old enough to play with me. Never play against a professional cricketer unless you don't mind parting with your money.

to do the talking. But I had never prescribed any course of action to an individual, and probably never will, and I wasn't about to start then. Daryll decided to take them on. It was obvious to me that it wasn't working and he was inflaming a situation that was already stacked against him, but there was nothing any of us could do about it.

It was a sad and frustrating situation, made even worse by the knowledge that Warney's stranglehold only really applied in Australia. There were several times, notably on our 0-6 tour of Pakistan in 1994, when DJ played Warney as well as anyone could have. But then Warney loved a crowd and very few have played up to one, and raised their game for one, as well as he did.

Hit wicket in Adelaide

We had a real chance of drawing the Test series in the third match at Adelaide, which was played after the one-day finals, the last match of the tour. Despite having a score of 500 on the board our chances were set back hugely when Allan was injured very early on. But Shaun bowled like a hero, more than 70 overs in the match, and we began the final day needing eight wickets to win and square the series.

We dropped some sharp catches at critical times and, to be honest, we probably lacked the mental toughness you require at times like that. It was the end of a long tour, it was dangerously hot for most of the match and our concentration wavered on that final day.

Mark Waugh made a brilliant, match-saving century although there was a moment of high drama and controversy when he ducked into a short ball from Shaun and swivelled away in pain before knocking the bails off with his bat. He was given 'not out' on the basis that his movement was considered to have come after he took evasive action and was therefore not part of the shot. Needless to say, that isn't how we saw it.

Hansie was livid. I have no idea why he was carrying a souvenir stump at the end of the game but the umpires' door on the way back to the change room ended up impaled by it. It was not acceptable behaviour from the captain but I do feel it's worth pointing out that the door was made from barely reinforced cardboard – a five-year-old could have put his fist through it. Hansie was merely intending to give the door a whack and was pretty surprised when it disintegrated.

But it wasn't just the Mark Waugh decision that had got to him. We all felt the umpiring was routinely shaded towards the home side and this was merely the culmination of weeks of frustration in which a number of key decisions didn't go our way.

I'll never forget sitting with Craig Matthews in the change room, tired and dejected after the game, when Darrell Hair walked past. We just stared at him. We were probably the calmest two members of the team, so he wasn't going to get any comment from us. We just looked at him.

'What the hell are you looking at?' he snapped as he walked past. He looked, and acted, so guilty. We took no satisfaction from his behaviour but we did treat it as confirmation, at least, that 50-50 decisions in Australia always went the way of the home side and that it was more than subconscious behaviour on the part of the

Sledging – we all do it

umpires.

The fact that it was the captain administering the damage and it was the umpires' change room rather than the players' made the story more interesting but if every 'damage to change room' incident was made public there would be no space to write about the cricket. The change room is, after all, your first port of call after every bad decision or bad shot and there is inevitably a great deal of anger and frustration that needs to come out. I've seen some fearful damage inflicted on innocent pieces of furniture and walls over the years and almost inevitably there will be an attendant on duty smiling ruefully at a sight he's seen many times before.

Mark Boucher's hole in the Eden Gardens change room wall will remain a particular 'highlight' as will Nicky Boje's complete destruction of both his bat and helmet after an innings at the Wanderers.

The most serious piece of damage I ever caused was to myself because I had a habit of carefully laying down my bat, however angry I was feeling, and then furiously throwing my gloves, pads, thigh pad and box with increasing anger in all directions. On one occasion I threw all the soft stuff a bit too hard and had to have my shoulder treated. This may sound crazy but why, after all these years, has nobody ever thought of hanging a large punch bag in the middle of the change room?

But it didn't take long to learn which team mates were safe and which weren't. Everybody, and I mean everybody, vacated the room when Bouchie was out while Jacques usually only needed a little corner of privacy and it was safe simply to keep out of his way. Herschelle was 'safe' – he just sat down and kept very quiet for about ten minutes, but with Graeme it's important for someone to hear all about how bad the decision was, or how unlucky he was. Smithy needs people around him, even if it's just to listen to him swear.

Similar to that at Lord's, the Adelaide Oval dressing room has a stunning Honours Board that hits you straight in the face as you walk in. You can't help reading it every time you walk in and out of the place and, also as at Lord's, it reads like a Who's Who of cricket legends. I can't believe there is an international cricketer who hasn't been just a little more inspired by Adelaide than most other grounds and that was certainly the case with me during my second innings century, an innings that included a slog-swept six off Warney. I hit very few sixes in my career and I can certainly recall all of the ones during my 101 Test matches. Most were top edges over the keeper's head against Wasim Akram, so hitting one in front of square and from the middle of the bat gave me enormous satisfaction, as did the little half-smile that Warney couldn't keep off his face.

Number four

The tour ended in bizarre fashion just hours after arriving back in South Africa. A month earlier, halfway through our time in Aus, I was struggling badly with bats and couldn't find one that worked for me. (Bad workmen always blame their tools.) Herschelle had a reputation for having the best bats in the squad and he always owned more than anyone else, so I asked him whether I could borrow one.

Hersch has a habit of numbering them and he becomes quite attached to all of them, like pets. He ummed and ahhed a bit before deciding I could have a go with 'number four'. It was a beautiful piece of wood and I immediately set off on an amazing scoring spree with innings of 103, 89, 44, 44 and 70 against Australia and New Zealand. It became obvious to Hersch that 'number four' had found a new home and was being well looked after by its new owner. It was now mine and I couldn't wait to start using it on SA soil.

My mother picked me up from Cape Town airport and we decided to go straight out for lunch to catch up on family news and take advantage of a beautiful day. I would go home and unpack later in the afternoon.

Nightmare. Mum's car was broken into during lunch and all my cricket kit was stolen, everything.

It was a desperate situation and desperate measures were called for. I had been writing a column for the *Cape Times* newspaper for about two years and I decided to abandon all personal pride, get down on bended knee and make a desperate appeal for the return of the bat. The pads, gloves and boots, I said, could be kept by the thief but I wanted the bat. Sadly, I never saw it again. I hope the thief made some runs with it.

Glenn McGrath (Australian bowler): *Gary was always the sort of bloke that I respected and admired. You always try and target the opposition's best batsman or a batsman who can make a difference to their line. Gary was always the type of guy the whole Australian team respected. Just his stats could tell you that. To knock him over we felt had a big effect on the rest of the team and yes, I was lucky enough to have a bit of success against him.*

Bowling to left-handers is something I've always done reasonably because my natural delivery was hitting the deck and going away from them, which brings the slips and keeper into play a lot.

We always felt he was the key player for South Africa. That's why I targeted him and it was funny how with the guys I targeted the Australia media helped me out a bit. We respected him so much that we wanted to knock him over as early as possible. Throughout my career I felt I lifted my game when I was bowling to the batsmen classed as the best in the world, and Gary was certainly up there. That was a true indication of where you stood as a bowler. Guys like Sachin, Brian Lara and yes, Gary Kirsten – bowling to them was the truest test of your ability.

The psychological part of the process was absolutely huge. The fact that he picks up a newspaper a day or two before the first Test and reads that I'm targeting him, he's already thinking about me and the fact that I've knocked him over a few times before.

If I could get him once in the first Test the papers say 'McGrath's got his man again.' That psychology builds and puts more pressure on the batsmen, I believe. I was always happy to do that and, at the end of the day, if they were good enough to beat me at my own game I could live with that.

When I first played against Gary I bowled a little bit fuller and maybe a little bit wider to get him driving which brought the gully into play, but mostly it was just hitting

Sledging – we all do it

that critical length. A lot of people have asked: `What's the secret to bowling well and taking wickets and, as Gary will confirm, it's pretty simple - if you can land the ball 99 times out of a hundred where you want to land it, generally hitting the deck and hitting the top of off stump, then you'll do well.

I tried to hit the deck about off stump to Gary, which meant he had to commit himself to play. The natural movement off the wicket was away from him, so it was hard work. Building pressure like that, or coming around the wicket and angling the ball in to the batsman and then straightening it off the deck was another option. It worked well against Brian (Lara) but Brian's a slightly different player, more aggressive. You felt he gave you more of a chance than Gary.

The other reason we targeted Gary was because of his mental toughness. We knew that he could build a very long innings if allowed to settle. He wasn't the type of guy who would go out there and destroy you by scoring really quick runs but he could build an innings and bat for a long time while the other batsman worked around him. We felt that South Africa's preferred game plan was to set a big target with Gary batting all day and walking away with another hundred, so obviously we tried to disrupt that as quickly as possible!

I never had a great deal to do with Gary socially but I must say I always found him to be extremely friendly and genuine. Perhaps when I call it a day we can get together and chat about the good old days.

Shane Warne (Australian leg-spinner): *Gary was the rock for South Africa - everyone batted around him. They've had a lot of stroke-makers over the years, Herschelle Gibbs, Jacques Kallis, Jonty Rhodes, those sort of players, but Gary's been the backbone of their side.*

In team meetings we always discussed how we were going to bowl to him. We always felt that if we didn't get him out early he could waste a lot of balls. He could waste a lot of our energy bowling over after over to him.

From a personal point of view I found it a real challenge to bowl to him. He never, ever gave his wicket away - you really had to earn it. He's one of those old-school players who gets bagged when he bats all day and makes 90 not out but the team knows how well he's done for them.

Gary and Mike Atherton were the type of guys who were hard to get out. They would hang in there and tough it out, no matter who was bowling. If you start blocking and hanging in there you do get sledged a bit. But Gary had the respect of everyone he played with and against. The way he went about playing the game and conducted himself was a great credit to him. We called him the consummate professional. We think there is one in every side and Gary was South Africa's. Jason Gillespie is ours.

In his preparation and the way he goes about every aspect of his game, he does everything right. He very rarely misfields, he runs properly between the wickets, he's calm under pressure...everything.

This is not a slight on him but he hasn't got much flair. He was determined, dogmatic, professional. He left no stone unturned and gave everything he had every single time he played. You can't ask for any more than that, and that's Gary Kirsten to a tee. You'd love to have him your side.

The more I bowled against him the more I realised that he didn't pick everything I bowled all the time. I tried to drag him wider of off stump and get him driving. So I'd get him wider and wider and then I'd try to get him driving at that big leg-spinner and bowl him through the gate, nicking to slip or caught bat-pad. But I didn't get him out a lot. Five times isn't a lot in 18 Tests, but I know I earned every one of them!

He scored a very good hundred in Sydney in his last innings against us when Stuart MacGill and I were turning the ball big time. Stuey was going over the wicket and I was going around probing and testing him, but he played extremely well and finished with 153. It was a terrific innings.

Socially I had a lot to do with Gary. He was often such a quiet guy but he was good fun to have a beer with and he was the type of guy you loved to play against because you could play as hard as you liked but off the field he'd be one of the first people you would go and sit next to in the South African rooms.

South African guys are very similar to Australians. They and NZ are the two sides we socialise with, go into the change rooms for a beer and that sort of thing.

Gary and Jonty were the two guys I would always sit next to and have a beer and a chat with. We talked about families, life, kids…that sort of stuff.

The story about Gary that will always make me laugh happened in Adelaide on the 93-94 tour. All our wives and girlfriends were there in our team hotel and he was talking to them but he didn't know they were our partners.

He invited a few of them to the track one evening and also to the cricket, and they played him along a bit saying: 'Okay, we might come down. We'll see you down there.'

The girls told us about it and we had a great laugh. The next day, when he came out to bat, I said: `Righto boys, let's get Tom Cruise, let's get old silver tongue out.'

Once he realised they were our wives and girlfriends he was pretty embarrassed actually. So anyway, 'Tom Cruise' stuck. Every time he came out to bat it was `Righto, Tommy, let's go buddy, what's on today?' For 10 years he got 'silver tongue' or 'Tom Cruise.' It was very funny.

But if I had to pick a characteristic to sum him up it would be his determination. I was surprised he wasn't captain of South Africa at some stage. I thought he would have been a very good captain because he commanded such respect.

I'm proud to have him as a friend and I fully intend to stay in touch and have a few more beers with him in the many happy years of our retirement.

Sledging – we all do it

19

Technology – please use it

We have a big problem in world cricket and I've never understood the reluctance to try to fix it. When I hear talk about the authenticity and integrity of the game being linked with the 'traditional' role of the umpire, the only appropriate emotion is one of despair.

Fighting to maintain umpires the way they have been for 100 years makes no sense. The rest of the game has moved on, bowlers are faster, fielding is sharper, running between the wickets is quicker, and yet umpires are supposed to be able to cope as they did 50 years ago. Umpires made mistakes 100 years ago and they still make them today. The difference between then and now is that they didn't have an alternative; today we do.

The argument that 'traditionalists' put forward about umpiring mistakes forming part of the rich tapestry of the game is absolute crap. Mistakes are not 'quaint' and they are not 'harmless'; they are mistakes. In how many other walks of life or professions will you find people tolerating mistakes because 'we've always had them'?

The TV third umpire was the best innovation to hit the game in my career and every effort should be made to advance the research into further contributions that technology can make in improving the quality of umpiring decisions.

Professional cricket is big business and the stakes have become very high indeed. Players are under huge pressure and they seek every piece of assistance they can obtain, from wherever it comes, to help them gain an edge. Umpires are also under huge pressure and they, too, deserve every piece of assistance they can get. Yet we deny them because we are worried about tradition and aesthetics? It doesn't make sense.

If it is obvious to a television audience of a million viewers that a batsman hit the ball before being given out lbw, why is the batsman still walking back to the pavilion? The beautiful game of cricket makes a mockery of itself sometimes. I have always battled to understand why so many cricket people remain immune to common sense.

At the very least we should have a system where the television umpire can over-rule a decision made by an on-field umpire. It would only have to be in the most extreme cases but if we do not move in that direction then our sport will continue to look like a joke. Two instances come instantly to mind. Jacques Kallis became Courtney Walsh's 500th Test wicket during our 2001 tour of the Caribbean and within five seconds the whole world knew that he had virtually middled the ball before it had hit the pad. Over-rule.

The second occasion saw a player given out lbw when the ball really did hit the middle of his bat...and nothing else. Nasser Hussain dug out a yorker in a Test match at Newlands in the 1999-2000 Test and, amidst the flurry of boots, bat and dust, was given out lbw. The first replay instantly showed, without a fraction of doubt, that he had hit the ball and his pads were nowhere near it. And to be fair to South Africa that day, we didn't even appeal. The bowler – Lance Klusener I recall, cut off an appeal and groaned with disappointment only to turn around to see the umpire's finger in the air. It was embarrassing. Over-rule.

I have no desire or intention to criticize the men who perform such an important and often thankless job. Players routinely take them for granted and, while bad decisions are never forgotten, many very good ones are instantly cast aside until the next bad one comes along. I couldn't do the job, but if I had to I would want as much assistance as I could possibly lay my hands on.

If the technology exists to track a ball towards the stumps, or to see whether it pitched outside leg stump in determining an lbw, then it should be perfected to the point where it can be used at international level. Technology makes cricket better; it doesn't ruin it. If technology was bad for the game then we would still be playing it with curved bats wearing blazers and cravats. Cricket people should not be afraid of advancing the game to the point where it becomes fairer to the players and a far more genuine contest. Good and bad decisions may even themselves out over the course of a career as long as mine, but bad decisions can still have devastating consequences. We lost a five-Test series to England on the back of one man's dreadful umpiring, and the backlash was still felt five years later.

A more concerted effort needs to be made to establish mutual respect between players and umpires. Far too many umpires don't enjoy the respect of the players and they either don't care or don't know how to gain it. Players really don't mind a mistake, particularly with a difficult decision, but inconsistency is what really hurts. An umpire should be competent enough to be consistent in his application of the laws of the game, but there are far too many who will give some batsmen out lbw playing a sweep shot and not others, or they are 'out' on Wednesdays but not Saturdays.

No ball

Another innovation screaming to be introduced is the electronic surveillance of the crease for no-balls. That duty must be taken away from the umpire to allow him to concentrate on what's happening in front of him, not below him. Not only does the technology already exist to make that happen, it's already a part of television coverage. The third umpire should be calling no-balls; it's that simple.

The argument that using the third umpire will slow the game down too much doesn't stand up to scrutiny. Provided the television producer can provide replays instantly, which they have been able to do for years, then a decision can be made in a matter of seconds. And if the third umpire needs more than two replays there's obviously sufficient doubt and the original decision stands. The on-field umpire should also have the ability to give a batsman out lbw subject to confirmation from the third umpire who can check for obvious mistakes, like the ball pitching outside leg stump and the batsman hitting it first.

I have also heard a theory that on-field umpires will become lazy and over-reliant on the third umpire and that their authority will be compromised. In my humble opinion, if an umpire becomes lazy and relies on technology to make his decisions for him, he will be found out very quickly. All it needs is for a single technological error when a replay is unavailable and he will be severely embarrassed. An umpire will always make his decision in the traditional way, but there is nothing wrong with having that decision endorsed by a man in a less pressurized situation.

It is impossible to continually judge correctly whether the ball has pitched outside leg stump or whether it hits the pad outside the line of off stump. Mistakes are inevitable, but if they can be reduced to a minimum with the simple assistance of television replays, then I cannot comprehend how people can be opposed to the idea. Everyone, from the players to the umpires to the sponsors and spectators will benefit from improved standards.

Run out – blind

One of my favourite umpiring stories (name withheld) concerns a provincial umpire standing in a Western Province game in the early years of my provincial career. I was running a hard second run but, fortunately, heading for the non-danger end. It was always going to be touch and go for my partner and the umpire clearly knew it because he had taken up position very early to study the line. Unfortunately, he was standing on the wrong side of the stumps and my partner's desperate lunge for safety happened behind the umpire's back. Nonetheless, he gave him out. When we asked him how it was possible to give the batsman out when he couldn't even see him, he replied: 'That's exactly why I gave him out – he wasn't even in the frame.'

Even earlier in my career I was playing a game for UCT and facing a useful off-spinner who bowled me an arm ball that I didn't pick. I padded it away and immediately knew I'd made a fateful error. It was hitting middle stump, probably halfway up. A batsman always knows. Fortunately, I was the recipient of such a bizarre piece of luck I had to find out what logic, if any, the umpire had applied. At lunch-time I asked him and was treated to this memorable answer: 'I gave you the benefit of the doubt because you were covering all three stumps – I couldn't see where they were so I couldn't give you out.'

Sorry – not out

The only umpire to call me back after changing his mind was my dear friend Barry Lambson, and he was quite right to change his mind, too. WP were playing Free State in Bloemfontein and I was facing a left-arm spinner who had a couple of men around the bat, although there really wasn't much turn. Or bounce, for that matter.

One delivery bounced straight from the middle of my front pad and into the hands of short leg, who cleared his throat and tossed it back to the bowler. Then I saw Barry's finger in the air, so I started the long walk back to the pavilion making a big show of shaking my head as I passed the umpire, like all aggrieved batsmen. In those days you could be a great deal more animated about your feelings on a decision, unlike today when all emotions must be suppressed.

My display of disgust seemed to have failed because I was about three-quarters of the way back to the pavilion and preparing to launch my kit at a change room wall. Then I heard Barry's voice: 'Come back, come back and bat!' he was calling. The fielding side were not amused – they had quickly forgotten how poor the original decision was and were now firmly in the 'take the rough with the smooth' mode of thinking. But Barry was right to change his mind and he slept better that night for doing it. I think I bought him a beer, too. I hope I did.

In another game against Free State, in my third season for WP when I'd established myself with a good season and was regarded as one of the more important wickets, I was the recipient of an equally bizarre decision that had the country talking to such an extent it made front-page and back-page news for a couple of days.

Bradley Player was bowling his usual, lively mix of swing and seam and I flicked at one delivery that was heading down the leg side. Once again I made no contact with the bat but the noise of the ball 'snicking' my thigh pad was enough to convince the Free State players and, more importantly, the umpire. So off I trudged, once again grumpy and shaking my head. This time there was no call back. I crossed the boundary rope and headed up the change room stairs ready to tell everyone about my misfortune.

But when I walked in there was already an atmosphere of outraged chaos. I knew it was a bad decision but this display of togetherness from the boys was quite a shock. I was surprised it had been so obvious from the change room. But then I realized what had happened. The Free State 'keeper, Philip Radley, had dropped the ball.

It was still the early days of television coverage, at least the kind of extensive coverage that picked up 'details'. And there it was, clear as daylight. Philip takes the ball diving to his right, drops it onto the grass as he lands, rolls over the top of it and then jumps to his feet with the ball back in his glove and claims the catch. I was completely dazed as I watched it. For a second I thought the umpires would have to call me back – we had proof, after all. But it was a situation none of us had ever encountered before, so I wasn't thinking very clearly.

There was quite a fuss the next day. I can't remember what Philip said, if anything, because the TV footage was so damning it would have been impossible to claim any kind of innocence, or even extenuating circumstances. Eventually it blew over although I'm afraid I think some of the mud stuck to Philip's reputation.

We've had a couple of laughs about it in the years since then and as far as holding a grudge was concerned, if I did it lasted about 12 hours. I expect he regards the moment as one of the silliest things he ever did in his career and it should serve as a reminder to everyone that dishonesty – and I don't mean excessive appealing – just isn't worth it.

I have a small confession to make, too, however. When Free State batted, and Philip came in to bat, we behaved terribly. The whole Province team had been so outraged

Technology – please use it

by what they had seen that it was difficult to contain the anger.

The normally calm, assured, sensible Eric Simons was bowling and it was the only time in 15 years of playing together that I saw him lose control. He told me to field at short leg, which I duly did, and it resulted in another unique occasion. It remains the only time I indulged in full-on verbal abuse of an opponent, and I kept it up for every ball until he was out.

Eric bowled the first ball and followed up until he was a few feet from me and Philip when he said, loudly: 'Have you apologized to him for your cheating behaviour yet?' Poor Phil. He certainly didn't do it again.

White coats

From men in white coats to…more men in white coats. At least ten people have been credited with coining the saying: 'Cricket is 90 percent mental and ten percent physical' and it's true, whoever said it first. At least, it's true for successful players. For a game that revolves so much around psychology it amazes me how little use is made of experts in the field.

Other sports that require a combination of physical and mental fitness, and training in both, use sports psychologists as much as physiotherapists and coaches. I don't believe there is a single golfer in the top 100, or even 200, in the world who doesn't 'train the brain' and make use of a sports psychologist. We experimented a little when Bob Woolmer was coach and inevitably there were teething problems, although I felt it was well worth persevering with. Even if players learn no more than the simplest visualization technique it would be worth every cent.

There seem to be few limits to what administrators are prepared to spend on the hard skills of the game – every province has an academy and there are ongoing efforts to build new practice and playing facilities throughout the country – but when it comes to the 'soft' skills there is a definite reluctance to invest. It is the area of the game that most needs to advance and move with the times. Professional cricketers spend so much time 'on the road', even at purely provincial level, and they need someone to be with them to help confront a range of mental issues that crop up repeatedly.

Steve Waugh said his team could produce 'mental disintegration' through sledging but nothing, and I mean nothing, can produce mental disintegration quite as efficiently as a 12-week cricket tour. Ever since cricket teams started touring 100 years ago there has been talk of 'good tourists' and 'bad tourists': those who get on well with their team mates and those who become sulky pains in the backside. Unfortunately, the system simply doesn't allow for individuals who suffer from homesickness, moodiness or any other perfectly normal reaction to being away from home and family for that long. Many a good career has been ruined by the unfortunate use of labels, and they're often handed out by people who really don't have the first idea of what it feels like to be a player on a three-month tour.

Just as unfortunate as the players who aren't picked for a tour are the touring players who are picked to play but have to suppress their emotions and wear a happy smile for the sake of the team and team spirit. It is hard enough getting through the back end of a long tour without having to slap everyone on the back and pretend life is rosy and you don't have a care in the world. Sometimes a player needs nothing more than a couple of hours to himself, a bit of private time, but the practicalities of that have never been built into cricket tours. If there isn't a practice then there's a team meeting, and if there isn't a team meeting then there's a sponsors' function, or a press interview. And if you do make it to a genuinely free day, and you spend it by yourself or with a friend, then you run the risk of being labelled a sulker and a bad influence on team morale. It's an area of the game I would love to contribute to in the years ahead.

20

The media and sponsors

The media form a crucial part of every cricketer's life these days and I defy any player to say he hasn't picked up a newspaper to see what has been written about him at some stage, good or bad. Actually, those that claim they don't read the papers usually read them the most.

My relationship with 'them', I hope, improved with every year of my career. I understood more and more of what their role entailed and how their responsibilities to their employers sometimes dictated their actions.

It also became apparent that most journalists merely 'called' a match, a moment or a scene as they saw it and didn't apply as much 'spin' as players sometimes thought. They were there to relay information from a particular day and that information, if inaccurate, wasn't always their fault. Besides, I learnt that today's information is ancient history by the time the next day's newspaper appears and therefore stopped allowing myself to become upset. Or as upset as I used to be.

In an ideal world the cricketers should be able to form relationships of trust with all the regular newsmen but that isn't possible. As a result I learned who I could trust and who, deliberately or not, might divulge something that was 'off the record' or clearly an innocent throw-away line.

But I also came to understand that public figures, such as I was, had to accept the good with the bad, and to do so with a genuine acceptance, not through clenched teeth. It was important - and it took a few years – to understand that the press had a right to do their job, and a part of that job was to pass opinions and interpret situations. If you were playing badly, then you were playing badly. It hurt even more to see it written but the harsh truth is that the public wants you to score runs and for South Africa to win matches. They may have a passing interest in the reasons you are performing poorly, and they may even be marginally interested in how hard you have been working to put things right, but basically – if you're not producing then you have to go. And it's the media's job to say what they see and believe.

What annoyed me the most were people who criticized my performance who weren't qualified to do so. There are two forms of 'qualification': those who have played the game at the highest level and those who have been involved in the game for a long period of time and had spent years watching and talking to people who have first-hand knowledge.

I understand the need to sell newspapers, and I also understand the necessity for media organizations to appoint 'young blood' to a beat, but when those new young men arrive on the scene and make bold, sweeping statements about people who have dedicated their last 15 years to the game, it can be hard to stomach.

A good relationship between the media and the players will always lead to a good, and more accurate, flow of information to the public. It often perplexed me that journalists made so little effort to know the players better. Then again, players could – and should – make a greater effort themselves.

Cricketers will all have their share of 'unfair' media attention. We are sensitive, after all. We put a lot of effort into what we do. But almost all of it disappears very quickly. Relationships should be rebuilt as quickly as it takes for the next day's newspaper to appear.

There is only one moment that I will remember for the wrong reasons, and perhaps it is because of the way the 2003 World Cup ended. A large story in a national 'paper had me slamming the team for their negative attitude and for their lack of belief. The article also alluded to me not backing Shaun as captain and to having delivered a team talk to boost team spirits. It was extraordinary. It was the only thing I had ever read about me that did not contain a single shred of truth.

The next day I approached the journalist at an airport between venues and asked, without a hint of confrontation, where the story had come from. He replied that I had 'misinterpreted' his story and that he had been 'misunderstood'. Unfortunately that is the kind of incident that leads to long-term mistrust, and both parties, media and players, should work hard towards avoiding that. Write a 'hard' story by all means, but base it on fact.

I had some hard press, and it hurt. But I also had an enormous amount of fabulous press that I will cherish for the rest of my life. Or at least, for my son Joshua's life (and those of any siblings he may have). My Mum kept numerous scrapbooks of the early stories of my career and, one way or another, I have an amazing collection of golden moments preserved. In my 'real' retirement I will cherish the reports written about me. I will know I did a good job, but I will also know it was just a job. Or was it?

A short career

Throughout my professional career I asked myself how important what I did was. I usually doubted that it was very important at all. Certainly it was important within the cricket community, but the cricket-playing world sometimes felt very small. Within the context of the rest of the world, Gary Kirsten was a genuine, bona fide 'nobody'.

That's not to say that I doubted my worth to society, certainly not. I regarded myself as an entertainer (or perhaps a valuable assistant to the entertainers) and that was always good enough for me. Putting a smile on people's faces and giving them something to look forward to is every bit as important as filling the holes in their teeth

The media and sponsors

or administering their bonds. But the attitude and approach to my profession that came most naturally to me meant I was never going to acquire lofty notions of my own importance.

People read the newspaper the morning after a game and throw it away. They don't give it another moment's thought until the next game, often in 48 hours' time. There's no time for anyone to dwell on a Test series win because the one-dayers start three days later, or there's another tour starting ten days later. I do find that sad and I believe the game is poorer for the lack of reflection time. But I'm not one to stand in the way of progress – it's simply a sign of the times.

The older you get the more you realize that you are a quick fix in the business of providing entertainment. I feel fortunate that I was always aware of the short nature of my life on the stage. (I thought it would be much shorter.) It's vital for young sportsmen, cricketers in particular, to realize that no single individual rules the game. He may do so for a short time during his career, maybe even for a large proportion of his career in the case of the very best players, but the game survives and continues just as it always has.

Mostly, people watch cricket because they want to watch South Africa against Australia, or England against the West Indies, not because they want to watch a certain individual. There are exciting fast bowlers, dynamic batsmen and great fielders in every team, and they are replaced as surely as goods on a supermarket shelf, and that's the way it should be. The only time this causes a problem for players is when they start to believe the game owes them something. Yes, many do dedicate the 'best' years of their lives to cricket but if they end up feeling bitter or resentful when it comes to an end it probably means they have never developed a healthy sense of perspective during their playing days.

Jonty Rhodes was the greatest hero of my generation and he was forgotten a few months after retiring. I don't mean 'forgotten' literally – most South Africans know exactly who Jonty is when asked and will do for the rest of their lives, but none of them watch the national team and pine for him. It's the men on the field wearing the shirt that command the attention, and if you're not there, you're forgotten. People will always be excited about next Saturday, with or without you in the team. I wish more sportsmen would realize that.

Much as I will spend the rest of my days being grateful to cricket for the quality of life it has given me and my family, I will never spend a single day expecting anyone to treat me differently, because there is a new generation of stars every few years.

Interviews

Media interviews varied around the world. England could be the hardest because they were the most 'forthright' and unashamed of seeking the story they wanted. The media reacted at the speed of light when an opportunity presented itself to run their own sportsmen down. At the same time they weren't shy to have a dig at the opposition.

It was probably the sheer quantity of newspapers, and therefore the competition amongst them, that made the English media the most 'feared' for South African teams.

(And probably not just us.)

The concept of 'good' stories – and I mean stories that might sell newspapers rather than interesting cricket stories – is one that I can understand in terms of market forces, but it doesn't make it any easier or less intimidating to live with. There is a constant fear that something you might say will be twisted to fit the headline and that often resulted in a tendency to say virtually nothing in press conferences – and that neatly fits into the English pigeon-hole of 'dull, uninspiring South Africans'.

In Australia the media form a crucial part of the whole psychological machine that clicks into action the moment the opposition arrive. Or maybe a day after arrival. There are always exceptions to every rule but generally the Australian media have a critical role to play in 'writing up' their own players and providing as much sledging material as they can for their team to attack the opposition.

One of the most classic cases came ahead of the 2001 series when we were herded, reluctantly, into a room to be quizzed by an assortment of television, radio and print media. The concept of a 'media afternoon' is a good one in theory – a chance for cricket writers to have one-on-one interviews with every member of the squad over a period of two or three hours and to store information for the weeks ahead.

Amongst the problems, as we saw them, were that several players had already had their comments regarding Hansie wildly misinterpreted and exaggerated and there were an endless number of potholes into which we could be led. There were also a good number of players who had little or no experience of the open-forum style session that we were being asked to participate in. Each player was required to sit in front of a table around a room and wait for interviewers to 'pick' him. It was uncomfortable, to say the least, and potentially dangerous.

So we opted to face the audience in groups of two or three. But the 'solidarity' approach didn't work either because, as we suspected, the Aussie media will get their 'line' whatever you do.

Jacques Kallis was asked a seemingly innocent question about his mental approach to batting and he responded, equally innocently but a great deal more sincerely than his questioner, that he always thought positively and tried to approach every innings believing that he could score a hundred. At some point he was led to mention that Don Bradman had probably thought along similar lines.

The tabloid newspaper headlines the following day were a joke. 'Don Kallis' and 'Jacques Bradman' were the obvious ones but the extremes to which headline writers and tabloid 'hacks' were prepared to go to ridicule Jakes were amazing. Perhaps we had been overly cautious to start with, but the end result simply confirmed everything I'd experienced on two previous tours. You face a brilliant team – the best – and a media machine prepared to do anything to help them.

I must say that certain newspapers, the broadsheets in Melbourne and Sydney, were often brilliant and impartial in their analysis of both players and matches and employed some of the best cricket writers around, but I always had the impression that the majority of the crowd at the SCG and the MCG preferred the 'smaller' newspapers.

Sound bites

Radio interviews were less risky in the sense that they were quickly over and not often repeated, but they were amusing in a different way because they always, always wanted some affirmation of how great the Australian team was. How good was Steve Waugh? How good was Glenn McGrath? How great is this team? Aren't we great, Gary? If they'd asked even slightly more subtly I would probably have replied, routinely, that they were very great indeed. But they always sounded so frustrated and disappointed when I simply used the word 'good' that I just had to continue doing it. But they were, and still are, a great team. There you are, Aussies. They were great. Much better than us. At the time.

Interviews on the subcontinent were interesting in a different way because, often, it wasn't possible to understand the questions. And it wasn't just the language, it was the style of asking a question that flummoxed me. I understood all the words, and they appeared to be in the right order, but I still didn't get the question. It seemed fine to ask for the question to be repeated once, but after that it became awkward and embarrassing – for me – not the questioner. So the best option seemed to be to answer anyway, and hope you were close to the mark.

The worst experience however, across the board, was being asked the obvious – the really obvious. 'How does it feel to score your first hundred?' 'How does it feel to captain your country for the first time?' I don't mean to criticize journalists because I know they just need a quote to fill a space and finish their preview or report, but it was so much easier to answer genuine questions and I'm certain it resulted in better quotes. 'It's a great honour and privilege to score a hundred/captain my country and it's a day I'll never forget.' A different and 'real' question, however, might produce something like: 'I first dreamed of this day when I was seven years old playing back garden cricket with my brothers, and my back garden was Newlands.' Or: 'I can't deny the honour but, to be honest, captaincy was never my goal. I'm not natural captaincy material – it's a job for other people, not me.'

Actually, the hardest question I was asked – and I was asked at least a hundred times – was about my thoughts on Sachin. I formed a genuinely friendly relationship with the Indian media because I'd done well there, and they called me often for a thought on whatever the latest talking point was. Followed by the inevitable question on Sachin. What can you say? 'He's very good'? No, that was for the Aussie press.' 'He's the best in the world.' Too obvious. It was virtually impossible. I would open my mouth and nothing would come out. 'He's just Sachin.' Perhaps, in time, the word 'sachin' could be coined as a term of excellence in cricket. That would solve a few problems for us mortals when asked to comment on him.

Sponsors

I can understand when players regard the media as a chore, but I've always struggled to comprehend why sponsors would ever be regarded as burden. The professional game would barely exist without them and I willingly did whatever I could to ensure they had full value from me, and from whichever team mates I could influence.

Above: I scored a few runs to third man in my time...

Above: But, contrary to popular belief, could score in other areas too!

Top: Nudger? Lance Klusener couldn't hit it any harder than that. Which is why I missed it.

Middle: That's better. Single to long leg and get Lance back on strike.

Right: The other great, South African cricketing dynasty. Graeme Pollock was a wise and welcome visitor to the change room during his time as a national selector.

Eyes wide shut... this was safely pouched. Hylton Ackerman told me the difference between those who 'made it' and those who didn't was the same difference between those who were still alert in the field after five hours in the hot sun and those who had nodded off.

Antigua: Far too perfect to be true. Snow white beaches, turquoise seas and deep blue skies. King prawn snacks, three 'bald, body beautifuls' and one very happy couple.

South African Breweries were a magnificent asset to South African cricket and I'm proud to say I formed a special bond with them through their representatives, Di Southey and Rob Fleming. The importance of the relationship between players and sponsors can never be overstated and I'm proud of myself for recognizing that fact and never taking them for granted.

There were numerous golf days and assorted functions that I enjoyed to the full – and rightly so because they were supposed to be enjoyed – but I also never lost sight of the fact that our hosts were bank-rolling the game I loved so much and keeping it afloat. I spoke to as many of the sponsors' guests as I possibly could and I did so sincerely and happily, not merely in the 'two minutes of polite chat' manner that can be tempting when you are either tired, distracted or uncommitted.

The nature of our relationship resulted in a spectacular, surprise farewell party held at my brother Paul's restaurant in Kenilworth a few weeks after I'd retired. I know I'm often the last to 'click' but I will always be staggered that over 100 people knew about the party for two weeks beforehand and I never picked up a clue.

Debs said we were meeting up with some old friends of hers at Porky's 'Bardelli's' restaurant and I was still asking her what the couple did and where they lived as we walked into the restaurant. The place was packed with virtually everyone I had ever known well, and the video highlights package on my life is something I will always cherish. I'll enjoy rewinding the tape when Joshua wants to know what I did for a living. Actually, I'll always enjoy rewinding the tape.

21

Smoked up in Antigua.
Let the players have their say

SACA and West Indies 2002

The South African Cricketers Association was formed to give the players an official voice in affairs that directly concern them, both on and off the field. Although its formation was treated with suspicion and apprehension by the old guard of administrators and ex-players, it was not a new or even radical idea. Players' associations exist in many sports and in most parts of the world and have done for years.

If anything, we were disappointingly slow in getting the organisation up and running. Nobody was, or is, pretending that an opening batsman or a talented all-rounder should be making executive decisions, just as the executives who administer the game have no place telling cricketers how to win Test matches. But everyone should be allowed and encouraged to engage in open dialogue.

In today's professional environment, with so many players dedicating the best years of their lives to playing the game, the players' associations are speaking with a stronger and stronger voice and becoming increasingly influential; and rightly so. As a result of South African sport's rapid rise from amateurism to full professionalism in under a decade, many of the administrative structures, practices and attitudes are outdated and unable to cope.

The notion that players are rich, greedy and selfish is, frankly, ridiculous. There may be one or two individuals whose primary concern is themselves – isn't that true of every profession? – but when players stand together and speak with a single collective voice, the tone is one of care for the game and the simple desire for a fair deal. Playing professional cricket requires a huge commitment and plenty of sacrifice, and the vast majority of men making that sacrifice would be better paid and better looked after in terms of medical insurance and pensions by working in an office doing a 'proper' job. It shouldn't be that way, and it doesn't have to be.

While medical aid, labour law and pensions should be standard options amongst all professions and careers, cricket players should have their most important say in the actual playing of the game – our working conditions. If the employees of an insurance company can object to smoking in the office, or the mineworkers at a gold mine object to 12-hour shifts, cricketers should be able to have a say, for example, in how many matches are played in a certain period of time, how long tours are and whether bouncers are permitted in the one-day game.

The Association has a critical part to play in the future of the South African game and the safeguarding of its most important assets, the players. The very best players will always be OK. Sponsors enjoy success and are attracted like moths to a candle when the glamour cricketers become involved, but cricket involves 11 players per team and they all deserve to have the same, basic rights. It's extremely difficult for any cricketer, let alone a young one with limited experience of the 'real world', to sit down in front of an administrator and negotiate a contract that is fair and reasonable.

SACA's formation was greeted with scepticism and suspicion by most administrators but the relationship between the players and their officials had become polite and cordial by the time I retired. Warmth, if it ever becomes appropriate, can come later. The association was in its infancy, but it is a strong baby with an excellent footing. Everyone involved in SA cricket should be hoping it thrives.

A major goal for SACA would be the establishment of a financial structure that would allow provincial players to benefit and share in the success and revenue generated by Cricket South Africa. If the country's professional players were made genuine stakeholders in the game, then their responsibilities towards promoting, caring about and uplifting the game would increase dramatically.

A similar structure exists in Australia and the professional players in that country know they stand to gain – or lose – by the profile and success of the game in Australia. It should never just be about the national team; the professionals just beneath the top level are just as important as the big names in keeping the game alive and well.

Performance and results-related bonuses have been in place for the national team for many years, and they are extremely welcome when the team succeeds. It's difficult to say whether they serve as an incentive because, in the heat of battle, I can't believe anyone I've ever played with has been motivated by money. But success deserves reward and players have always appreciated reward. Now is the time for those rewards to be shared amongst all the professional players in the country.

If Cricket SA's projected revenue for a year is 100, for example, and the professional players' budgeted share is 30, then they should be entitled to a split of the additional revenue in a successful season that yields a net income of 120. Every professional player in the country would then be incentivised to make his 'job' both a passion and a career.

Until SACA was formed the dealings between players and administrators were inevitably one-sided and therefore extremely frustrating. Players and administrators have clear and separate roles, but they are mutually dependent. Through much of my career there were times when players, on the whole, felt frustrated and even angry at what was perceived to be a dictatorial approach from their bosses. On many occasions we might have reached a very similar decision if we had been involved in the process, but it was the fact that we weren't consulted that upset us the most.

There were times when a certain aspect of a certain competition wasn't 'working' for the sponsors, the broadcasters or the spectators. Perhaps it was the starting time of a match, or the length of a day-nighter – whatever it was, it would inevitably be resolved by non-playing administrators who then informed the players of what they would have to do in future, however impractical or unpopular the new conditions were. That is far less likely to happen today – if it can happen at all.

In the world of golf the PGA plays a pivotal role in the administration of the tour and the same applies to tennis with the ATP representing the views and best interests of the players. Why should cricket be any different? If it is because of the ethos of cricket then I'm afraid that is old-fashioned nonsense. Tennis used to be an 'old-syle' gentleman's game – it was still fully amateur and played by men in long trousers 50 years ago but the world changes. Golf, too, has kept all its old-world charm and character while still managing to move to the forefront of professional sport.

Antigua

Discipline is critical to the success of any sports team or individual and the best kind of discipline is that which is self-imposed. That, of course, is not always possible and it also has the potential to backfire with horrible consequences as it did during the dope-smoking 'scandal' following the Test match win in Antigua during the 2001 tour of the West Indies.

Understanding the background and build-up to any moment in history is as interesting and important as having a knowledge of the incident itself. It is difficult not to lose concentration and focus on the job of playing international cricket when you travel through and stay in some of the greatest corners of paradise you can imagine.

Even in Trinidad and Jamaica, which have self-sufficient economies outside of the mainstream revenue of tourism that all the other islands rely on for their survival, there are beaches, bars and…beach bars. Everywhere. Cricket has a 'coolness' and an appeal that doesn't exist anywhere else and many teams – notably Pakistan and England in recent decades - have been caught out by the Calypso 'sex, drugs and rock 'n roll' atmosphere.

For the decade that I was a national player the South African team enjoyed a better team spirit and shared each other's company more than most other nations, but that doesn't mean to say there weren't disagreements, arguments and even the odd bust-up. They are a normal part of life in any society, but embattled sports teams living in each other's pockets for 24 hours a day can be particularly prone to them.

The relief at winning the Test series in Antigua was enormous and it led to some animated celebrations. Seven members of the squad decided to 'do as the locals do' and smoke some dope – marijuana.

Disaster

The incident was a spectacular managerial disaster. The worst part about the whole thing was the sinking feeling we experienced when it finally went public - not another scandal, please. I couldn't stand the thought of more controversy, especially as we'd been playing some great cricket and were tentatively beginning to heal the public's scepticism after the match-fixing period.

Something needed to be done once the incident had become known to us and the guys involved had been told often enough that they were ambassadors for their country and should behave accordingly. But perhaps it's important to judge the behaviour that evening with some understanding.

We celebrated immediately with a couple of beers after an historic win, and it was barely mid-afternoon. Several hours later the 'silly seven' decided to ask one of the locals (who was actually assigned to look after the team) if he could find a 'joint'. He did. They smoked it in the privacy of their hotel rooms and were not otherwise behaving in an anti-social or irresponsible manner. They were extremely stupid, but in essence it was a largely harmless thing to do. Nonetheless, they were representing South Africa and despite local custom, it was, in fact, illegal. So they had to be punished and everyone accepted that.

The procedure we followed after that was a disaster and it led to severely strained relations between Daryll Cullinan and the rest of the team because he felt especially strongly that an example should be made of the 'guilty' players and that they should not, in any way, be allowed to 'get away' with anything.

The team management, however, made a decision to keep the incident 'in-house', which made sense at the time but, in retrospect, was crazy. A 'story' like that was always going to leak out, particularly with one team member so set against it, and when it did leak it was always going to be a media feast – which it was. Apart from the actually incident, which allowed newspapers to paste DRUGS SCANDAL headlines on all their stories, you also had the added allure of the cover-up. We inadvertently doubled the scandal by making it possible for reporters to throw words like 'deceit' and 'lies' into the story.

It was a serious enough offence to have been made public, but I was a part of the decision-making process to try to keep it quiet. I accept my part of the responsibility for the bitter taste it left in many mouths and for the damage it did to a game that had taken one of the biggest body blows of all time just 12 months earlier.

The decision of the internal disciplinary committee, which comprised captain Shaun Pollock, coach Graham Ford, assistant coach Corrie van Zyl and manager Goolam Raja, was to levy the highest fine ever imposed on players – a massive R10,000 each. We then tried to move on and put it behind us.

Daryll's objections and unhappiness at what he saw as the leniency of the team's actions may have flown in the face of the team's decision, but they were understandable. While he understood the 'need' for everyone to let their hair down and do something crazy once in a while, he felt that players on national duty should carry out their craziness well away from the team and somewhere 'safe'. And when they were 'caught', he believed they should face the consequences. Full consequences.

It was ironic how the 'bust' actually happened. The girlfriend of one of the players had seen the boys smoking their 'joint' and had mentioned it to another girlfriend. Word spread fast and that was that. It wasn't even supposed to be a bust.

We all learned a few painful but valuable lessons and poor old Herschelle was beginning to wonder whether he was ever going to make it through a tour without being fined. I don't believe anybody could honestly accuse Hersch of being malicious or intentionally troublesome, but he simply cannot stay out of trouble. He can't even be accused of being a bad influence, but if he is your friend and you do go out with him, the least you should do is expect the unexpected. And look out for the crossfire.

Macky flashes leg

The scandal aside, however, Antigua will always be remembered with an increasing sense of disbelief. The Jolly Harbour Resort in which we stayed was closer to a tropical paradise than any of us had seen or imagined before. Upon arrival we were issued with a hospital-type wristband that entitled you to, well, anything and everything. From king prawns to pina coladas, and sailing boats to rump steaks, the wristband got you it all – no cash required.

This may sound peculiar, but one day we decided we actually needed to escape this microscopic world of luxury to see if there were any signs of a life we recognised on the island. So we drove to English Harbour on the opposite side of the island and sat down for a relatively normal pizza – and even paid for it.

We returned to Antigua after the Test match for the one-day series and played the game during Antigua Regatta week when yachts from all over the world converge on the Caribbean island for a week of racing and partying.

The evening after the game I went for a walk around the harbour with Justin Kemp and a couple of other guys just to see all the boats and to soak up some of the atmosphere from what looked like the biggest party I had ever seen. It was still a very warm evening and the walk made us very thirsty, so naturally we had to stop for a beer. Or was it two?

There was hardly a boat without a South African crew member aboard and, as I've mentioned before, meeting up with fellow countrymen abroad is (mostly) one of the great pleasures of touring. The ensuing conversation was as informative as it was humorous and by the end of it I had decided that I would rather face Courtney Walsh and Curtly Ambrose in bare feet and without pads than cross the Atlantic in one of their boats. I always thought sailing was supposed to be luxurious – or at the very least, comfortable and enjoyable. Not a form of torture.

As usual on tours like these it can be a good idea to spend the evenings in the company of those who are likely to provide the best entertainment. Consequently, Neil McKenzie wasn't short of friends when it came to dinner time. There was nothing better for spirits than a bit of Neil Mac unpredictability.

It was the night of the pizza meal in English Harbour. We were standing outside the restaurant waiting for a taxi ride back to Jolly Harbour and Neil suddenly disappeared to the other side of the road with his shorts rolled up provocatively high and his t-shirt pulled suggestively off his shoulders. It was almost impossibly funny to cope with. In the few minutes we had before our car arrived, he thought he'd see if he could attract a 'client' from the passing traffic.

A couple of cars slowed down on their way past but perhaps his 'luck' would have been better had it not been for the five guys on the other side of the road heaving with hysterical laughter at the sight of Maccy flashing a leg at bemused cars passing by. The things you do on tour.

Charter

Soon after Eric Simons took over as coach the players decided that a disciplinary 'charter' was required and that it should include a code of conduct which all players agreed to abide by. It was drawn up by the players themselves.

It included everything we felt was relevant to the way we conducted our lives and played the game while on national duty – and in some cases even when we weren't.

If we had had that charter in place during the Antigua 'crisis' it would have been crystal clear what was required and there would have been no room for doubt or confusion.

Management encouraged the team to read up on the charter during my last year, especially on tour, to remind themselves of the values and 'ethics' we had all agreed upon as a group.

Whatever happens in the future, I hope the charter survives.

22

Relationships

The perspective one gets watching international cricket from the stands, or on television, is obviously restricted and one-dimensional. One of the questions I'm most frequently asked concerns the relationship between the players off the field. What's Merv Hughes really like? Does he want to kill you off the field, too?

The answer is invariably: 'Yes, we do socialize after the game.' At least, we try to. It doesn't happen nearly as much as it used to in less professional times (a source of great frustration and sadness for the players of the 60s, 70s and 80s) but I always used to make an effort. Without my sounding like an old fart, the players from that era are right. It is very sad how little we get to know each other off the field now.

The easiest guys to have a beer with immediately after the game were the Aussies. It's a big moment in your career when you first realize that your opponents go through the same worries, pressures and insecurities as you do. That's really the definition of not being intimidated: when you can accept that everyone gets out for nought and bowls bad balls, no matter who they are.

Sitting and relaxing in the dressing room with a cold beer and asking an opponent how he was feeling at a particular moment is amongst the best learning tools I ever discovered. I was always amazed when I told great players how calm they looked when the heat was at its highest and they invariably replied: 'Oh really? Well, I was shitting myself.' As my career went on and I became a senior player I learnt that it was important to look calm and collected, especially if that was the last thing you were feeling. I always found an ice-cold opponent far more intimidating than one who was waving his arms around screaming. But either way, if you take the trouble to find out what their perspective was on a particular situation you'll be far wiser and more successful cricketer – and person.

Shoaib

I had a particularly interesting relationship with Shoaib Akhtar. We played against each other a lot. The first time I encountered him was on our 1997 tour to Pakistan when he was picked for a President's XI to play us in a three-dayer at Peshawar. Abdur Razzaq was selected, too.

We'd heard about this wild, tearaway fast-bowling kid a few days earlier and how he could already be the quickest in the world. It wasn't the first time we'd heard a story like that, from Lilac Hill to Montego Bay (and even sometimes in England). We'd hear rumours about someone who was supposedly lightning fast but they rarely materialized. We didn't think much more about it.

But I thought quite a bit more about him once he'd clanged me on the head early in that game. He wasn't as fast as he became later, but it was clear he had the potential to be very swift, and dangerous.

After the game he approached me and asked, quite humbly I thought, what I thought of him and whether there was anything I could recommend for him to improve. Was there anything I could see that would make him a better bowler? I was a little flattered, I must say. So I gave him a couple of pointers about the lines to bowl to left-handers and what length to bowl to suit different conditions around the world. I find it extremely ironic and amusing to think of what he became, one of the best and quickest the world has seen, and he did it all despite getting advice from me. In retrospect I should have told him that nobody gets wickets by bowling short. I should have strongly recommended that he keep everything pitched up.

On my penultimate international tour, again to Pakistan, Shoaib struck me quite badly in the face. I was down on the ground and there was plenty of blood, and the swelling was impressive. But I never lost consciousness and I wasn't really disorientated. I was completely aware of Shoaib and his concern and appreciated it greatly. He didn't regret bowling the ball or that I'd missed it, because we both knew it was part of the game, but it was encouraging to see a man like him remember, in the heat of battle, that there are more important things in life than a game of cricket, the most obvious being your health.

That evening he phoned my hotel room to see how I was doing and to make sure the injury had been stitched up neatly. It was another genuine touch that I appreciated greatly. He asked if I was going to be fit enough to bat in the second innings and I said I wasn't sure because I couldn't really see out of one eye. He said that wasn't a good enough reason to stop him bowling bouncers at me and I replied that that was fair enough. We both had a good chuckle.

Athers

It was occasionally possible to spend time with the England team and I was always keen to put aside the fierce and traditional rivalry we enjoyed in pursuit of common interests away from the game.

Graham Thorpe and Michael Atherton endured mixed reputations as players and as tourists. The media portrayed them as grumpy more often than not and they probably were. Ironically, they were two men whose company I thoroughly enjoyed whenever our paths crossed.

It started after the Port Elizabeth Test in 1995 when I'd been named as man of the match after scoring a couple of 70s in a low-scoring game.

The South African team had gone out for a post-match party and I decided to extend the celebrations when the others returned to the hotel. As usual, the choices are not always so plentiful for a late-night glass of wine and cricketers tend to head for the same sort of places.

I found an anonymous but very pleasant bar and cruised in for a nightcap only to bump into Thorpe and Atherton. I knew neither beyond a cursory 'Hello'. Athers had really established himself in SA as a dull, moody captain with few good words to say about anything, on or off the field.

I had honestly started to feel frustrated and slightly sad about the lack of interaction between the teams by then, particularly when compared to the Aussies. Even in England a few months before we had hardly visited each other's dressing rooms.

I headed straight for them, fortified by my belief that we should be mates off the field (and by several drinks). They were in a similar mood and welcomed me to share a very good bottle of wine, not their first.

We chatted into the early hours of the morning about anything and everything: a cricket conversation constantly broken up by opinions and arguments about completely immaterial, irrelevant issues – nonsense basically. The strength of the English pound was certainly one topic but, more importantly, it ensured a steady flow of the best wine in the house. Which wasn't fully appreciated, of course.

Comfortably the most important part of the night, however, was the confirmation that people are so often not what they seem or how they are portrayed. I admit I'd fallen for some of the negative press about Atherton before that night but, although he wasn't exactly dancing on the bar, he was highly amusing and great company. That was subsequently confirmed on several further occasions when we weren't quite so thirsty. Fortunately, that was the only time we finished chatting at three o'clock in the morning.

Lara

There has been very little communication or socialising between South African teams and West Indian teams over the years. The contests have been hard on the field but, sadly, have ended there. It's a strange scenario in many ways because the West Indians who have played in South African have, to a man, become social and cricketing icons in the regions in which they have settled.

The 'sanctions busters', like Sylvester Clarke, Ezra Moseley and Alvin Kallicharan did far more than merely survive in apartheid South Africa; they flourished and did a huge amount to break down social and cricketing prejudices. I was at school and Varsity during that time, however, so you should listen to their accounts of life in SA for a more accurate reflection.

But in my experience of the post-isolation era Frankie Stephenson will always be a legend in the Free State as will Eldine Baptiste in EP and KwaZulu-Natal and Otis Gibson in the Border. But the greatest impact I have ever seen, on the greatest number of players, was made by Desmond Haynes during his time at Western Province. Herschelle Gibbs, Jacques Kallis, Paul Adams, myself... the list goes on and on. Dessie made the world of difference to all of us, and many more, and the lasting legacy of respect will remain for several generations.

But outside of domestic partnerships there was sadly little interaction between ourselves and the West Indian cricketers. The single, very special occasion was Ernie Els' wedding which occurred on 31 December 2000. I'm not sure many other cricketers were invited but it was a fabulous evening. Everyone had their own drivers but Brian's appeared to have been commandeered by someone else, so he asked whether Debs and I could share our driver with him and his fiancée when the evening seemed to be drawing to a close. Naturally it was a pleasure.

Ten minutes later, after a great chat about cricket and the lifestyle – pros and cons – that accompanies the job, we decided that a final nightcap would be appropriate and redirected the driver to an appropriate spot for a *loopdop*. It's remarkable how few moments there were in ten years of international cricket to chat and share thoughts with fellow professionals, let alone one of the greats of all time, but on that evening there were no barriers, no ranks. Just two professional cricketers and their partners chatting about what they did and how it affected them. Spending a couple of hours with Brian Lara was just another example of how popular perceptions can deceive. Arrogant, aloof... not then. In fact, on the evidence of that night, it was hard to believe he ever was.

Quicks

Fast bowlers and opening batsmen have a natural affinity for each other. It must be the attraction of opposites. After openers have been sticking around for a year or two, facing the new ball and enjoying the occasional success, even the nastiest, meanest guys can't help developing a respect for them. Facing the new ball isn't easy, physically or mentally, and the opening bowlers always back themselves at the beginning of a match or innings. They know that's when they are at their best and if you're the guy who constantly has to face them they have a certain empathy. Not that it ever shows on the field. Afterwards, though, they are usually the first to offer a greeting.

I've always maintained that no batsman actually enjoys facing the short ball. Some have managed to create an illusion that they do, and that takes fantastic PR work, a lot of bravado and quite a bit of bullshit. Perhaps I'm wrong. Maybe there are, or have been, a couple of players who actually enjoy an occasional bouncer but a barrage of short ones from a couple of genuinely fast bowlers isn't fun. However, it's how you deal with them that determines whether you are successful or not.

I don't believe you need to be a great player of the short ball to succeed at the highest level, but you do need to have an extremely efficient way of dealing with it. The method must be tried and tested for hundreds of hours in the nets and you need to be able to rely on it. The first step is to make sure the short ball isn't going to get you out, and if that means making sure you can leave them all alone, then practise that. Only then can you start learning how to score against them. I fell into this category – not a great player of the short stuff but good at dealing with it so that I knew it wouldn't get me out regularly.

There are some things in sport and life that are simply not enjoyable at the time, but immensely rewarding afterwards. Sprinting up the side of a hill during pre-season training is not 'fun', but you do it year after year because as soon as the pain goes away the results are worth every ounce of discomfort. Facing fast bowling was similar. In some ways, it held a huge charm for me. Whether it was the challenge of my skills or the adrenalin rush, or both, I'm not sure, but it was certainly a combination of love and hate that was addictive. Perhaps there was a bit of masochism thrown in there, too.

I was never, ever scared of being hurt physically. Being hit on the body or arms and feeling pain simply didn't bother me because I'd accepted a long time earlier that it would be an intrinsic part of the job. Besides, the masochistic part of me used to say that feeling pain was good for you; it focussed the mind and made you that much more determined. As long as it didn't result in the loss of my wicket, I didn't care how uncomfortable I was.

It was actually more difficult facing bowlers like Glenn McGrath who bowled in exactly the right place for four or five overs before you even had a scoring chance. It amazes me that more fast bowlers don't concentrate on making the batsmen play every ball, or at least think about every ball. McGrath and Shaun Pollock are two of the most successful bowlers of their generation, of all time for that matter, and their success is based on wearing batsmen down mentally more than physically because there is no respite. A fast bowler that gives you two or three balls an over that you can ignore from the moment they leave his hand is effectively giving you two minutes off, plenty of time to bring the heart rate down and compose yourself for when you do have to work again.

With the greatest of respect to Polly and McGrath (they are the hardest bowlers I ever faced and how much more respect can I show?) they reminded me of the 60-year-old golfers you see at every club who play off a nine handicap, don't hit it very far but never miss a fairway and routinely break 80. Consistency is what makes them great and consistency is what the rest of us strive for.

Sachin, Rahul

The profile of people like Sachin Tendulkar, Rahul Dravid and other Indian superstars is something South African cricketers will probably never experience, no matter who they are and what they become. Only Jonty came close to cult status if not quite the deification that Sachin experiences, but only in India itself, certainly not in South Africa.

When you see the size of the crowds waiting outside the Indian team hotel, and hear the noise, see people fainting with excitement (as well as heat and dehydration, probably) it's very difficult for us to imagine what it might feel like. Yet the old adages are so true – reputation is only skin deep. Sachin is modest, extremely polite and very enjoyable company, not that I've ever spent more than five or ten minutes with him at any one time.

Rahul is equally genuine as a person without the slightest sign of airs or graces. Both men are humble about the game and what it has done for them. Humility is something I tend to look for very closely in individuals. I have only ever had a desire to socialise and spend time with people whose feet have remained firmly attached to the ground and there's something even more pleasing to see that quality in a superstar.

Allowing your status to affect your perspective on ordinary life can happen to anyone in the public eye and it takes plenty of self-reminding to bear in mind that being a good sportsman does not make you a better person, or more entitled to a place at the front of the queue, than a good gardener or a good plumber.

Ridley Jacobs (West Indies wicket-keeper): *I always admired watching Gary play. What I admired most about him was his patience. He was someone you would always want in your team because he would stick around and the others would bat around him. Once he got to the crease, he didn't mind taking a few knocks, but he wouldn't give his wicket away. In a difficult situation he would really stick it out and come out on top most of the time.*

Brian Lara (West Indies captain): *He's been a great servant to South African cricket. A lot of us are preoccupied with style and flair in batsmanship. He didn't care about that but always managed to succeed in the same job that we had to do. It may not have been stylish. But it was almost always very effective. As a captain, you would have thought that this guy looks like someone you could get rid of pretty quickly, but he got stuck in and was a patient cricketer who achieved a lot of team goals.*

Michael Atherton (England captain): *The evening to which Gary refers in PE was indeed a drunken affair, I'm afraid to say, but a huge amount of fun. It came at the end of the 1995-96 series and was certainly very unplanned. In terms of consequence or conversation I would have to say there wasn't much to report except that there was much drinking of very decent red wine and an equal amount of bitching by fellow opening batsmen about how hard the job was.*

But actually it was far more important to me than just that. I didn't really know many of the SA players well, and was quite suspicious of them at that time because I saw them conveying this very righteous public image which didn't sit at all well with my more cynical nature! Gary, to me, represented the more human and laid-back face of South African cricket. As for his batting – well, I truly believe that he was one of the most underrated batsmen of my generation. In terms of openers I would place him in the very highest rank. I could barely name two other openers I would have been as happy to have in my team as Gary. Utterly dependable, good technique, brave, and greedy for runs. He had the perfect temperament for opening the batting.

Sachin Tendulkar (Indian batsman): *Gary Kirsten was a brilliant player. He knew exactly how to pace his innings. He had all the right shots for an opener. Once he got in it was difficult to get rid of him. He knew when to score and what pace to bat at and I think that made all the difference. He was pretty much always successful against us and scored two hundreds in Kolkata that, I think, were very special to him.*

Contrary to what some people say, he was not a frustrating batsman to bowl to. He was always an attacking player. He was very, very smart and shrewd in the sense that

Relationships

he knew when to attack and when to defend. But, at the end of the day, he was an attacking player. He did not believe in simply blocking.

Shoaib Akhtar (Pakistani fast bowler)**:** *I regard Gary as a true gentleman, a decent cricketer and a good friend. I'll never forget the first time we met: it was during a three-day match in 1997 when I was a youngster playing for a Board XI against the touring South Africans. He had scored a lot of runs in the 12 months before that and was establishing himself on the world stage. I went up to him and asked what I could do to become a better cricketer. He said: 'Just be yourself and work very, very hard.' I have lived on that advice all my career.*

One of the saddest days of my career was when I hit him on the helmet in Lahore during the first Test of the 2003 tour. I forgot both my manners and his age! When I went up to him afterwards he looked so ugly...no, really, I am just joking. That night I called him to make sure he was all right and he said to me: 'Why am I trying to hook you at the age of 35?'

But in the next Test he showed his true courage and skill by scoring an amazing hundred. He is not only an example to all South Africans but to all cricketers and I would like to wish him the very best of luck for the future. I hope to 'bump' into him many, many more times when we are both finished with playing the game.

23

A world of change – Finding Deborah and finding faith

The contributions and 'fingerprints' on the my life left by Duncan Fletcher, Alan Solomons, Hylton Ackerman, Robin Jackman, Eric Simons, Jonty Rhodes and so many others are recorded elsewhere in the book but I'm sure none of them would mind if I said they were small compared to the influence on my life that my wife, Deborah, has had. She really helped me gain an understanding of the way I wanted to live my life. Until I met her I was living a single man's subsistence existence, a slash-and-burn lifestyle that centred on me and revolved around me. It was a lot of fun at the time but very shallow, not that I noticed. There was nothing to sustain me outside of cricket, and there's only so long a man can be sustained by his job. Besides, I really didn't want to be sustained by cricket.

But I had no idea of what it meant to really love someone and to care for them. Everything had been about me, me and me. Debs had the patience, for some reason, to teach me that life doesn't work like that. It would have been much easier simply to write me off and find someone less self-indulgent.

We met at the infamous Green Man pub. As self-appointed, part-time manager of the establishment I was generally able to hop out from behind the bar counter to join the clientele if and when there was a good reason. The day I saw Debs for the first time was the best reason I ever had to stop serving drinks. A little research resulted, reasonably quickly, in an introduction. We chatted briefly and I was very quickly aware that she was wonderfully different. Obviously she was beautiful, but there was a lot more. But she had a boyfriend at the time, so that was that. Until about five months later.

I walked into a restaurant and couldn't believe my luck when I was met by Debs just inside the door. She was my waitress. I tried to engage her in conversation but it must have come across terribly. Actually, I know it did. She told me herself. Sports 'personality' in restaurant, chatting up waitress… oh dear. And Debs was having none of it. Having initially thought of me as 'just another boring sportsman', she thought I was a complete creep when I tried the 'I'm not like the others' line on her.

But I had decided to be brave in my pursuit and not to be deterred. The second time I asked her out on a date, a few days later, she just laughed at me. But the third time she didn't laugh, so I knew I was making progress. She just said 'No'.

By the fourth time (or was it the fifth?) my perseverance paid off and she agreed to go on a date, although I think she was a little reluctant. She was certainly wary of sportsmen.

She wasn't convinced of my lifestyle, and rightly so. Debs had been a Christian all her life and came from a strongly Christian family in which her father, Michael Cassidy, was an evangelist, the founder of African Enterprise, a Christian Mission Organisation working in the cities of Africa. Frankly, I don't think she saw too much of this sort of interest or concern in me. A happy-go-lucky cricketer with a bit of a 'reputation' going out with the daughter of a preacher – it wasn't everybody's idea of the perfect match. And it wasn't Debs', either.

When she looked at me she must have seen either a blank canvas or a hopelessly lost cause because, though I was fun, I had chosen to enjoy life in a hedonistic way and I was something of a spiritual vacuum. If you'd asked me why I was put on earth and what I thought I could achieve (outside cricket) I would have stumbled for an answer. Once Debs decided she could take me seriously, and even wanted to, it was obvious that I needed to understand her life, her values and the beliefs that had guided her life up to that point, and would continue to guide her life.

I almost fell off my chair when Debs first told me her father was an evangelist. And I wasn't the only one in for a shock when it became known that Debs was going out with some hillbilly, hard-living cricketer called Gary Kirsten.

But as Debs and I fell in love she really wanted me to have some understanding of God and where he fitted into her life. I had fallen in love with her because of her nature and her kindness and also the respect I quickly had for her values and now I wanted to understand everything else.

Whilst meeting Debs brought huge changes to my life, the real transformation happened from within me. Debs might have been a catalyst for it, but ultimately there is only one way that a leopard changes its spots and that is with a shift of heart, mind and spirit. And a story of my life and my cricket career would not be complete without explaining the one thing that has had a profound effect on my life – in every aspect.

Finding faith and developing a relationship with Jesus Christ is without doubt the single most important discovery and step that I have taken in my life. When I met Debs and came into touch with her faith and her way of life, I noticed something distinctly different – a peace perhaps. It was something that I knew I wanted in my life. So I began finding out what it meant to be a Christian. This meant taking time to read and question. I also attended an Alpha course at our local church. Neither Debs nor her family put pressure on me to take this step, but I began the process and gradually realised that this was what I had been missing in my life. The final piece of the puzzle. It was the simple realisation that there was someone out there controlling my destiny, someone who cares and wanted me to be the best possible person that I could be. It was this relationship that came to affect every area of my life – both on and off the field.

Top: Nothing beats the look on a young fan's face when he or she has the signature of their hero. But the professional 'bounty hunter' autograph collectors can be a different matter.

Above: The Kirstens, Trisha and Shaun Pollock and Isabelle and Lance Klusener enjoying a traditional Moroccan dinner of lamb targine in Tangiers.

Top: Great mates on and off the field, Herschelle and Bonamy take time out to join the usual Kirsten exploration trip – this time in Sydney harbour.

Above: It wasn't just cricket, of course, but the patronage of Nelson Mandela probably did more to inspire us than any other, single factor. Here we are *en route* to India in 1996.

Left: Taking a slow cruise up Keurbooms river with his brother in law Martin and his wife Sam. One of my favourite holiday destinations.

Above: Fishing with Mark Boucher in Florida. Can you feel the tension? Do we look stressed? Relaxation and escape between duty is crucial to performing at your best.

Left: The bandana again, this time in a four nation tournament in Nairobi. Because we played in white clothes match referee Mike Denness ruled that I was contravening clothing regulations and fined me.

Below Left: Hit in the face for the third time in my career by Shoaib Akhtar, this time seriously. He called me later in my hotel room to see if I was OK.

Below Right: Man of the match at Headingley in 2003 following one of my best centuries. From 21-4 we made 340 and won the game.

On the field…

My whole understanding of success began to change and suddenly scoring runs no longer became the ultimate yardstick for my happiness. I began to ask myself questions. Was I of any value to the system and the players around me? Did I make a difference as a person or did I just arrive, hold my catches (sometimes) and try to score runs?

The 'new me' discovered that there is much more to life than bowling or hitting a cricket ball, but also that having a realistic sense of values didn't mean you had to care any less about the little red ball. In fact, I cared more and became more effective because I knew that my life and happiness didn't depend on my results on the cricket field. I felt I was able to deal with the disappointment of not scoring runs so much better and that my life didn't begin and end between 22 yards of white paint. I began to see the importance of conducting myself, on the field, in the correct manner. Abusing and sledging the opposition was something I never felt comfortable doing even at the start of my career. Although it might have formed part of team strategy, I was convinced there were other ways I could add value to the team.

When I became a Christian the relationships that I had formed with my team mates over the years never changed. Actually, I believe they improved. Many of the guys used to joke about how they planned one day to change in a manner similar to mine. My answer to them was always not to wait for too long, because no one knows what tomorrow will bring.

Off the field…

I'd like to think that my relationships with my family and friends have also become better, that I've become a little more consistent and reliable and that I'm able to offer something more and beyond the odd two-minute international phone call. I want to give to others in whatever way possible and I would like to assist others in their careers, especially sportsmen, helping them to realise their true potential as people.

Naturally, my focus is on cricket. Being able to assist young players in making the dream of playing for their country come true is something I feel strongly drawn to and I really hope I have the opportunity to do exactly that.

I also have a responsibility to my community and my church, to be a good example to those who might look up to me and who aspire one day to become top sportsmen. The many people I've met at church, people from all walks of life, have been a real inspiration to me and are always on call to listen and pray as well as to support.

I have had the massive and unexpected privilege of playing cricket for my country for 10 years. I was blessed and given incredible opportunities to pursue my passion and make a living out of it. God has been by my side through some incredibly difficult times as well as the good times. I still get things very wrong. I still make plenty of mistakes and I'm definitely in no position to tell people how to live their lives. I can only share with you my experiences and what an incredible difference coming to know God has made to my life.

Such lifestyle changes could have been intimidating for a person in my position but they never were. As with all life's projects and challenges you start with the simple things because they matter most. Debs has always been a 'simple things' person and, although she has been part of most of the biggest life and career decisions I've ever made, she never forgot to put a little note in my suitcase that I'd find a week after arriving in Australia, or wherever we were touring.

She has been an incredible source of support and encouragement. On several occasions she has talked me out of retirement. At other times I would just be moping around feeling sorry for myself and she would knock some sense into me and tell me to start thinking positively.

Fortunately she loves travelling and seeing the world, so there was an added incentive to make certain I completed the natural course of my career. She certainly wasn't going to let me finish prematurely and run the risk of having regrets. When I needed my confidence and self-belief to be boosted, she did it. And when I just needed a good old-fashioned kick up the backside she did that, too.

Golf, please

One thing we agreed on without hesitation or condition was that we would delay the start of a family until I could be at home to devote the majority of my time to the home and the children. We were lucky in being able to plan a family, and we had time on our side and the ability to lay the foundations. Few people have that luxury and we are both grateful that Joshua - and his potential siblings – won't have to endure Dad being away from home for months at a time.

If the Kirsten genes are as well represented in Joshua as they are in all my generation, he is likely to pick up his first cricket bat at about the same time he starts walking. He will have difficulty in gripping it, however, whether he is left or right-handed, because I will have slipped a golf club into his little hands a few moments earlier. The prospect of the exciting years ahead, watching our kids grow up and sharing their lives makes the decision to stop playing cricket seem as simple as taking your next breath. I know I'll miss playing cricket, but I've been able to plan my exit and Debs has been there, if not physically then in my thoughts, every day for the last seven years.

As a father I now regard my family and my faith as my life. Joshua and Deborah are the future and the future excites me enormously. But, at the same time, I hope I never forget how much I owe to cricket: the opportunities the game has given me, the people who worked so hard for me, the chance to travel and see the world and the chance to lay a solid foundation for the rest of my life. I hope I'll always feel humbled by my good fortune and grateful for the quality of life cricket gave me and will continue to give me and my family for the rest of our lives.

Playing cricket was a passion for me from the age of seven and I was able to indulge myself in my passion until the age of 36. Artists and musicians, presumably, are passionate about their work but very seldom do they get the chance to represent their country, to stand in front of 20,000 people, listen to the national anthem and then hear the crowd cheering for you to win. And for the last seven years I knew Deborah, the most special person I've ever met, was a part of that crowd, too. It simply couldn't have got any better.

My in-law family…

Debs' side of the family may not have been avid cricket lovers before I arrived on the scene but they became ardent supporters as the years rolled by. Mum, Dad, Mart, Sam, Jonathan, Cath, Grandpa and Gran and the whole extended family have been massive supporters of cricket, not just of me. A small 'regret' of my retirement is that they may lose a little of the enthusiasm they developed for watching the game now that I'm gone.

On the other hand, I trust the cricket 'bug' has bitten them deeply enough to make sure they continue supporting the great game. Cath's husband, Jonathan, was a committed baseball fanatic (he is American) but has now, after watching or listening to ball-by-ball internet coverage, been converted to such an extent that he sends e-mails asking why certain players aren't scoring runs or haven't been included in the latest squad. A few tales from me about the trials and tribulations of the players involved should make certain they all have enough personal interest in proceedings to overcome their deficiencies in the finer points of the game.

My parents-in-law, Michael and Carol Cassidy, became particularly fascinated with cricket. Although 'Dad' loves his sport it was a very new experience having a 'famous' sporting son-in-law and he did everything he could to support me, even to the extent often of praying for me before every delivery I faced during crucial innings. This was especially true during the century I scored at Lords in the 2003 tour. He says he'll find out from the Lord later about the correct theology of all that. In any event Dad so existentially entered into my batting career that he says he feels he has personally 'faced' every fast bowler in the world who ever bowled at me. He also still wears with the utmost pride every piece of South African team kit that I gave him.

Apart from the e-mails and phone messages of support, Dad provided a source of inspiration himself through the work of African Enterprise, an organisation he founded over 40 years ago that conducts missionary work throughout Africa. He used to tease me about the amount of time I was away from home and the amount of travelling cricketers were required to do. But he routinely did more miles per year than I and he was going as strong as ever at the age of 67 when I was looking forward to putting my feet up and staying at home.

Cricket aside, the Cassidy family must be amongst the warmest, most sincere and hospitable people I have ever known and they accepted me into their lives without question as I gradually became part of the family. I have the deepest affection for every single one of them, which is why I don't mind telling a story about my brother-in-law, Mart.

When Debs and I first started dating, Mart, who was at Varsity and a typical student, thought our relationship was a fantastic idea. Not that he had necessarily thought about my suitability as a partner for his sister, but I was a cricketer who ran a bar in his spare time and Mart had worked out that if he stayed close enough to me then he wasn't going to have to pay for too many beers in an evening, short of money as he always was as a student.

So whenever Mart spotted an 'opportunity' such as a function, dinner or just a night

A world of change

out at the Green Man, he would always latch on to his sister, usually with a group of mates, and angle for an invitation to come along. Debs greatly enjoyed these moments of extra sibling 'closeness' and, to be fair, so did I. If Mart's crafty student ways were contributing to my chances of staying with Debs, I was all for it and happy to buy him and his mates whatever round of drinks they called for. Today Mart and I still enjoy a special friendship and he has grown into a remarkable man of accomplishment and responsibility.

At last the Big Day...

The day we married, 18 September 1999, was the best day of my life.

I was very aware of how lucky I was to experience such an occasion, with all our best friends and family there. The memories will last my lifetime. It is still difficult to describe how deliriously happy I was throughout the entire day.

Even a couple of weeks later, when we realised just how profoundly we had exceeded our budget, I was still buzzing with the success and joy of the day. We simply couldn't help the guest list expanding during the planning phase and we both felt strongly that the more people could be there, the more fun we would have. And we were right.

The reception was held in a marquee hoisted on the old Keurboom Sports Club, now part of Western Province Cricket Club, and we prayed hard for good weather – which we received. An afternoon spent having a great time with nearly 300 friends and family, starting at 11 am and finishing at 11 pm, was followed by a night in the incredible Cape Grace hotel. From there we caught a 7.00 am flight to Harare and went on to spend a week on Lake Kariba, followed by another week on a beautiful island in Mozambique.

The beauty of the wedding and the happiness of the honeymoon, the friendship of so many people – perhaps it would have come my way cricket or no cricket. But in the quiet moments I still give thanks to the Lord as the ultimate giver, and most especially of Debs.

24

Who read Duckworth Lewis?

World Cup 2003

In the weeks building up to the 2003 World Cup tournament in South Africa it became obvious that I had missed the boat. What was always going to have been my one-day swansong had passed by. I'd missed selection for eight successive one-dayers as selection convener Omar Henry and his colleagues, including my mate Symmo, searched for the right balance in both the team and the squad.

We had back-to-back one-day series against Sri Lanka and Pakistan as preparation for the World Cup and a couple of opening partnerships hadn't worked in the first eight of those ten matches. An early wicket or two was routinely cramping the attacking potential of the middle order, and players like Jacques Kallis were having to spend too long rebuilding the innings rather than compiling a substantial score.

I was thrown a last-minute lifeline with two matches of the series against Pakistan to go. It was in the Boland, a ground known as much for its scenery as for the awkward slowness of the pitch and the outfield. Runs scored in Paarl were generally hard earned.

I couldn't help feeling a bit like an old boxer being given one last shot at the title, a final payday to end a long career. I also knew that I had to score runs – if I failed the selectors would be justified in going back to their plan 'A'. I knew I needed runs, at least 50 but probably a lot more than that; seventy or eighty would be more convincing.

It felt ironic that I was under so much pressure to prove myself again after playing over 170 matches and scoring over 5000 one-day runs, but I wasn't upset and I certainly didn't object. While I believe experienced players deserve to be treated with respect, you can't simply allow them to keep playing on reputation alone. I had a good record, sure, but everyone's time comes eventually and if the selectors felt I had lost my edge in the one-day game then at least they were being true to themselves and doing the job to the best of their ability. But anyway, they had given me a chance to prove them wrong and I was grateful for it.

We were chasing a modest 214 for victory. As always, I knew I would have a great chance of shaping the innings and making the runs I needed if I could just survive the opening spell from Waqar Younis. Fortunately Wasim Akram wasn't playing. There was no need to force the pace or play high-risk cricket, but I needed to get through Waqar's spell with the new ball.

I had scored two when a Waqar 'special', delivered with a round arm, angled into me, straightened and kept low. I had hardly moved. It hit me on the shin. My team mates later told me it looked as if it would have knocked middle stump out of the ground but when I finally saw a replay I couldn't agree. It had straightened enough to hit off stump as well.

I felt the familiar cold shudder down my back and tried not to look at the umpire too quickly. Acting calm and casual on this occasion felt like a futile gesture but it had become second nature after all these years. When I looked up I knew what was to come. At least, I thought I did. His head was shaking from side to side. 'Not out,' he said.

Those are the chances you must never, ever allow to get away. I had been unusually tense but I settled quickly after that and began to play with fluency and freedom. I was enjoying it, really enjoying it. As we passed 200 and I reached the 90s I finally allowed myself to believe I'd make the squad and be a part of a third World Cup. We won the game and I returned to a very emotional dressing room, 102 not out. Herschelle, in particular, was pleased. Very pleased. We'd opened a lot together over the years and he was keen to have me back.

The opening ceremony was unquestionably one of the great highlights of my career. Rarely, if ever, had I felt more proud to be South African and I spent every day of national duty feeling proud. Walking on to Newlands that night as part of the national team, and to hear the roar of Cape Town's finest, was wonderful enough, but to be hosts to the rest of the world and see the greatest cricketers on earth standing on what had been my back garden as a kid…it was difficult to breathe.

The opening game against the West Indies the following day was also very special, although we lost. It was thrilling cricket for much of the day, with Brian Lara making a century and us falling just three runs short of an imposing total. The team was understandably nervous and it had been a jittery performance, with bat and ball.

The biggest single mistake we made, however, was starting the tournament in the belief that we were going to win it. The hype about winning it on home soil had started about six months earlier and there seemed to be hundreds of people quite happy to talk about winning as though all we had to do was turn up to collect the cup.

My personal view was that it was going to be harder to win at home rather than easier. The weight of expectation was massive and it certainly affected most of us. I felt we should have focussed our attention on getting into a position where we had a chance of winning rather than thinking of the final, but I didn't say much for fear of bursting the bubble or being accused of aiming too low. UCB president Percy Sonn was absolutely convinced we were going to win, and never missed an opportunity to say so. I don't think it helped much.

Our early performances were inconsistent and several teams were playing better cricket than we were. As the tournament progressed I felt we'd fallen increasingly into a 'hit and hope' situation in which we were relying on sporadic bursts of brilliance to carry us through. It was so unlike the heyday of our one-day game when we believed we knew how to win games from almost any situation, even when things had gone horribly wrong.

There were some bizarre situations to deal with, too. Much as home ground advantage lifted us, it inspired our opponents equally. Lara's innings at Newlands was magnificent and I doubt whether Stephen Fleming will ever play better than he did at the Wanderers when New Zealand chased down a massive score. We simply couldn't control games in the way we could before and the key games slipped from our grasp in a deathly, painful drip of runs and wickets.

Not again

The final nail in the coffin came with another tied game. I still can't believe we were knocked out of successive World Cups after tied matches. Sri Lanka at Kingsmead. Mark Boucher blocked what turned out to be the final ball of the match in the belief that we would have won the match on the Duckworth-Lewis method should the rain, which was heavy by then, have prevented a resumption of play. It was a debacle.

The reason there was such a mad scramble to find out what the D/L target was, and why we got it wrong, was that there had been a management and senior players decision to concentrate on the full game and not become distracted by the complications of the calculator. There are constant dangers that come with trying to stay ahead of the D/L target – a batsman plays a high-risk shot to the last ball of an over because he needs four runs to stay ahead, he is dismissed as a result and the team start the next over 15 runs behind the target.

The local weather bureau was consulted and every Durbanite that had an opinion was adamant that the light drizzle predicted for the evening would, at worst, come and go but would only delay the match, not seriously affect it.

Nonetheless it was a debacle. The policy made sense at the time but we should have been prepared for all eventualities. I looked at the sheet of paper with all the D/L target numbers on it and I must admit I didn't read the single line of small print tucked away at the bottom of a fully-printed sheet of A4 paper. 'These scores are to tie,' it said, helpfully.

Mark hit a six off the penultimate ball of the 45th over certain in the knowledge that he'd reached the D/L number – which he had. But like the rest of us, he didn't know the number was to tie.

Suddenly there was a desperate scramble in the dressing room as the reality dawned on us. There was chaos, and panic. I have no idea who realized the terrible truth, but Nicky Boje – the official 12th man – went sprinting onto the field, screaming at Bouch and trying to get the message across. Umpire Steve Bucknor wouldn't let Nicky onto the field; he was shooing him away as though he was a streaker. Everything started happening in slow motion. At that stage we didn't know for certain that we would be eliminated, because there were still five overs to go. We were screaming from the balcony, shouting our lungs out: 'ONE MORE RUN. GET ONE MORE RUN!' But Bouch couldn't hear a thing. The stadium was packed and the crowd, evidently, were as confused as we had been. All he was thinking was: 'Don't get out, don't get out.'

Mark safely blocked the last ball and then the umpires brought them off.

The next 30 minutes, or however long it was, were amongst the longest of our lives. The 46th over was lost, then the 47th. Then the 48th. Eventually, the reality began to sink in. It was agony. The magnitude of that one run was impossible to comprehend at the time, but we all knew that something horrible was happening, and it was something we'd never forget for the rest of our lives. For those of us who'd been involved in the 1999 semi-final, the outcome defied our ability to understand. It just couldn't be happening. It just couldn't.

We had played some excellent cricket at times but never really dominated. Perhaps we would have 'clicked' if we'd progressed to the Super Sixes and the semi-finals. Perhaps, maybe…what if. But it was a sad way to bow out.

Jonty

Equally sad was the end to Jonty Rhodes' career. He was comfortably the finest role model of his generation, an inspiration to aspiring cricketers – throughout the country, black and white, Christian and Muslim – for over a decade.

As far as I was concerned it wasn't the legacy of being the best fielder in the world that counted most, or one of the most consistent middle-order batsmen the one-day game has ever seen, but the way he played the game that mattered most and the person that he was.

He was consistent, always reliable and invariably someone to turn to in times of need or difficulty. He was not only willing to help others at all times of day and night, but would go out of his way to.

Amongst the hundreds of cricketers who had their lives changed by Jonty was Mark Boucher. In the early years of his international career, having established himself at the tender age of 21, Bouch would retreat into a shell of self-punishment during a loss of form and his team mates were ignored. Although he was suffering and was desperate to put it right, he also came across as selfish.

Jonty changed that completely on the West Indies tour of 2001. He told Mark how important it was to continue making a contribution to the team, even if you were dismissed for a duck. Jonty used to throw balls to other batsmen, offer words of encouragement, fetch a drink for the batsmen waiting to go in – anything to contribute. He was the least selfish person in the dressing room. Mark was not alone in benefiting from his example.

Jonty never compromised the very strong Christian principles that he lived by but that never, ever made those who lived by other faiths – or none at all – feel uncomfortable.

Jonty played with a commitment and a passion for his country that was unmatched by anyone who ever played alongside him. He also loved doing what he did. There were times when he was homesick and a little miserable, perhaps more than most, but I never heard him complain in all the years we lived in each other's pockets. That summed him up – a sense of priorities so well organized that we all looked to him for perspective and he never failed to remind us that, however bad the lbw decision might have been, or the sleepless night hunched over the toilet, we were extremely lucky to be travelling the world playing cricket for a living. Making friends like Jonty during your playing career is one of the reasons there will be no regrets entering retirement. Besides, we're not retiring. As Jonty always said, even as a 22-year-old, 'The real world starts once cricket has finished.' Life is just beginning, not finishing.

Not finished

As Jonty began his new life working for Standard Bank I had one tour left and it was one I was seriously excited about, five Tests in England. At least, I thought I had one tour left until Graeme Smith rounded up the senior players and persuaded me to carry on to include Pakistan and New Zealand. I will never complain – without those tours I would have reached neither 100 Test caps nor 20 centuries. But I had been very serious about calling it a day after the England tour, especially if we'd won the series. I couldn't think of a better way to finish. The fact that I'd scored a couple of hundreds and had enjoyed it so much, not just the cricket but the fresh, young, fun atmosphere in Graeme's team made it much easier to carry on. I have no doubt I would have quit if I hadn't justified my place in the team or if it had ever felt like a chore.

The Pakistan tour began just eight days after we returned from England. That should have been a good enough reason to stop. There was a lot of debate and discussion about security on the tour and even whether we would go or not. Eventually the 'safe' venues were agreed to by the United Cricket Board, which meant there would be no return to Peshawar. Understandable but a shame for those who had never been there. Mind you, I am not the kind of tourist to ignore security warnings or travel advice. But also not the kind to be negative or pessimistic.

Apart from the day I travelled to Australia 10 years earlier to make my debut, my journey to Pakistan was the only time I was a 'solo' tourist. The team had come back from 2-0 down to win the one-day series 3-2 in a fantastic fightback and I was the only Test specialist required to make the trip. After a full day connecting in Dubai, which I loved, I made the trip to Lahore where I was collected by a not very subtly armed delegation of officials and guards.

The trip to the hotel was made with a three-vehicle escort that made very little sense to me. If there were any disgruntled terrorists around wanting to let off steam by taking potshots at officials, I felt like the perfect target. Not big enough to be intimidating but big enough to make it clear I wasn't 'just anybody' – which I was!

The security for the whole tour was daunting and distracting and it was a difficult tour both on and off the field, but despite all that, I'll always be proud that the team went and showed an example to the rest of the cricket-playing world. I'm not suggesting any cricketer should ever put his well-being at risk for the sake of the game, but if independent security experts say that venue X is as safe as London, Sydney or Johannesburg, then for the sake of the game, they should consider what the game has done for them and what they can do for cricket. The Pakistani people were delighted to have us there and, guns and armoured vehicles aside, we couldn't have had a warmer reception.

The warmest reception, at least on the field, came from Shoaib – as always. I top edged an attempted hook into my face and went down like a felled tree, blood everywhere. What an idiot. What was I trying to do?

But I returned during the second innings acutely aware that I was, potentially, facing one of my greatest moments. To go out and face him again two days later, and to perform, would have done a lot to define me as a person and a cricketer. I was intensely irritated to have got out for 46 because I was seeing it well, albeit through one eye, and could have pushed on. Yet another 'what if'.

Mark Boucher (South African vice-captain and wicket-keeper): *For the last two years of our careers we shared the distinction of being one-Test captains though mine was against Australia, so that obviously made my Test more important than Gary's. But his Test was way, way more memorable.*

On the fourth night of Gazza's Test, against Pakistan and the Wanderers, he was just settling in for a beer with Ernie Els at the bar of the Vilamoura at the Sandton Sun. This wasn't usual during a Test but it had been raining all day and the match was destined to be a draw. I was still very much the youngster of the team, so I didn't dare join Gary.

But he saw me sneaking past and called me over. 'I'm captain now,' he said with a big grin on his face. 'You can have a beer if you want. Besides, have you seen the weather forecast. It's going to rain all day.'

The next day it was beautiful and sunny. I'll never forget the talk Gary gave himself as he was preparing to go out and face Shoaib Akhtar. Anybody who thinks Gary couldn't be hard when it was necessary should have heard him dealing with himself that morning!

Five years later he was facing Shoaib again in Lahore in his penultimate series when he was hit in the face and went down with blood all over the place. We were desperately worried for Gary in the change room – you just don't know how serious it is and the worst thing is the unknown. Eventually he staggered back into the change room and let out this great laugh: 'What the *** am I doing trying to hook the fastest bowler in the world?'

In the second innings Gazza was batting through one eye and we were together when Shoaib pulled a hamstring and limped off. Gary gave thanks all round and tried not to smile too obviously. The next over was bowled by Mohammed Sami, who suddenly seemed to find an extra 10 kph to make up for Shoaib – he bowled a couple of balls at 155 kph.

I'll never, ever forget the smile on Gary's face at the end of the over when he said: 'I should never have let you guys talk me into carrying on. That's it – I'm definitely retiring now!'

But the greatest legacy I think he'll leave the team, and hopefully South African cricket, is the idea of recognising when your hour has come and being able to respond and seize your chance. He called it 'stepping up to the plate' and it's a phrase that is used time and time again by the team.

He explained to me that if you played 100 Tests there might only be five or six innings where you could define your career, win a Test or a series and make a massive difference. He used to tell us that, when those moments arrived, form was completely irrelevant. It didn't matter how you'd been playing beforehand, it became about something else, about passion and determination.

Gary did it in his very last Test innings. How good is that? Afterwards I presented him with a plate from the Eden Park dining room. It was just a lunch plate but we did a little ceremony and took pictures of him receiving his plate. We all knew what it meant, though we had some funny looks from the change room attendants.

Gary and Jonty had the greatest influence on my career and my outlook on life and the game, and Gary and Allan were the two senior players that related most easily to the kids on the team – age didn't matter to them as long as you pulled your weight and showed you deserved to be there.

It'll be very, very strange being in a team meeting, fines meeting, team bus and certainly playing a game without him. But we're close friends and that's far more important to me.

25

Life on the road – touring the world

There are certain characteristics that repeat themselves the more you tour a certain country and they become the fingerprints by which you recognise them and know you're back. In over 40 tours with province and country I came to know the cricket world intimately, but that does not necessarily mean I knew the rest of the country very well.

Sydney, to me, means Darling Harbour and the Rocks, the Harbour Bridge and the Opera House and a run around the Botanical Gardens. Yet Sydney is a massive, sprawling city that stretches for 20 or 30 kilometres in every direction. I barely know Sydney at all, but the part I do know, I know very well indeed.

There have always been, and always will be players who spend an entire tour, even their entire careers living in hotel rooms and ordering room service between net practices and matches. I never judged or criticised those players who chose to do that but I couldn't help feeling it was a pity and a waste of valuable opportunities. I love nothing more than meeting new people and experiencing different cultures. That doesn't mean to say I head towards museums and art galleries on my days off (although I certainly have to if Debs is on tour with me) but just a long, anonymous walk around a city gives me a great feeling for the place.

It felt extremely important for me to absorb as much as I could. My approach probably stemmed from the fact that I felt, at least for the first three or four years, that every tour could be the last, so I wanted to make each one count. The memories and experiences I was gaining by interacting with people and feeling their way of life became a strong motivation to make me keep performing and improving, to make sure I was on the next tour.

Golf

Being a golf fanatic helped make sure I wasn't going to be one of the guys more inclined to stay in the hotel. There were seldom the right number of players to make one, two or even three four-ball teams and that gave me another opportunity to meet and play with a couple of local members. We played on some magnificent courses around the world and that, too, provides me with memories to last the rest of my life.

One that particularly stands out is The Capital in Melbourne where Shane Warne had arranged a round on our behalf through a friend. It was privately owned and consequently so immaculate and beautiful to look at that I still remember it as though it was last week. We have been fortunate enough to experience five-star treatment at hotels and golf courses around the world, although not regularly, but this just took our breath away. The drive up to the clubhouse must be Australia's version of Augusta.

None of the squad had any idea of what to expect and, having played a match the previous day, many chose to rest – and regretted it badly when we arrived back. But there is usually a minimum diehard quota of six that will play whenever and wherever possible. When we walked into the pro-shop there were six sets of clubs with our names on them and a hot towel to freshen up before our round.

Usually there is a mad scramble to choose the best set of hire clubs because they can be a bit 'used' at most clubs, but here were six of the best, either Calloway or Titleist, I can't recall. But each set was absolutely perfect. My preferred tactic on arrival at golf clubs on tour was to hang back and wait until everyone else had chosen their clubs and then take what was left. What nobody ever seemed to realise was that I would often have the best set of all. Either the hire clubs would run out or the professional would be so embarrassed at what I had to play with that he would almost always lend me his personal set – or, at the very least, his assistant's. This time, however, we had identical Porsches.

There is little to say about the course itself other than 'incredible'. Every blade of grass looked and felt as though it had been cared for individually and the water and trees were almost too perfect to believe. It is always important who wins and loses on a golf course, particularly amongst cricketers, but this time I honestly can't remember. Although it is unlikely that my memories of the course would be so good if Pollock or Boucher had taken my money, again. So I think I must have won that day.

The second-best round of my life was also played in Melbourne, in 1994, but it took place at Royal Melbourne Golf Club just a week or so after the Australian Open. Playing off a nine handicap, I shot 76 and spent the rest of the tour on the receiving end of snide and sarcastic comments about the legitimacy of my handicap. You can only imagine the abuse I was subjected to when I produced my best round four years later, a 75 at Brisbane – off an eight. I was instantly cut to a six by the on-tour golf committee, which oversees fair play in circumstances that often prevent cricketers who are casual golfers from obtaining 'genuine' handicaps.

Mark Boucher eluded the grasp of the committee for all six years I played with him, however, continuing to claim five or six shots despite shooting 75 every time we played. But next to Brian McMillan, Bouch was a saint. Big Mac steadfastly played off a 15 and won every single tournament we ever played in. I understand that the world of business is less tolerant and he's now been cut to a seven.

Professional sportsmen are accustomed to harnessing the tension and adrenalin of a 'crunch situation' and it's not uncommon to see a cricketer raise his game to amazing heights in response to the prospect of paying R50 to a team mate. Graeme Smith, for example, is the kind of 12-handicapper who can make four sixes in a row followed by an eagle when he's about to lose the game.

But the worst kind of cricketer is the one who arrives at a course telling everyone how he hasn't played for three months and that he can barely remember the rules. That is the second clearest sign you will ever get that you are about to lose your money. Final confirmation that you are about to lose your money comes when you ask the man what his handicap is and he replies: 'Well, I'm probably around…'

The Vines course in Perth is another special venue. On the 2000 tour we had almost a week between the Test series and the start of the one-day series and we loved the golf course so much we went on two consecutive days, the second after a full morning's practice. The bowlers hired carts.

As a general rule golf was discouraged the day before a match and if it was sanctioned then it was compulsory to hire a cart. Five hours on your feet before the possibility of a full day in the field can have its effect, no matter how fit you are. But if we played on a beautiful golf course the day after a match, especially if we had won and had done our travelling that morning, then 18-holes followed by a cold beer and chat about the game (either cricket or golf) represented some of the happier days of touring life.

Allan Donald was as keen a golfer as anyone – even me – and, being the unofficial King of Birmingham, he organised several rounds at two of the best courses in the English Midlands, The Belfry and The Warwickshire. Sadly, I always seemed to play like a dog when we went there, and never worse than during Al's benefit day at The Warwickshire. Actually, I have my suspicions about my golf temperament. The bigger the occasion the more I seem to hit the ball, which is, of course, a good thing in cricket. But not golf. It is a problem I intend to address during my retirement.

New Zealand

New Zealand is the most beautiful country in the cricket world (apart from South Africa, of course) and one of the most beautiful countries I've been to. It's a lot quieter than people might realise but the scenery can be spectacular and it's usually possible to find a very good restaurant. Provided you look around and don't want to eat after 9 pm.

But nowhere in the world do you feel more of a second-class citizen playing cricket than in New Zealand, or perhaps that should be 'second-class sportsman.' Cricket is such a distant second to rugby that there isn't a pretence at competition between the sports. In fact, why am I pretending cricket comes second? Netball, yachting, equestrianism, triathlon…they all enjoy many hours in the sun while cricket's spotlight turns off altogether unless the national team is successful.

During our second tour in 1999, the governing bodies of both cricket and rugby hadn't consulted their respective fixtures committees and our schedule clashed with several Super 12 appointments. The only people who came to watch the cricket were those that couldn't get tickets for the rugby. The beginning of the Super 12 season clashed with the start of our tour in the beautiful and amazing town of Queenstown where we were supposed to be playing our first match. Except that Queenstown's only playing field had been booked by the Highlanders for a few stretching exercises and a bit of touch rugby. We had to drive an hour and 20 minutes to the next town to play the game.

At the Basin Reserve in Wellington, the country's only dedicated cricket ground, the atmosphere can be very different and very special, but it's the exception that proves the rule. Coming from a country in which rugby and cricket enjoy equal prominence, we found it extremely difficult playing international cricket in a rugby stadium, even a very pleasant and famous one like Eden Park in Auckland.

The most amusing moment of rugby madness actually happened at Eden Park following one of the more remarkable test matches I played in. A fungal infection had ruined the pitch ahead of the first Test of the 1998-99 tour. The grass had died and, consequently, there was nothing to hold the soil together. Fears were rife that it would disintegrate and turn the match into a farce so, in an act of desperation, the groundsman spread wood glue all over the pitch and immediately killed all life, movement and bounce.

I helped myself to 128 and Daryll Cullinan broke Graeme Pollock's national record score of 274 with an unbeaten 275. Hansie declared just one run behind the national team record which was set in the 1969-70 Kingsmead Test against the Aussies. I'm not certain why he did that but I strongly suspect it was as a mark of respect to Ali Bacher's team because it wouldn't have seemed right to break the record on that pitch.

We managed to bowl the home side out once but it took forever and the task of doing it again on the flattest wicket any of us had seen proved beyond us. I expect we would have needed another two days.

So we shook hands at the end of the fifth day and returned to the dressing room and a cold beer. As we were leaving the field, I spotted the ground staff moving *en masse* towards one end of the ground. They were riding a couple of tractors and had some heavy machinery. I didn't think much more about it.

Daryll, however, was more curious and didn't reach the dressing room for another five or ten minutes. When he did, he called me to the door with a curious grin on his face. 'Come and look at this,' he said.

One set of goal posts had already been erected and the other was being hoisted into place. The man with the white-lining machine was halfway down the first touchline and there were a couple of Blues players throwing a ball to each other. Professional sportsmen are used to the quick passage of time and we have all felt the sting of a backlash, but here we were – 10 minutes after a match in which we'd scored 621 and 275* - and you would never have known it had even taken place.

It was very clear to all of us that we weren't going to beat the system so, given the schoolboy sports careers of most of us, we were only too happy to join it. We walked back out onto the outfield, or what had been the outfield ten minutes ago but was now a rugby field, borrowed a ball and started a little kicking contest. I'm happy to say I slotted my three points for South Africa at New Zealand's home of rugby. And a few more, though I didn't venture too far from the 22-yard line. There were some serious kickers in that team – Allan Donald could land them from the halfway line all day.

Easter Jonty

The last one-day match of that tour was washed out and the reserve day was threatened by continued bad weather. We were facing a logistical challenge of some note. Or at least, team manager Goolam Raja was. If the reserve day was called off early enough, and I recall the 'cut-off' point was about 3 pm, then we could catch an evening flight that day and reach South Africa, 30 hours later, just in time for the Easter weekend. Of course, that is not the way we should have been thinking. But it was. And nobody more than Jonty.

It was the one and only time in Jo's career that he didn't want to play a cricket match. It was a question of arriving home on Friday afternoon or Monday night, virtually the whole of the Easter weekend gone. We were leading the series 3-2, it was cold and we were all yearning to get home. Especially Jonty.

He's bound to be appalled at my recollection of the event, but I had the distinct impression that Jo was networking big-time. Every time the umpires inspected the ground Jo was at their side and I'm sure I saw him chatting to the match referee on a couple of occasions. Clearly Jonty would never have dreamt of influencing their decision, but he was a constant presence in case advice was sought or needed. And he wasn't shy about reminding them that the World Cup was just around the corner and that it would be a shame if anyone missed the tournament through injury.

The pitch was wet, no doubt, but we had played on worse. The outfield was squelchy but not necessarily dangerous. Perhaps it was in a few areas, but more at deep cover than on the bowlers' run-ups. It was touch and go. The hours ticked by and then the minutes as our final departure time came closer. We had all packed our kit and our personal bags in hope and the luggage was waiting in a truck outside the hotel.

We sat in the dressing room while Jonty and Hansie, who was taking a rare back seat, discussed the situation with the match officials. Finally, just after 2.15 pm, Jo came hurtling back into the dressing room with a beaming smile on his face. The man who had inspired us to be enthusiastic throughout his career, even in the most desperate times, had forsaken all that zest for what felt like the greatest victory of the tour. We'd been hanging around for 30 hours for a match that didn't matter, and we were all aware of the potential travel arrangements. Jonty Rhodes might have played half of South Africa's greatest one-day innings, but as we dashed for the bus with two and a half hours to make our flight to Sydney, and onwards to Jo'burg and Cape Town, that felt like one of the best. There is no doubt that Jo would have given his all if we had played the match, and made sure the rest of us did, but there was a wonderful irony in seeing the world's most enthusiastic cricketer, for the only time in his life, trying not to play a game.

Oz

The best country to tour, purely from a cricketing rather than cultural or geographical perspective, is Australia. The facilities for playing and practising the game are unrivalled anywhere in the world and the passion for sport that characterises virtually every top sports event creates an awesome environment to play in.

Every one of the cities in which cricket is played (I haven't been to Darwin or Cairns) is extremely attractive, with plenty of trees, lakes and rivers which isn't just pleasing to the eye but makes for fantastic road-running, another hobby vital to a successful tour.

At the start of a warm-up match against Western Australia in 2000 I was dismissed early and set off on one of my customary 'I'm-not-going-to-sit-around-here-for-the-next-six-hours-without-doing-any-exercise' runs along the banks of the enormous Swan River. The air was so clear that, to the naked eye, the distance between the two bridges I crossed looked about two or three kilometres, perfect for my purposes. In fact it was more like ten and I was far stiffer than I should have been when I took the field for the last few overs of the day at 6.00 that evening.

Waterfront property has its premium all over the world and Australia is no different. Sydney harbour, Melbourne, Brisbane, Perth and Adelaide, all have their 'favoured' residential suburbs near water. Houses are often double the cost of those in the suburbs behind them. They may seem overpriced, but Australia is the ultimate proof of that old estate agency motto: Location, location, location.

There is never a shortage of entertainment and leisure options, from movie theatres to Chinese quarters, from sushi bars to shopping malls. You have to be pretty careful where you cross the road – always use the green flashing light – but strict as the local by-laws are, life for a cricket tourist in Australia is good.

Every tour begins with a festival match at Lilac Hill on the outskirts of Perth and the crowd figure has been announced at around 10,000 on both occasions I've played there. There is only seating for about 7,000 but the rest seem quite happy to stay at the bar and fall over by the middle of the afternoon.

Despite the festival atmosphere the match is played competitively and even the ageing stars that make comebacks for the day do so with much pride at stake. Dennis Lillee opened the bowling against me and Adam Bacher in 1998. He was 48 at the time, or at least in that region, and produced a master class – every ball in exactly the right place and 10 overs that cost 28 runs. Amazing.

The MCG is, quite simply, the most physically imposing and awesome stadium a cricketer will ever play in anywhere in the world, and a Boxing Day Test match there is amongst the three greatest 'must dos' in a cricketer's life, the others being a Test at Eden Gardens and one at Lord's. In London and Calcutta, however, you can't have dinner on Melbourne's South Bank - probably the most diverse and mouth-watering collection of restaurants I've ever seen.

The downside to a tour of Australia is the amount of time it requires – in our case, because of the protracted one-day triangular series, about ten weeks. That is a very, very long time to be away from home for anybody in any profession. On a smaller scale, and this always comes as a shock to people who haven't travelled there, it takes an entire day – door to door - to get from one side of the country to the other and the long flights do become wearing. We'd have a wake-up call in Perth at 7.00 am, fly at 9.30 and arrive at our hotel in Melbourne at 8.00 that night after adding on the three-hour time difference and a battle through the evening rush hour.

But everything is forgiven and forgotten on New Year's Eve, which has been spent on all three of our tours in Sydney harbour watching the annual fireworks display from the harbour bridge and the Opera House. Absolutely magnificent. Apart from death and taxes, the one thing you can always rely on is for the Australians to organise a good party.

England

Road transport is often perceived as the worst chore about touring England but, in three full tours of the country I found travelling by road was one of the best things. It's one thing being stuck in England's famous traffic jams if you're behind the wheel and have a job or a family waiting for you, but a very different thing if you're in the back of a luxury bus listening to music or watching a video. On the last tour in 2003, in particular, we bonded very closely under Graeme Smith and genuinely looked forward to the next road trip.

Every town has its own character and history and you experience it from the moment you arrive. I've always been interested in history, so the sight of city walls and cathedrals that are five or six hundred years old start painting vivid pictures in my mind. The whole concept and culture of the village green and Sunday afternoon social cricket is one that I imagined to be urban legend and myth until I saw it. I realise that English society is changing and people tell me that social cricket is dying away, but it only takes the sight of one village green next to the village pond and the village church and the village pub for a visitor to have all his preconceptions ratified.

The media can be overwhelming, however. Apart from the sheer number of radio stations and television programmes that require sports input, there is a greater variety of newspaper and magazine journalist than exists anywhere else in the world. It can be intimidating hearing a question from a tabloid journalist, knowing exactly what answer he wants you to give, and then trying to answer honestly but without giving him anything he can 'interpret' to fit the story he has already probably written.

London

Another very obvious highlight of an England tour is the chance to visit London, usually three or four times per tour. London has more energy than any other city I've ever visited, apart from New York, and it can be an invigorating experience simply getting from A to B, whether it's on the bus, by underground or even by taxi. Part of the reason that being in London is enjoyable, to be honest, is that you are aware you don't have to spend your whole life there. And because I've only ever been there in summer. I'll always love going back, but I'm pretty sure I couldn't live there. I'm not sure I could do much more than a couple of weeks, in fact.

In complete contrast there are the rural areas of the Midlands and further north, such as the Yorkshire Moors and the Lake District. There isn't much to see of the little towns scattered amongst the fields and trees of the countryside from the window of the team bus, but with every tour bus comes a couple of cars that we can use after practice and between matches. More than any other tour in the world, a trip to England offers at least a few days to explore and unwind. However crowded England's cities have become, there is still plenty of greenery and country pubs and inns to make 'escape' a real pleasure.

In 2003, a few days before the Headingley Test, we had a complete day off. Back-to-back Tests meant most people chose to put their feet up in our Leeds hotel but I was in need of a deeper kind of rejuvenation and refreshing. Neither of the team cars was being used by anyone else so, having had my invitation to travel turned down by everyone else, I drove myself to the city of York which I'd last visited in 1994.

I parked and walked down the high street, stopping at all the oldest buildings and appreciating their longevity and history. I picked up historical leaflets and brochures and, of course, went back to one of the most amazing buildings in the world, York Minster.

I even stayed the evening and had dinner by myself in a small restaurant in a building that was 400 years old. It can be a bit lonely exploring by yourself but it makes the experience no less rewarding for me. By the time I got back to the hotel room that night I was fully reminded of how lucky I was to be doing what I was, and how fortunate I was to have had the playing career I'd had. I didn't have a regret in the world.

Four years earlier I'd enjoyed similarly uplifting experiences with Debs when we visited Stratford-upon-Avon to see where William Shakespeare was born and infused ourselves with the whole 'Shakespeare thing'. A little later we had the chance to visit Debs' parents in Cambridge where her father, Michael, was on a sabbatical and working at the famous University. It was a short visit but, once again, the chance to step off the treadmill of the tour was a fantastic release. If anyone took a photograph of Gary Kirsten's embarrassing attempts to steer a punt down the river Cam I would give them a lot of money not to publish it.

Both the '94 and '98 tours of England included short trips to Amsterdam which, to me, were glorious revisits to my early cricketing youth. It was a staggering feeling passing on tips about where to go for beers and food to the national squad when my experience of those places had been gained as a journeyman youngster trying to make a living from the game, let alone aspiring to higher honours.

My great friend from The Hague, Wulf van Alkemade, became my surrogate uncle during my season playing there and he remains a fabulous friend to this day. But when I returned as a professional a few years after leaving, with Allan Donald and Co in pursuit, it was a great reminder of how far I'd come. But also a pleasant reminder that I hadn't changed too much. After a minute or two, Wulf could see I was still who I was when I left.

But back to London. I have a certain sympathy for the England team with regard to their results at Lord's. Newlands is to me what Lord's appears to be for them, a bogey ground that actually becomes harder to play at rather than easier because of its popularity. Your focus can be diverted and distracted by everything on the periphery of the Test. In London it's playing at the home of cricket while Newlands in Cape Town, with the greatest of respect to the other SA venues, is invariably the most popular ground with the tourists and there are inevitably good crowds. Anyone who wonders whether 'atmosphere' and a sense of occasion helps to raise a player's performance need look only at what some of the best players of the last decade have done at Newlands. Centuries by Sachin Tendulkar and Ricky Ponting come to mind immediately, but there have been many others.

West Indies

In its contrasting ways the Caribbean was everything and nothing like I expected. From a cricket point of view it was fantastic to experience the passion of Barbados, for example, but difficult to imagine how the great teams of the 70s and 80s actually became so good. Practice facilities are hopelessly limited and nobody really seems to care much about preparation. I cannot believe that generation after generation of brilliant, naturally skilled cricketers simply came along for 20 years. They must have worked hard and achieved that success in spite of the lack of what we regard today as adequate nets and other training facilities. And perhaps the generations that followed them, towards the middle and end of the 1990s, took success for granted and became lazy. It's only my guess but it seems logical.

Away from the cricket field, however, the West Indies actually exceeded my expectations. The beaches in Antigua seem too 'postcard' to be true: snow-white beaches and a turquoise sea that you can see straight to the bottom of. All the islands, apart from Jamaica perhaps, feel small and sparsely populated, which adds to the feeling of 'paradise lost' when you have the chance to explore and enjoy the beach. If the ocean and sea life is your passion, and you also happen to be a professional cricketer, I imagine it could become hell.

Although it may be difficult to appreciate for those who have never been to the Caribbean or spent two or three months away from home, there is a very real danger of monotony and boredom setting in, and those can be the most disruptive forces a touring party can experience.

Most of the islands are geared towards tourism and the 'targets' that tourists enjoy are not what suits a professional sports team every night of the week. No doubt most squads have been carried away by the rum punch and beach party scenario in the first week after arrival (and we were no exception) but once the novelty has worn off there is the realisation that there isn't actually very much to do. Cheerful Italian restaurants serving a simple bowl of pasta are thin on the ground – I can't recall any, in fact – so players can become hotel-bound. And like zoo animals that have spent too long in confinement, cricketers also develop cabin fever after too many days in their room; behaviour becomes unpredictable and sometimes moody, eating habits are sporadic and telephone bills are astronomic. Paradise can be a very ordinary experience after too long there.

I expect plenty of English cricketers have been back to the Caribbean to experience it purely as a holiday but it's a long journey for South Africans, via New York, Miami or London, so I'm very fortunate to have had the 1992 experience when as an unashamed tourist I watched the one-off Barbados Test with Kenny Jackson. Through a carefully planned series of research experiments, we ascertained that it was possible to stop partying at the first glimpse of the morning sun, sleep, have breakfast and still be at the Kensington Oval for the start of play. OK, maybe half an hour late. But a snooze in the afternoon was essential.

Before I played my final Test at Wellington's Basin Reserve I was quick to remind everyone that it's impossible to plan fairytale endings in sport, and probably more so in cricket than in any other game I know. I'll never forget the sight of Allan Border bowing out in his final Test facing the ignominious bowling of Jonty Rhodes, and then Jonty, years later, denied the appropriate stage that he so richly deserved. Instead of leaving the game in a blaze of World Cup glory on home soil, he broke his hand in the field, left the squad early and watched us from home make an early exit.

But the reason I was most sceptical about my own prospects of leaving on a high, apart from the fact that I'd just scored two singles in the previous match, was because of what happened in my only Test at the Kensington Oval.

Having developed my passion to play for South Africa on the Test stage during the '92 experience when Kenny and I were bunking down as shameless backpackers on brother Peter and Adrian Kuiper's floors, it was an especially poignant moment when I returned in 2000, almost a decade later. My career and my life had come full circle from wide-eyed, open-mouthed fan to senior player, and I was about to cap it all with one of the most emotional centuries I could imagine. It was a decent pitch, too. Everything was set.

I made a 'pair' - the only one of my career.

Zimbabwe

Goodness knows where Zimbabwe will be in its painful, contorted cricketing journey by the time this is published. Even as far back as the 2003 World Cup I said that I would seriously have considered whether or not to travel if we had been scheduled to play in Harare or Bulawayo. It simply would not have felt right.

My views on the country are based on happier times when cricket was played, for the most part, free from the controversies that have threatened its survival in more recent years and free from political interference.

It is a beautiful, rugged country. I loved the place so much I added four holidays to my three or four tours there and would love to go back if, and when, visitors feel safe and welcome once again.

Zimbabwe offers South Africans the things South Africans love the most – the rivers, the wildlife, the fishing and, of course, Lake Kariba, which is one of my favourite places in the world after spending three different holidays there, including half of my honeymoon. It may not have much to do with cricket but when I imagine complete and total relaxation, I don't think of masseurs or soft beds. I picture myself on the deck of a houseboat on Kariba, the quiet of the early evening disrupted only by the sound of a distant elephant uprooting a tree, with my fishing rod in one hand and a cold Zambezi in the other. I believe my heart rate may have dipped into single figures at times.

The second half of our honeymoon was spent in Mozambique, which was everything we had hoped it would be. A few days in the bush were followed by four days on a remote, semi-desolate island in the Mozambique archipelago snorkelling the reefs and eating grilled fish on the beach. Once again I had a lot to be grateful for. During every sunrise and sunset over the ocean, and every other moment of luxury and beauty, I never forgot to be thankful to the game of cricket.

I was not away from for it for long, though. We flew back to Cape Town, married, honeymooned and blissfully happy, and I was gone again 12 hours later. Ironically it was straight back to Harare where I joined up with my WP team mates for the last match of the pre-season tour. It was against Mashonaland, who had eight Test players in the XI and we managed to beat them by an innings. I loved Zimbabwe.

India

Touring the subcontinent is very different and, occasionally, very difficult for both 'Westerners' and Africans! On long tours it becomes harder and harder fitting into a different culture and the frustration levels rise more and more. The passion for cricket is greater than anywhere else in the world but, awesome and inspiring as that is, it can be inhibiting, too.

Debs loves India – she would put it top of her list if you asked her where she enjoyed touring the most. The markets, shops, spices, clothes, saris…she could immerse herself for hours, probably days, in the back streets and markets of Mumbai. I expect we'll go back at some time in the future – it'll be a fantastic experience to see the country as 'Joe Public'. India is the only country in the world where cricketers will, certainly, be recognised walking down the street.

When you experience the hype generated outside a Test match ground and see the crowds screaming at the arrival of the team bus, it's difficult to believe, and I mean that seriously. I wondered whether a film was being made and the crowd were just 'extras' being paid to behave like that. Then I thought the Prime Minister or perhaps a couple of Bollywood film stars must have turned up. It took a while before I could believe they were screaming and cheering because the South African cricket team had appeared. A few minutes later the India team arrived and I realised the crowd had barely performed a warm-up for us. There were tears in people's eyes, their faces were contorted in ecstasy, or agony – I'm not sure – but it was clearly an overwhelming experience being so close to their heroes. The noise was incredible.

A walk down the street lasts about two minutes before you're recognised and very soon your new friend is joined by two or three others. After another two minutes you feel like the Pied Piper with a group of 20 or 30 people following you. It's a novel experience and I will always be able to picture the looks of grinning bewilderment on the faces of team mates experiencing it for the first time. But the truth is it becomes depressing to face the choice of staying in your room all day or putting up with the chaos that ensues if you visit a market or a temple. We all tried dark glasses and caps, but that just extended the recognition time from two minutes to about four.

Apparently Sachin is known to use false beards and wigs, but it seems a bit of an extreme measure. In his case, however, it makes perfect sense.

I may have found it hard work touring India but the country had a deep and profound effect on me as a person. In other chapters I've described the severity of the poverty that exists everywhere but it isn't the pitiful sight of destitute families that is so moving, it's the way they conduct themselves and handle life. They have a smile on their faces and they don't demand things in the way that more privileged people do.

Many, many times in the years after touring India I would hear people saying 'I want', 'I deserve' and 'I need', and I would feel a deep sense of pity for those people because they didn't know what those words meant. I would always think back to the people of India and remember the look of total contentment on the faces of ordinary people who had gained a pair of sandals that had not worn through to the road. They were their most valuable possession and yet they rejoiced over them, and I had friends and colleagues around me moaning about the fact that Adidas or Nike had 'only' given them ten free shirts and three pairs of shoes.

Sri Lanka

Sri Lanka is a thoroughly enjoyable destination and, in many ways, completely unlike the other subcontinental countries. Much, much smaller than India but with many of the best Indian qualities – friendliness, genuine hospitality and a completely absorbing style of life and society that made you feel it was possible to 'fit in' rather than just pass by.

The size of the country is also what makes it so appealing to tour. Other than in Colombo, Test matches are played in the mountain city of Kandy – Murali's home town – and Galle, where Murali appears to take 12 wickets per match as part of his normal routine. Both trips are about two and a half hours drive from Colombo and about 100 kilometres. Enough said about the width of the roads. Throughout the drive you never quite seem to leave the city and the road is constantly crowded on both sides by dogs, donkeys, children and bicycles. Road travel is a lot less hair-raising than in India and Pakistan, though, because you rarely travel fast enough to do any damage.

Undoubtedly the hardest aspect of the country is the weather, which is sensational if you're lying next to a swimming pool just outside an air-conditioned hotel, but intimidatingly hot and humid if you're required to bat or stand at mid-on for six hours. Fortunately the hotels are excellent, really comfortable and relaxing, and the availability of a wide variety of food and drink means it's easy to feel at home. Sandwich shops, coffee bars and western-style restaurants mean that feeding yourself is neither dull and predictable nor risky – and the presence of Royal Colombo Golf Club makes the tour 'down-time' even more pleasurable.

26

Captain, my captain.

I trust Mark Boucher will forgive me for not including him amongst my international captains, but I played under him for only a couple of matches and a fine job he did, too. But my career was divided into four very distinct periods, led by Kepler Wessels at the start and followed by Hansie Cronje and Shaun Pollock in the middle. I finished my career under the leadership of Graeme Smith.

National captains, by definition, must share some characteristic similarities but in terms of what they brought to South African cricket and the way they approached the job, these four were very different men. Each led the team for long enough to create a legacy of their own (even after a year and half in Graeme's case) and each can honestly claim to have contributed a great deal towards our status in the cricketing world.

Kepler Wessels

Kepler brought a hardness to our game that most of us were unfamiliar with. He was a tough man anyway but his experiences in the Australian team gave him an even more steely edge. There are many ways to captain a team and Kepler's method was to lead by example. He did things in a certain way and he expected people to follow. He wouldn't spend much time talking through issues or problems with his players; if you had a problem he expected you to resolve it quickly and without fuss. But if you ever had any doubt about what you had to do on the field, and how much you should be prepared to sacrifice to win, you had only to look at Kepler.

His knowledge of the game was so superior to the rest of ours simply because he'd played 24 Tests before South Africa was even readmitted to the international game. He was the first man to explain to me the difference between Test cricket and any other form of the game, simply that there were no hiding places in Test cricket. In other forms of the game it is possible, with enough experience and street knowledge, to take a breather during an innings, to escape to the non-striker's end or simply 'switch off' for a while against a non-threatening bowler. But in Test cricket he explained that pressure and stress were virtually constant companions for an opening batsman and helped me prepare for that reality.

After the emotion and joy of the 1994 victory at Lord's we had a monumental party,

Kepler included. We celebrated long and hard into the night safe in the knowledge that, having won in four days, we had a full day off to recover. Then Kepler called an official practice session after breakfast. It was very typical of him. He didn't believe in lingering after a victory; it was a case of getting back to the office as soon as possible and concentrating on the next job.

You always knew where you stood with Kepler and there was never any room for negotiation or debate. He was hard and uncompromising. A couple of days before the 1994 Durban Test against Australia he called another practice session that clashed with a golf day that had been organised months beforehand. Coach Mike Procter objected and the two of them exchanged heated words before Kepler turned back to the team and said: 'Fine, either you can play in the golf day or I'll see you at nets.' It was abundantly clear that he expected to see us at nets and there'd be hell to pay if we weren't there. I don't think anyone played golf – probably not even Proccie.

Kepler wasn't a fan of being in the public eye. He believed that his responsibilities as far as the media spotlight was concerned started and ended on the field. He wasn't a fan of talking to the press or making speeches at dinners, so a lot of that work fell to the manager or coach and I believe that attitude was one of his greatest attributes because his focus was entirely on cricket and the potential for distraction was cut to a minimum. And that is the way I believe it should be. From the day Kepler retired I watched the captain's commitments burgeon out of control.

Yet for all his seriousness, Kepler was not shy of the odd practical joke. During the 1994 one-day tour of Pakistan he and Hansie ransacked the room shared by me and Eric Simons and practically destroyed it. Beds were overturned, drawers emptied, sheets out of the window... But when we finally confirmed that it was them and I confronted the captain about it, my timing could not have been worse. I don't know what the problem was but he was all set to call upon his skills as a boxer until I made a hasty exit and kept a low profile for a couple of hours. Kepler was never shy to have a box.

Hansie Cronje

Not many people know that I was Hansie's captain in the SA Universities team in the late 1980s – but it was never going to stay that way. It was obvious, to me anyway, that he was natural captaincy material and was destined to have a remarkable career. In fact, he was such a natural leader that I'm probably in a club of about three people who can say they ever captained him, from under-10s to the national team.

For the majority of his time in charge he was very much the full package as captain. It is easy for some people to think that the scandal which ruined him somehow obliterates all the success he achieved and the respect he enjoyed in the earlier years of his leadership, but it doesn't. It may be difficult to believe, but even during the years when he must have been involved with bookmakers, he appeared to fulfil every role and task that came with the captain's portfolio.

His man-management skills could be excellent, too. He allowed and encouraged each player to believe he was the best in his position and the man to lead the team to victory in times of crisis. He also expressed great faith in his players and helped them to believe in themselves. There were a couple of occasions in the early years of my career when I felt vulnerable and had doubts about my ability and my right to be in the team. He instilled the confidence in me that I badly needed.

We were experimenting with batting orders during the 1995 series against England in an effort to drag our one-day game into the modern era. As most people will agree, we went on to position ourselves at the forefront of one-day tactics. Pinch-hitters were in vogue at the time and there was much conjecture about whether they were best used as an opener or at number three. For a couple of games Richard Snell had opened in my place.

I was being batted at number six (or even seven) and I felt completely useless. If things went well then I was coming to the crease at a time when we needed to hit the ball out of the ground, which wasn't my game. It felt as if I was being selected as a specialist 'disaster' batsman who was expected to rebuild the innings if we crashed to 30-4.

I took my concerns to Hansie and told him there really wasn't any point in picking me if I was going to bat at six or seven. But instead of being negative I asked him to put me back at the top of the order and promised he wouldn't regret it. He chatted to Bob Woolmer and, as a result, I was moved back to opener for the very next game. I was even more determined than usual to make a big score.

The game was played on a belter of a pitch at Centurion and England made 272. In later years there would have been a very systematic, unemotional approach to the run chase with everyone convinced we'd win, but in 1995 a total of 272 was intimidating, to say the least, and the dressing room was apprehensive.

Fortunately Andrew Hudson and I put on 150 for the first wicket and I made 116 in a seven-wicket victory that raised a few eyebrows. I think it's fair to say that most of the crowd had written us off at the halfway point and the atmosphere became increasingly charged as we laid the foundations for the win.

Hansie came up to me after the match and said: 'OK, you made your case pretty clear, didn't you?' We laughed together and I said 'Thanks, I know you backed me as an opener and I'm glad it paid off.' I also said that if I couldn't open then I honestly believed the team was better off without me. He assured me that there would be no more experimenting with my position again.

In cricketing terms it was very easy to communicate with Hansie. Any part of your game that was troublesome was open for discussion whether it was during a net session or in the middle of a game. He was a superb on-field captain, too. He may have dropped down the batting order a couple of times when the wicket looked green but that was because he sensed trouble and wanted to be the man for the crisis. He was never afraid to bring himself on to bowl at a time when wickets were desperately needed and he certainly wasn't afraid to counterattack the bowlers when they were starting to dominate. Even when the pressure was at its greatest, he wasn't afraid to lead from the front.

He had a priceless ability to rev his fast bowlers up, most particularly Allan Donald, who was wound up on hundreds of occasions, often to great effect, by his fellow Free Stater. For some reason Allan often started a match with a couple of wayward overs but Hansie always managed to get the very best out of him in his second and third spells.

Finally, Hansie was an outstanding cricketer. People can forget that, too. We needed 225 to beat Sri Lanka in a Test match at Centurion in early 1998 and we were all scratching around, struggling to come to terms with Murali, who was turning it a mile. There was pace and bounce in the pitch, too, making it even harder. The Test could genuinely have gone either way at 99-3 when Hansie walked to the crease. I'd managed to survive but never felt comfortable and I thought we were in for a long, hard slog. Hansie decided we were in for a very different kind of slog.

He hit Murali for a couple of the biggest sixes I'd ever seen, playing the slog sweep about as perfectly as anyone has ever played it. He reached 50 from 31 balls, just five short of Ian Botham's world record, with me watching from the other end without contributing a thing. I certainly didn't need to run for him. I didn't even need to call. It was a great show.

Before anyone knew it, we needed about 20 to win and the match was virtually over. I felt like a kid missing out on all the party cake. It makes me laugh now. But I walked down the pitch at the end of an over and said: 'Listen, can I join in the fun, please?' He just smiled and said: 'Have a go.'

So I charged down the wicket at Murali and tried to hit him 'inside out' over extra cover and managed to squirt a loopy top edge just over cover point's head. We ran two. The next ball was a bottom-edged slog sweep past the keeper's right foot and then we ran a bye after I had missed the next ball outright. Hansie just smiled. He made it look so easy.

Shaun Pollock

Kepler and Hansie both led by example for much of the time but Shaun was the ultimate captain in that regard. I doubt there have been many others who relied more on the example and standards they set to lead a team than Shaun. He was a clean-living, straightforward captain and a brilliant performer on the field with a huge workload to carry, particularly with the captaincy.

He believed players needed to be as ready as they possibly could before they took their place on the international stage because a captain can't be distracted by the task of protecting players, not that there is anywhere to hide in the international game.

There was no time or space for talking about performances with Shaun. You had to be prepared to 'do', not talk; that was his bottom line.

He took over at an extremely difficult time and, despite limited captaincy experience, learned very quickly and guided the team to new heights. His record as a Test captain, which shows a winning percentage of over 50 percent, will stand for years as proof of his ability as a captain, no matter what happened later.

Only Jonty could ever match Shaun's competitiveness. No matter what we were doing or playing, Shaun and Jonty needed to win more than anyone else. Even

Captain, my captain.

Boucher. Whether it was table tennis or putting a golf ball into a glass along a hotel corridor, it didn't matter. They played as though it was a Test match.

Touch rugby was the common form of competition amongst the squad because it was favoured as both a warm-up and a warm-down exercise. 'Touch' is a relative term, of course, and there were times when the competitive edge threatened to spill over into a couple of big tackles. Fortunately, they never materialised. But one thing that was absolutely accepted as part and parcel of these life-and-death contests was cheating, in every shape or form.

My abiding memory of touch rugby was of Jonty diving, full-length and at full speed, to stop a guy getting past him. That was fine in England, South Africa or Australia but Jo had a complete inability to adapt his all-or-nothing approach and the smell of burning skin as he landed on the gravelly outfields of the West Indies and India could be quite overpowering.

Shaun encouraged this atmosphere of competition as much as he could because he believed it would stand his players in good stead on the field. He believed if they coasted at anything as a team then they might do it at times during a match. But if the team was always competitive then there was never a danger of their being caught 'soft' during the heat of battle.

Shaun did himself an injustice with the bat. He had the potential to be one of the greatest genuine all-rounders the world had seen rather than one of the best bowling all-rounders the world has ever seen. And he may still achieve that status. But for most of my career he believed it was his duty to play aggressively at the bottom of the order and flay the bowling as much as possible while the ball was old and soft, and what a job he did. He was, however, good enough to bat at number five and make regular hundreds, and there were a couple of opportunities from time to time that he could have taken but he allowed himself to be talked into staying where he was.

Graeme Smith

Finally, to Smithy. I'm not a superstitious person but I am nervous about comparing his captaincy at the age of 23 with the others. Things can change extremely quickly in this game and he has a long, long way to go in his career, and that has to be borne in mind. But, like his predecessors, he has all the necessary skills to handle the job. He leads by example, thinks on his feet, handles the media well and isn't afraid of tough decisions or unpopularity.

But above all that he has a rare ability as a motivator. As rare as I've ever seen. Like everyone else, I found it difficult to believe his age when he took over as captain. He has a powerful presence in the change room – probably something to do with his physical stature – but he is unquestionably the kind of captain you want to fight for.

He has a similar presence on the field, too. He has the kind of attitude and approach that simply melts down even the most stubborn resistance from within a team and moulds the players together in a unit that will live and die for each other. The players in Graeme's team play cricket for him and the team, not for themselves, and that is surely one of the most precious assets a captain can have.

When I think back to the start of my career, how little I really knew about international cricket, how limited I was as a player and, in a few other ways, how naïve I was, I'm proud of the distance I travelled. Yet Graeme started his international career four years younger than I did and still hadn't turned 23 when I retired. There are many hurdles still facing him but the mind boggles at the knowledge he will acquire and the records he might break if he lasts as long as I did.

Yet, as befits the strangeness of cricket, I learned as much at the end of my career, in my mid-30s, playing under the captaincy of a 22-year-old, as I did in my mid-20s playing under Kepler. I thoroughly enjoyed my time in Graeme's service, most prominently the amount of passion, commitment and drive that he brought to the job of representing one'scountry. That was never something I lacked, I hope, but playing under Graeme made me realise that there is always more if you want to look for it. Sixteen years a professional, ten an international, and a kid takes over the reins and asks me for more. Asks everyone for more, all the old pros. Was there a raised eyebrow? Yes. Did we find more? Yes. Was there a raised eyebrow then? No.

I have no doubt South African cricket, internationally, will be in fantastic hands while Graeme retains his drive and belief. Passion is already an overused word in Graeme's vocabulary but that is inevitable – he believes in telling the truth. Passion is the only word appropriate to describe the way he approaches his job and plays the game.

On my last tour for South Africa, to New Zealand in early 2004, things started badly and went from bad to worse. While I was at home taking my turn changing Josh's nappies and enjoying the early days of parenthood with Debs, Graeme was trying desperately to stem the flow of miserable defeats in a one-day series that was eventually lost 5-1, the first series South Africa had ever lost to the Kiwis.

When I arrived for the Test series I could see Graeme was taking an enormous amount of strain. I wanted to do everything in my power to turn the tour around, not because I felt sorry for the young captain but because I could see how much the reputation of SA cricket meant to him and I would have felt ashamed to feel any less passionate about reversing our fortunes.

Before the first Test in Hamilton Graeme gave a team talk in the evening that was so intense, and delivered with such conviction and passion (there's that word again) that he had tears in his eyes. It wasn't over-the-top or awkward, and he wasn't shouting or waving his arms around. He was just very serious about the level of commitment and determination he required from everyone in order to turn a disastrous series around and restore the pride to South African cricket. When he talks about playing for the people, he means it. Of course he is young, and cynicism may yet creep into his approach, but somehow I think not. Graeme will change as a person in many aspects of his life, but as a cricketer and a captain I believe he will stay loyal to his principles.

His tactical awareness was sometimes exposed and he still has plenty to learn in that regard after a year in charge but that is hardly surprising at the age of 23. It is no different from what Hansie experienced when he took over at a similarly young age. Both men had been captain of every team they ever played in but international cricket,

Captain, my captain.

particularly Test cricket, contains more sub-plots than any other level of the game and requires greater subtlety and concentration than any other, as they both discovered.

Shaun Pollock (South African captain): *Gary was the ultimate professional. He probably wouldn't have described himself as a flamboyant batsman, but that was to his advantage because he identified that and stuck to what he was best at. He had a great record and just got on with it without any fuss.*

His facial expressions are what I'll remember most; they were quite a sight. He had a big broad smile but would also take the mickey with po-faces and funny noises. And then there were his lucky underpants, but I had better not say too much about that!

Graeme Smith (South African captain): *When I first arrived in the team he was going through a tough time against the Aussies and was under huge pressure to perform. There was a lot of stress and tension around during the first Test at the Wanderers when I was 12th man. I made my debut in the second Test at Newlands and we had a good partnership in the second innings when Gary made 80 and I made 60. That was the first time I experienced his 'experience'. He had his box split right down the middle by a delivery from Brett Lee, something that would have caused most guys to lose their nerve for a while. But Gary just wore two boxes from then on!*

It was also the first time I saw the determination in his eyes and saw how hard he was prepared to fight. As a kid I'd always thought of him as 'the banker' but he was a street fighter, too.

Something that surprised me but made a huge impact on me was how he was always prepared to look at himself, criticise himself and try to improve – always. He was honest with himself. He might have been the right man for the job but he wanted to be an even better man for the job. It didn't matter that he had played 80 Test matches and scored 6000 runs.

When I became captain he was one of my greatest allies. He doesn't say a lot but he gets on with whatever the job is at the time and does it well. It's the example he sets that makes him so special and so respected. The way he trains, prepares, thinks…He has a calming influence on people.

In my second Test, against Australia in Durban, I was batting at number three and it was already getting dark when Gary and Herschelle walked out there. Gary was being peppered with the short stuff and had been hit a couple of times and taken a couple to the ribs. It was obviously a hard and painful battle. Then, finally, he managed to tuck one from Brett Lee away down to fine leg to earn himself a breather. Except that he didn't just trot down to the other end, he ran as hard as he could and turned almost blind for the second run. I think Herschelle was a little surprised but not unhappy about going back to the non-striker's end. That just summed Gary up. You can't put a price on what effect that has on the team – almost everyone else would have trotted the single. We won that Test…

27

A few good men

Friends, colleagues ... and others.

When Debs and I planned our wedding we decided on a guest list of 80. We finished with about 260. When I decided to write a chapter about a few of the people – friends and team mates – with whom I've spent many happy years, I thought immediately of four or five. A few moments later it was closer to 45. Unlike my wedding, however, I am not in charge of the length of this book. So, without pride or prejudice, let me tell you about some of my best friends and team mates, starting with Eric Simons.

Eric Simons

It's impossible to overstate how important the role was that Eric played in my life and career. I learned a lot from the way he lived his life and what was really important to him. He helped me define and then understand myself as a person, not just a cricketer. Eric is a principled person and, although he's certainly not inflexible, he lives life according to those principles and won't allow himself to be compromised.

I provided entertainment for him, too, by having too much to drink during a fines meeting or generally being stupid. The enduring image I'll always keep of Eric and me during our playing career is of him shaking his head at me in a dressing room with a smile on his face that reflected a mixture of care and despair. What was he going to do with me?

Obviously he also saw in me a person who could contribute in more ways than one, someone who also cared about those around him and was interested in what was below the surface of a professional cricketer. We all have a tough exterior and wear a public face in the business of professional sport, but with Eric I could cut straight to the heart and soul whenever I wanted or needed to, and he could do likewise with me.

In the earliest days at Western Province Eric was a combination of big brother, step-father and best friend. I looked up to him enormously, a genuine fast bowler who could also bat superbly. In many ways it was an unlikely friendship. In retrospect we had virtually nothing in common and lived opposite lives. I was disorganized, partying, single and living life in the fast lane. He was focussed, married, settled and successful.

And a non-drinker. But we got on from the moment we first met and became the best of friends within a few months.

One of the passions we did share on tour was going to the movies. We formed the infamous (and extremely unofficial) South African Movie-Goers Association (SAMGA) and membership within cricket circles – with all its perks - became highly sought-after. Once a new member was accepted he faced a rigorous induction which included the ritual of arriving late for his movie as a member of SAMGA and calling out from the back of the theatre to locate the rest of the members, so he could sit with us.

Clearly there were few cricketers in the Western Cape with sufficient pride to refuse this humiliating initiation and soon our ranks had swelled to at least 20 members. The initiation ceremony, I must say, was far less anti-social than it sounds because there was one further criterion for membership. Participation in the club required members to find, and then watch the worst movie that happened to be showing in whatever town we were in. Reputable and even good movies were reserved for viewing with wives, families and friends, and SAMGA members watched the dregs that nobody else would watch if they were paid to. I can reveal that 'movie of the century' as voted for by SAMGA members was a classic called *A weekend at Bernie's*. I doubt if many video stores have a copy these days, but it will forever remain a magnificent example of just how bad movies can be. Brilliant.

Eric had a complete tolerance and respect for everyone around him. He never judged people by his own standards but he lived his own life by the qualities he believed were important and right. He was certainly never guilty of prejudging anyone, an easy mistake to make in the egotistical and righteous environment of the entertainment/sports industry.

Even as a young, hard-living man whose own values were still 'settling', I was intensely moved by the love and devotion Eric had for his family and for the institution of the family. It was clear to me that, although there is no such thing as the perfect family or parent, Eric and Caron were making as good a job of it as I'd ever seen and I'm happy to say, now that Debs and I have started down the family road with the birth of Joshua, that I would consider it one of my great achievements if I come close to emulating Eric as a husband and father. I'm happy to admit I've tried to model several other aspects of my life on his but I'll be particularly happy if I can manage this one.

Alan Dawson

My admiration and affection for Dawsy is no less than that I have for Eric although, this time, it was Alan who arrived at Newlands as a wide-eyed youngster while I was a 'seasoned veteran' of three or four years' standing.

Like me, Dawsy underwent a massive career change operation, having made his debut as an opening batsman alongside Terence Lazard in the 1992-93 season. I was batting three. It was an early season game and the Newlands pitch was as green as the outfield. The opposition were Eastern Province and our immediate concerns, having lost the toss, were Brett Schultz and Rudi Bryson, the fastest and unboubtedly the meanest opening bowlers in the country at that stage. In fact, they probably still rank

Right: If you can't bat for a long time in the nets, how can you expect to in the middle?

Below: The last tour. Getting ready to say 'cheers' to three great friends and, I hope, superstars of the next decade. Herschelle, Jacques and Graeme.

Above: Eric Simons. Friend, confidante, role model and a man of honesty and integrity.

Above: Goolam Raja. The most selfless man in cricket, dedicated to making life for the team as comfortable and painless as possible in a decade of service as manager and assistant manager.

amongst the top three in both categories of those I faced at any stage in my career, particularly in conditions that suited them. Terence was out to the first or second ball of the match and I walked to the crease to join Dawsy.

We were both roasted. It was a baptism of furnace proportions for Alan, who had been thrown in at the deep end due to an injury crisis that had also resulted in my making my captaincy debut. I was hit on the elbow by one of the two quicks and had to retire hurt, coming back later in a painful attempt to save the match from a futile situation.

Before I went off, though, I was batting with Dawsy and concerned as much with personal safety as I was with protecting my wicket – as was Alan. I gently pushed a rare, full-length delivery from Bryson through mid-on and the only fielder in front of the wicket was Schultz, at mid-off. The bowler looked at the fielder and the fielder looked back at the bowler. Eventually, with extreme reluctance, Schultz set off after the ball without a hint of either speed or enthusiasm. He was always a very big man. It was the only occasion in my career when I ran five at Newlands without the aid of an overthrow. 'Bear', as Schultz was known, dived for the ball in exactly the manner his nickname would suggest and then performed an exaggerated parachute roll before struggling to his feet and, finally, throwing the ball back.

Being new to the game, Dawsy hadn't known what to expect and my call for a third came as quite a shock. The call for the fourth was even more of a shock but when he saw me charging back for the fifth I think both his body and brain refused to acknowledge what was happening. Fortunately 'Bear' Schultz was so slow that Dawsy managed to scramble back safely but it was touch and go. He was still puffing so hard and feeling so confused by what we'd just done that he promptly nicked the next ball to the 'keeper.

The second innings was no less torrid although Dawsy showed tremendous character and fighting spirit batting in an innings of sheer defiance that lasted over an hour. Nonetheless, just as I had realized four years earlier that my natural place was at the top of the order and not the middle, Alan realized that he wasn't an opening batsman. In fact, he faced the truth that he might not even be a top-six contender.

He bowled useful medium pace back then but didn't take it terribly seriously. So he could bowl a bit and bat a bit, and he was useful in the field. And to cap that, he was continually reminded that he was 'too small' to make it at first-class level. Not quick enough and not strong enough to succeed as a bowler or a batsman. As a final reason for his 'inevitable' failure, it was pointed out to him that he was sharing a squad with Brian McMillan, then regarded as the best all-rounder in the world, and Eric.

What Alan subsequently achieved in the next decade is amongst the most admirable careers I have ever seen. Even when Brian Mac and Eric were both fit and available for selection he forced his way into the team through the sheer power of his performances, at least in terms of runs and wickets – and remember, he wasn't 'big enough' to make an impact through his physique.

That he managed to reach the highest possible level in the first-class game left me feeling as inspired as I have ever been. He almost single-handedly won the '98-'99 Supersport Series final with an innings of 143, batting at number nine after Province had collapsed to 83-7 and then earned several opportunities to represent his country.

The greatest lesson I could possibly learn from Alan, however, was not the simple things like determination and will power – those I had already found from other sources. Where Dawsy differed from any other professional I knew was in his determination to find fault, reason and solution within himself before he looked anywhere else for blame. In fact, he never looked elsewhere, only at himself.

Dawsy's humility was a constant factor in my career. His approach to life was always to self-examine rather than blame other people, even when he was clearly the victim of prejudice and poor judgement. He was an example and an inspiration to everyone who played with him, however frustrated they may have been on his behalf. The two of us prided ourselves on being the fittest members of the WP squad. Even in my last season we both produced the best results on the 'beep test' and he pushed me hard on the many road runs we enjoyed during our careers.

There are many things you can't control as a sportsman, like how tall you are, but you can always make sure you are fit, and Dawsy did just that with rare dedication.

I captained WP during the Supersport Series final of 2002-03 against Easterns and bowled Dawsy through an entire session between lunch and tea. He didn't even cast me a sideways glance, let alone mutter a word of complaint, and he went for less than two runs an over. It was an amazing act of endurance, 16 overs at the same pace with as much control at the end as he had at the beginning.

Andrew Kalis and Alistair McKenzie

Dawsy and I were also two-thirds of a triumvirate of trouble that included one of Cape Town's finest club cricketers, Andrew Kalis. It was at a time in the mid-1990s when I had an involvement with a pub in Claremont called the Green Man. It was a hugely popular spot with touring teams and developed something of a 'sporting' reputation – albeit strictly recreational.

The three of us had birthdays within five days of each other and one year we decided to organize a 'proper' party at the Green Man. It was in the days when we were all single.

We even designed an invitation and had a couple of hundred printed, which was unusually well organized for us. We then set about distributing them to some of our best friends, but most went to people with whom we wanted to become best friends. So when the big day arrived the three of us were there early, looking our best. Two or three hours later, another 20 or so guys had arrived. And 160 girls. We thought it was a great party.

Andrew is a special kind of man. His passion for club cricket is incredible, and his desire to change with the times – and even help to change the times – is an inspiration to everyone. At a time in the early to mid-90s when a lot of people were frustrated by integration and unity he surged ahead and took his club Almar to the championship. He's a true and consistent friend and, much as we were bound by cricket, he was someone I could just as easily escape the game completely with.

Andrew was a groomsman at our wedding and Alistair McKenzie was my best man.

We played UCT under-20 rugby together and, if you've read the early chapters of this book, you'll know what that was all about. The two of us shared Varsity digs with a third student, Martin Brookes, who subsequently became one of SAB's principal brewers, no doubt assisted by the hours of research into the product conducted by the three of us at the UCT rugby club bar, amongst other venues. Martin has since moved on from Cape Town to become a master brewer overseas but Alistair is still in the Mother City.

The point about both Andrew and Alistair is the loyalty they have shown to a friendship that is not easy to maintain, not because it's me but because 'me' is a professional cricketer who has spent well over half his life away from our home town. It's difficult to maintain any kind of meaningful friendship or relationship in that situation and it requires a lot of effort from everyone, but whether I was away for ten days or ten weeks, it didn't matter to them. It was if I'd never been away.

In 1997 I had 18 days in Cape Town and in 1998 I was at home for 40 days. I have known cricketers to return home in those circumstances and feel like strangers in their own town, out of touch and out of the social loop. I'm extremely thankful that I had enough true friends to keep me sane and they didn't complain that I was never here.

As I have mentioned before, friends are extremely important to a sportsman gaining and retaining a balanced perspective on life and his own sense of worth outside the sporting environment. But they come a distant second to a player's family and, in particular, his wife or girlfriend. It may have been OK for cricket tours to be 'boys only' in the amateur days of 30 years ago, but professional cricket is remorseless in the 21st century and the least the modern player deserves is to be granted a semblance of normal life in the company of his wife for a few hours in the evening.

While I'm on the subject of out-dated thinking, allow me to digress to the topic of childbirth. I was asked on a number of occasions why I chose to miss a Test match to be at the birth of Joshua. I confess I find it a difficult question to answer because I have no desire to offend anyone or belittle their opinion, but I didn't ponder the decision at all. There was nothing to think about, no debate and no questions to be asked or answered. Outside of my wedding day the birth of Joshua was the most important day in my life. To miss it for a cricket match...? I'm afraid that argument, too, belongs to a different era.

Craig Matthews

There were also, of course, some very close cricketing friends who were away from home at the same time as me. Whether it was for South Africa or for Western Province, we spent so much time together that you couldn't help but become good friends. One of them was Craig Matthews. He was a long time vice-captain to Hansie and an extremely successful leader of WP, and I respected both his deep knowledge and understanding of the game as well as his ability to step away from it when appropriate and make an amusing, often dry observation about life and its fickleness. .

October was Craig's favourite month of the year. Early season nets at Newlands were inevitably green and juicy and he would seam the ball into the right-handers and hit the inner back thigh with regular monotony. There was a scream from Craig's net every sixth delivery, at least, followed by some furious rubbing and swearing. Salt did not need to be rubbed into this collection of bruises although Craig often couldn't help himself.

It was a very different story for us left-handers, of course. I think I once played and missed at 25 deliveries in a row, a situation that resulted in a furious exchange of grins.

Brian McMillan

I played as much cricket with Brian McMillan as almost anybody else and I can honestly say I was more relieved that he was on my side than anyone else I played with or against, certainly at provincial level. He had a fabulous ability to rise to the occasion and produce a big performance, with bat or ball, whenever it was really needed.

Big Mac never admitted defeat, particularly while he was bowling, because he could surprise any batsman in the world, no matter how well set he was. Mac had a ferocious bouncer that was so much quicker than anything else he bowled, it was impossible not to be caught off guard. Whether there was a slight 'bend' in the arm when he delivered it was irrelevant to us; it was an extremely effective ball. Like a magician making a rabbit disappear, those watching Mac – including every umpire that ever stood in a match with him – was left thinking: 'Did that really happen? How did he do that?'

It's true that he didn't enjoy bowling as much as batting but that didn't mean he was any less effective at the job. He was also the finest catcher of a cricket ball I have ever seen, and probably amongst South Africa's top two – ever. I can recall him dropping only two catches in over a decade of playing together but the number of absurdly brilliant ones he caught is too high to count. We took them for granted.

The first of those two drops came in a pre-season match against Border in King William's Town. He was standing at first slip. When the ball hit the grass there was a protracted period of stunned silence. Mac stared at his hands as though he'd never seen them before. Nobody could quite believe it. Inevitably the shock was broken by the sound of a muted laugh and eventually there were smiles all round. It took another seven years for Mac to drop one.

Dave Richardson

'Swinger' had a profound and very positive effect on me when I first joined the national squad. He did more than anyone else to make me feel welcome and not overawed, and that I belonged there. And I would like to think it wasn't just because he was my room mate at the time.

I thoroughly enjoyed every minute I spent in his company and we found huge areas of common ground for conversation though he, like Eric, came from a completely different 'corner' of life. He was older and wiser than me, a lawyer, and married with children. I wasn't old or wise and, although I did have a girlfriend at the time, I certainly wasn't able to chat about families or social responsibilities.

Dave remained someone I looked up to for the remainder of his career, which ended four years later, also in Australia, when he called it a day after the third Test in

Adelaide. When he was calm, which he was for most of the time, Swinger was the dispenser of wise and sensible advice, a man to soothe inflamed situations or tempers. But when he wasn't calm, he could be very uncalm indeed. Whenever anybody was on the receiving end of a fired up lawyer's tongue-lashing, they generally remembered the advice they had been given by 'Grandpa', and acted on it.

Goolam Raja

Goolam Raja was probably the most unsung hero I have ever encountered. Having toured for the first time in 1994 when we travelled to England, I beat Goolam into the national team by just a couple of months and outstayed him by just a couple more, and I can categorically state that I never met a more selfless person in the entire decade we were together.

Goolam's approach to his job - he started as assistant manager and became manager - was to add as much value and make life as pleasant and as trouble-free as possible for the people around him. Goolam's own goals and ambitions were never apparent and the solitary target he set himself on tour was to allow his team to focus all their mental and physical energy on cricket. If they were worried or distracted by anything else, Goolam treated it as a personal failure on his part.

Having been around the cricket-playing world a few times, sometimes with the team and often on solo reconnaissance missions, he allowed no detail to escape his attention, however small or seemingly unimportant. And he was a shrewd deal-maker, too, whether it was discounted laundry rates, telephone simcards, e-mail connections or waived excess baggage charges.

Far more important than the money he saved us though, was the peace of mind we enjoyed whenever our partners were due to join us on tour. They almost always seemed to arrive in the middle of the night but Goolam made certain they were as comfortable as humanly possible from the moment they stepped off the plane to the moment they stepped back on to it two weeks later.

Sometimes I think we was generous to a fault. He never said 'no' to any request and was only ever unavailable for an hour or so on Fridays when he attended the local mosque. He would routinely travel two hours ahead of us when it was an airport day and in the subcontinent that would often mean a 3.00 am start. There were times when I wished Goolam would take half an hour for himself and just rest. But that wasn't his way. Besides, the next challenge was always just around the corner – like finding the best Indian restaurant in town and organizing a table for 14.

Alan Dawson (South African cricketer): *I'd be playing a club game in front of a crowd of three and I'd make some runs. After a shower and a beer at the end of the day there'd be a message on my phone saying: 'well batted – gk.' That would have been nice in any circumstances except that Gary was on tour in Australia and it was midnight there. You couldn't have a more genuine friend.*

He's also the most professional cricketer I've ever met, from his preparation to his execution and the recovery. His appetite for batting was insatiable; that's the most amazing thing you learn as a young cricketer when you meet someone like Gary. We opened the batting one day for Claremont Cricket Club at the national Club Championships and put on 330 for the first wicket in a 50-over game. Normally I would have been pleased with 60 or 70 and loosened up, but with Gary you pushed yourself as hard as you could and never gave up.

He was never a shouter or a table-thumper as captain but he gained more respect than anyone else I've seen. It came straight from the way he conducted his own life, on and off the field, and from the way he listened to and cared about his team mates. When he came back from an international tour to play for Province we would all raise our individual games by 20 percent simply as a result of him being back. There was never a time for coasting.

His long-standing association with the Red Cross Children's Hospital and his work with Cape Town's street kids was a constant reminder to the rest of us not to moan or complain and to keep a sense of perspective. If something, anything, was worth doing, it was only worth doing 100 percent. From net sessions to exploring a new city, it was worth doing it with Gazza because you'd always have the best experience.

28

Never mind 'my day'

Heritage

The structures within Australian cricket appear to be extremely formalized and organized and everything appears to be brilliantly designed to allow the best club players into first-class cricket and the best first-class players into the international set-up. I share the commonly held view that we are South Africans, not Australians, and we must do things our way, but I'm not shy to suggest that we emulate and adapt the best of the Australian system to suit us.

The most obvious difference between the two countries is in the history and the culture of the game. Incredible as it may seem, ours is, possibly, richer and deeper than theirs, but when we toured Australia we felt like paupers in terms of heritage.

Almost everywhere you look on a cricket tour of Australia, there is the inescapable presence of Donald Bradman and the great teams and players that represented Australia from the first Test in 1880 and onwards, from the 'Invincibles' in 1934 to the great teams between the 50's and the 90's.

Throughout my international career we were genuinely handicapped by a feeling that we lacked a similar history, and even when the brilliant feats of Trevor Goddard's 1963 team in Australia were rekindled, and the victories of the 1969 Springbok team, it didn't feel quite the same.

Every team I played in felt very aware of the political background from which we came and even the most 'straightforward' of our players were conscious that we were representing a new era. I never felt completely associated with the great Test teams of our past because, magnificent though they were, they weren't representative of the whole country. It was made extremely clear to us that this was a different era and we had different duties and responsibilities, and whilst many guys regarded themselves as merely players and either 'above' or 'below' politics', I was always aware that it was our duty to participate in our 'new' history and to promote it.

But after the initial euphoria of 1991 and 1992, it became obvious that we were handicapped by our lack of a popular identity.

In the early '90s we weren't even 'Proteas', or even 'King Proteas' as the original plan suggested, and we played under the badge of the United Cricket Board of South Africa, not the national emblem. It felt almost as though our own country wasn't ready to accept us.

The Australians, by contrast, were loudly, proudly and sometimes brashly aware of what it meant to wear their baggy green cap and how they were continuing a century-old legacy of Australian cricket tradition. It provided them with an edge more powerful than words can describe. It was something we definitely lacked during my career and it was extremely obvious when young players were drafted into the squad. They didn't have a sense of history, they didn't know who Tiger Lance was and, if they did, they were conscious of the fact that our past was tainted by a political system and way of life that was abhorrent. We often felt awkward being associated with the great Springboks of the past but there was little, if any, guidance to help us through.

In many ways we are only as old as Zimbabwe in international cricket. We haven't had time to build role models and heroes, or time to create an identity. Throughout my career it was more pertinent to celebrate our democracy, not our cricket team. Having said that, we progressed in 10 years as far as it takes other countries to move in 50 years.

Role models are important in every society and every sport; it's a little easier for everyone if you have a dozen banked away from forty or sixty years ago, but we had only a couple that made the transition from 'then' until 'now'. The creation of new heroes was, and still is, vital to the well-being of our game.

All my heroes played sport in apartheid South Africa and were 'advantaged' sportsmen. I never really had the opportunity to meet or identify with cricketers playing in the SACOS leagues. My only exposure to the game came at Newlands because it was where I lived and consequently the men I followed were household names only in white households - Garth le Roux, Steven Jefferies, Alan Lamb, Jimmy Cook, Graeme Pollock, Peter Kirsten.

It's desperately unfortunate that the majority of the population didn't even have the opportunity to represent their country and, while we can't change that, we can all make a difference by learning a little of our shared past. Or at least, of the past that we didn't share. Like all cricketers and supporters I will always wonder how good South Africa might have been during the 70s and 80s, and I mean a team selected from the whole of South Africa.

Makkie

Makhaya Ntini became a very special person in the closing years of my career. I don't believe it's possible to 'act' as an ambassador and a role model, you simply have to be as you are and trust that you 'are' what you are required to be.

Makkie had the toughest of starts to his career when he was charged with rape. But he was acquitted and, as far as his team mates were concerned, that was the end of the matter. After a period of natural uncertainty, he developed into an incredible star, a role model not just for the black children of South Africa but for his team mates who came from a more privileged background, too.

I'd like to think we became close friends during my last couple of years in the team. I spent more and more time standing at mid-on or mid-off when he was bowling and that resulted in plenty of chats about his plans for different batsmen and what he thought they might do next. Off the field I appreciated his culture and background and had nothing but respect for our differences and for the fact that he had had to work infinitely harder than I had to get where he was.

He was, and still is, an inspiration to all fast bowlers in terms of his physical conditioning and the way he has stayed in shape and bowled so many overs. As with Jonty's fielding, people can make the mistake of believing that some cricketers are just naturally quick, strong or fit. That may be true at amateur level but to be as good as Jonty or as fit as Makhaya takes hundreds of hours of dedication, pain and sweat. To watch him bowl, at the same pace, at both the beginning and end of a Test match day used to lift everyone in the team. Very few people can understand how much physical exertion that requires.

I also believe Makhaya is now South African cricket's supreme role model and there is an opportunity, if his profile is correctly marketed, to reach out to thousands of aspiring young cricketers, particularly in the black communities.

100 Tests

For the first time in 31 years the name 'Kirsten' will not appear on a South African scoreboard at either domestic or international level. It will be a while until that name may appear again, but I certainly do feel a sense of pride, having been one of four brothers to play first-class cricket in South Africa. (Peter and I played for South Africa and Western Province; Paul for WP; Andy for WP B. Peter and Andy also played rugby for WP. Peter coaches WP, and Andy coached Kenya at the 2003 World Cup.) My only regret is that my late father never had the opportunity to watch us play a little more. He would have been 78 when I retired and would certainly have enjoyed watching his sons play the sport he loved, late into his retirement.

Playing 101 Test matches for my country is an achievement I will always reflect on with massive pride. Did I ever think I would get there? No, I didn't think I would play even one Test match, so every one was a bonus for me. Playing a Test match is a very special experience and I treated all 101 with the respect they deserved. I will never forget walking off the field with Justin Langer before the first Test in Adelaide on the 2000-01 tour of Australia. His enthusiasm to get out there and play Test cricket was a lesson to all those fortunate enough to have the opportunity. Although I went through some tough times in my Test career, I loved being out there and playing cricket for South Africa.

I never felt I was supremely talented and therefore never considered such a record a possibility for most of my time in the national team. But once I was within sight, it was difficult to shift the thought. Only the 'legends' of the game had ever played 100 Tests and, though I never made the mistake of thinking I would become a 'legend', the idea that someone as ordinary as me could sneak into their ranks was an amazing thought.

Throughout my career our team struggled against the weight of experience of our opponents. It may be difficult for many people to understand, but sportsmen are often intimidated by experience and when you are playing against six or seven men with between 70 and 100 caps, and your most experienced player has 20, the odds stack up even higher against you. It was important for South Africa to break through the 100-cap barrier, so that younger players have something to aspire to. It's great to know that I was the first player in South Africa to achieve that, but I certainly look forward to many more players joining me. I think Shaun Pollock and Jacques Kallis are next in line to join the '100 club'.

Centuries

There are people who have no time for statistics, who feel they are irrelevant when watching for the pure entertainment of the game. But for many, it's the only way a player can be measured, the only way one can determine the greatness or effectiveness of a player. Any Test batsmen would tell you that scoring Test 100s is why they play the game. Test cricket provides the ultimate test of skill as a batsman. No stone is left unturned when the opposition bowlers are trying to get you out. Your competence in all areas of the game is constantly under scrutiny when facing the best bowlers in the world. So scoring a Test 100 is the ultimate individual achievement.

After two years in the national team, when I had finally started to feel established, I had a grand total of one century to my name. After another year I had a couple more. At the rate of one century per year I felt I was being extremely optimistic setting a career goal of ten centuries, but I did nonetheless. Sometime in 1996 I did an interview in which I stated my goal. I had hot and cold flushes when I read it later. Scoring the first hundred had felt like climbing a mountain and here I was saying I wanted ten.

After reaching ten Test centuries I had also reached a stage in my career where I didn't set any further long-term goals. I think I even went through times when the thought of scoring one or two more would have seemed a distant goal. After the second Test against England in 1999, in Port Elizabeth, I remember having a drink with Pat Symcox and discussing retirement. I hadn't scored a run in the series and I was ready to go. He suggested I set a goal of scoring 15 Test hundreds. He said if I were able to achieve that, it would place me in a top bracket of all-time scorers of centuries. I thanked him for the beer and left, not giving the conversation too much thought.

After the next Test and the 14-hour 275, the thought of 15 Test 100s came back to me and I suddenly realized it was not such an impossible task. I often remember that day and think how close I was to finishing my Test career. But God had other plans for me after testing my resolve and character during those times. My reward was 21 Test centuries. Amazing.

The last five hundreds all came in the final 12 months of my career during which, I think, I averaged over 70. I'm particularly proud to have finished on a high – no danger of hanging on too long.

One of those centuries, the 18th, came at Lord's. I'm sure every cricketer feels a slightly different sense of satisfaction achieving a landmark at the home of cricket but, as I mentioned at the beginning of the book, it had been a constant dream of mine since I first saw the Honours Board back in 1994, a decade earlier. It was now my third and undoubtedly last chance to score a Test hundred at Lord's. It was an incredible occasion for me, partly because of the way I handled the extra pressure that my 'obsession' had placed me under. I had about eight or ten overs to bat at the end of the first day and I played like a dog. No part of me felt comfortable. Fortunately, I survived without anybody noticing how bad I was thanks to the powerful spotlight of attention on Graeme at the other end.

That evening I unwound my frustrations with Debs and let a lot of the tension out of my system. The following day was the greatest chance I was going to get to write my name into the history of the game, literally in this case. We sat together for a long time, just enjoying the quiet of each other's company as I tried to get myself into a relaxed frame of mind. I needed to focus on the next day but I needed to do it calmly, not with anxiety or apprehension. I wanted to take my chance, not be overwhelmed by it. I couldn't afford to be afraid of failing – my best chance to put 'Kirsten' on that board was to be relaxed and focused.

The following day, when I scored the 100th run, I felt as happy as I had ever done on a cricket field. I was overwhelmed with a pure, uncomplicated, almost childlike happiness. I couldn't have imagined a better way to finish my career. Nothing had burned as brightly as the desire to score a century at Lord's, and now the job was done.

My next century, at Headingley, will also live long in my memory. At 20-4 in the first hour, I don't think many people favoured us to win. But three days later we did just that. I managed to score 134 and 60 in my two innings on what certainly won't be remembered as a flat batting wicket. It's amazing how often those really difficult batting pitches produce the most entertaining Test matches. I suppose it's the constant action with a combination of runs and wickets on a frequent basis – they're probably a little more fun to watch than play in.

Retirement plans

At the end of the tour a few of the players - as well as Eric, now coach - convinced me not to retire but to try and push for 100 Tests. Mark Boucher sat me down and told me I was crazy to consider stopping now. He spoke passionately about the significance of the 100-Test milestone and how important it was.

How right they all were. I'll always be grateful to them for persuading me to hang on for a few more months. One of the main reasons for my decision was the amount of enjoyment I was experiencing playing in the South African team under Graeme Smith's captaincy. This was a great bunch of guys who were all keen to work hard on their games and take their performances to a new level. Our new fitness expert – Adrian le Roux - was doing some incredible work with the squad and by the end of that tour most of the players, even the 'old' ones, were 15% to 20% fitter than they had ever been before.

The prospect of 100 Tests and 20 centuries was suddenly very enticing. But those targets would not have been sufficient motivation to reverse my original decision to retire after the England tour if I hadn't been enjoying my cricket so much, or if I had been unsure of my form or confidence.

If anybody had told me in 1993 that I would play 100 Test matches and score 20 centuries I would honestly have thought they were smoking something. Not in my wildest dreams would I have believed that was possible.

Even in retirement, however, there is some unfinished business regarding my Test centuries. In 1998 I was awarded a Benefit Year at Western Province. Amongst the memorabilia I gathered and was given, were ten stunning bottles of wine donated by the Groot Constantia winery. Each bottle depicted one of the ten centuries I had scored at that stage of my career with the date and venue as well as my signature; they were bought at auction by Gavin Varejes, a well-known memorabilia trader.

His successful bid was subject to one condition – that I would arrange another bottle for each century I scored after his purchase. I'm hoping he'll be happy to pay for them because another 11 bottles as good as the first ten will not come cheap. Having not heard a word from him for the first four months of my retirement gave rise to the slim hope that he had forgotten our 'deal' but he's too shrewd for that. One thing is for certain, however – neither of us believed for a moment he would require another 11 bottles to complete his 'set'. Three or four, perhaps, but not 11.

One of the strangest but most common questions I've been asked since retiring is whether I achieved everything I set out to achieve in my career. It's strange because I so far exceeded my craziest, wildest ambitions that I sometimes don't know how to answer that. There is not a single achievement or goal that I regret missing. The closest I could get would be to have played one more season of domestic cricket for Western Province after international retirement and commit myself to them totally as a way of paying back the time and faith the province invested in me. But the team is so strong and there are so many brilliant, talented young guys coming through that I would simply have got in the way. I will, however, be around to guide and advise whenever I am needed or wanted.

Changes

Cricket people must not be afraid of the future, and if the future means change – radical change – then it must be embraced for the well-being of the game. Test series, particularly long ones, are not as popular as they were and I can't see that situation changing. Test cricket is the greatest form of sporting competition I have ever known but that does not mean to say it needs to be preserved as a museum piece.

I believe a Test league needs to be properly structured in much the same way that every other team sport in the world has a champion team at a certain time, not simply a never ending roll-on system that has no start or finish. Of the various proposals that have been suggested, my favourite would be to play all the other Test nations in one-off fixtures, home and away, every year. Bonus points would be given for runs and wickets and also for the margin of victory in order to help a clear winner emerge.

The marketing potential could be enormous and the sense of urgency and significance that is missing from several of today's fixtures would return, and with them the crowds. England and Australia, of course, don't have a crowd problem (at least, I should say 'attendance' problem) but I'm sure that both countries would rather see the game flourish everywhere and not just when they are playing for the Ashes.

No doubt there would be resistance from a great many people, and there would be a huge list of problems raised. But where some people see problems, others see solutions and opportunities. Cricket has to adapt to survive – every other sport has. A compromise could be found, I'm sure, but the basic notion of long, bloated tours belongs to a different era. Perhaps the short, sharp, home-and-away Test programme could be played over a two-year period to accommodate certain series, like the Ashes.

Even more radical, perhaps, but just as sensible is the concept of two Test leagues with promotion and relegation each year or two, depending on how long the season was played over.

Below the top two leagues there could even be a third division to give aspiring nations something to aim towards. Much is spoken of the growth of the game in Africa, and rightly so, but there will always be a ceiling placed on players' and administrators' ambitions.

If, for example, it was possible for nations like Uganda to play in an international third division with the prospect of winning promotion to the second division, and therefore the first, it would at least be possible for young players to dream of playing a Test match at Lord's. Impractical yes, and many would say impossible, but dreams are an important part of sport.

This is not my original idea, but how about this as a starting blueprint for international cricket?

Division one:
Australia, South Africa, England, India, Sri Lanka, New Zealand, Pakistan, West Indies

Division two:
Zimbabwe, Bangladesh, Kenya, Namibia, Holland, Scotland

Division three:
Canada, USA, UAE, Nepal, Ireland, Uganda/Malaysia.

I envisage a play-off between the winner of the second division and the bottom-placed team in the first division to determine who plays in the first division for the next 12 or 24 months. It would add an undeniable edge to a series that might otherwise have attracted very little worldwide attention.

My day

From very early in my career I knew I didn't want to be one of those cricketers that harked back to the 'good old days' and constantly referred to 'my day'. The game changed so much in the decade and a half that I played it professionally and change is healthy for the survival and growth of any sport. Change for the mere sake of it can be destructive but change aimed at keeping up with the needs and demands of society is positive and productive.

I didn't retire only because I was 36. The game was beginning to overtake me. I wasn't getting any quicker or stronger – or younger, obviously. Batsmen were hitting the ball harder and harder and I felt I was relying more and more on my experience, playing from memory. The pace of the game was also becoming faster and consequently more entertaining and that, too, is a good thing.

I'm delighted that I can move off the field and yet stay involved with the game I love so much. Ten years after my retirement the international game will have changed as much as it did during my ten years of playing and I look forward to watching it and sharing in the drama and excitement that the players will be experiencing. And if anyone ever hears me yapping on about 'my day' or reliving anything that sounds like it might be coming from the good old days, I would like them to show me this page and claim free drinks for the rest of the night.

Jacques Kallis: *His legacy to the team members that remain behind, and to future generations of international players, is the work ethic that applied to his training and also the attitude he brought to the specialist batsmen. He formed the 'Top Six' club where responsibility was welcomed by all of us and hundreds were celebrated with a good cigar. Whether we smoked or not.*

He developed a culture where pressure situations were wanted by players, not avoided or dreaded. He used the expression 'stepping up to the plate' and we used it a lot to describe what we had to do in a crucial situation.

We were very similar in temperament when we batted and thoroughly enjoyed being in each other's company. We were both calm and didn't allow anything to rattle us and we concentrated well – that's probably why we had nine or ten century stands together. We understood what made each other 'tick'.

Neither of us 'lost it' very often and when we did we weren't very good at it. I tried to throw a fit in the change room at Headingley once and ended up flat on my backside, which caused Gazza no end of mirth. Then again, anyone who saw him throwing his gloves around the place after getting out couldn't help laughing, too.

We're very close. When he retired I told him that, if I ever lost form during a tour of Pakistan, I'd be sure to fly him out to be at my side and to put me right. He said: 'I'm not available, Jacques!' That's how close we are.

29

The final day

I was so focussed on trying to win the Test match against New Zealand that I barely gave a thought to the fact that it was the last day of my cricket-playing life, and thank goodness for that. If I'd felt a fraction of the emotions I experienced when I walked off the field for the last time then I wouldn't have survived a single delivery.

So much depended on that final day. It had been a disastrous tour in terms of results. The one-day series was lost 5-1 and we were 1-0 down in the Test series after being badly outplayed in the previous Test at Eden Park. We were resuming that fifth morning with a chance to salvage everything – the series, our reputations, the tour and the reception back home. There were still a few Smith-sceptics around who would, no doubt, have taken the opportunity to stick the knife in unless we could perform that day.

50-3 overnight, needing 233 to win. An early wicket would have made the Kiwis firm favourites and the pressure might have been too much for our lower order. Graeme and I were tense as we padded up. Smithy is almost always talkative, whatever the situation, but he was pretty quiet that morning.

After scoring a hundred in the first Test in Hamilton my last three innings had been worth precisely one run each. I didn't know whether I was out of form or not – I hadn't been around long enough to find out. I had a lot to think about. It was going to be a long morning session, too, stretched by half an hour because of bad weather earlier in the game.

This second innings did feel different to the 175 that had preceded it. I was always aware that it was my last innings. On my way to the middle I repeated over and over again 'stay calm, stay calm.' I was working hard to control my emotions. But it was also the match situation that was making me nervous. We just had to win – I couldn't even begin to think of the consequences of defeat. I can say, without a shadow of doubt, that I felt as much pressure during that innings as in any other I ever played. Every single felt like half a run and every boundary felt like a single. But we slowly started getting there and the victory post was within sight.

It was the final over before lunch. We'd added 161. Scott Styris was bowling and wobbling it around a bit through the air. I missed one. Out, lbw for 76. No reaction yet. Emotions under control. Disappointed, of course, but the match was won. I started walking back.

This was it. The last 17 years of my life were coming to an end with every step. The last 11 years of international cricket. I was never going to represent my country again. I felt cold and shivered. Suddenly I couldn't control the situation any more. Through all my life I had always had the next innings, and the next match, to put it right, no matter how bad things were or felt. Now there were no more innings. Ever. My whole cricket life was flashing through my head. I saw the boundary rope approaching and I felt light-headed and short of breath. This was it. The last time I would ever cross the rope, in either direction.

As I did so my entire emotional system collapsed and I began sobbing. I thought it would wear off quickly but it didn't. Everyone had come out to greet me, plenty of slaps on the back and kind words. But I was only vaguely aware – I was in a bad way.

The emotion inside the change room was incredible. No matter how it is described, or by whom in the years to come, it will be impossible to do justice to the atmosphere in the room that afternoon, and the memories will stay with me forever. It had been a long season and everyone was relieved to have won the Test, but Herschelle, Jacques and Bouch, and Shaun, almost everyone in fact, they all went through the emotional journey with me and shared my gratitude, sadness, relief, joy and ... just about every other feeling you could imagine. It was time to say goodbye to team mates who had become close friends for many years. We had a party that night.

Goodbye to all this.

Herschelle Gibbs (South African opening batsman): *The last day of his career was the most emotional day of my sports life. As he walked off the field he burst into tears and that instantly set the rest of us off. Gazza composed himself a little later and eventually most of the other guys got it together but I couldn't stop, and I didn't care! I cried for three hours, right through the fines meeting we had two hours after winning the Test and right up till we got on the bus to go back to the hotel. I hadn't cried like that since I was a baby.*

It was a combination of so many feelings and emotions after playing with Gary for 14 years since I made my WP debut when I was 16 years old. I had as much respect for him as anyone else I know, and to watch him finish his career with a match-winning innings to square the Test series was just a bit too much for us to take.

I thought of his early days when he caused chaos and mayhem with Kenny Jackson and how his life changed for the better when he met Debbie, and I thought of all the madness we shared opening the batting because, as Gary always told me, you can't be completely sane facing the new ball for as long as he did.

And I remembered Cochin, as I will for the rest of my life, when we both scored hundreds and we put on 235 for the first wicket. It was the closest I've ever come to death, on a cricket field. It was the hottest day in the world. To be fair to the old man, he stood up to it better than me, although he was out first. When he got back to the dressing room he was staggering about in a complete daze looking for his bags. He couldn't remember a thing.

Gary started the 'Top Six Club' that made us all appreciate our responsibility and appreciate the full value of a hundred and he left a legacy of professionalism and dedication that affected every single one of us. I'll especially miss his calmness and the soothing effect he had on me. He didn't just fulfil his potential, he probably exceeded it – if there is such a thing.

At the start of his last year he challenged me and Graeme Smith to a bet: the scorer of the most first-class hundreds would be taken out by the other two for the best dinner in the whole of Cape Town. We tied – all with five. I insisted on a play-off and that, I can reveal, is the real reason Gary retired.

The one thing I will make sure I have very close to me for the rest of my career is Gary's phone number, wherever he is and wherever I am. I will need to chat.

Graeme Smith (South African captain): *We were sitting in the dressing room padded up and ready to start the final day. We heard the five-minute bell and Gazza rubbed his head in that familiar way he does when he's feeling a bit of strain and said: 'I can't take this any more. I'm going to have a heart attack…people don't understand the pressure.' We both laughed a lot. It was half intended as a tension-breaker but it had also been a tough tour and we desperately needed to get something out of it, and he knew that.*

Normally I talk a lot to my partner when I'm batting. I'm quite chatty; it's just the way I am. But that day I was in a different world. I knew our partnership was crucial to the game. Not just the game, actually, the whole tour. Maybe even my captaincy. I'd been lying awake from 4 am thinking about it. I lived and died every single ball that either of us faced that day.

After a couple of overs from Daniel Vettori, Gazza quietly said to me that he was going to 'take him on' and try to hit him over the top. I very nearly had a heart attack of my own. But this was Gazza, so I didn't say 'No'. All I could say was 'Pick the right ball,' and then silently prayed for him. From then on I had my heart in my mouth every single time Vettori bowled a ball.

When we were about 40 runs short of victory Gary stroked four boundaries in the space of two overs to take us past 200 and then I knew we were safe. I knew we'd won and had saved something from the tour. We'd done it, me and Gazza. Well, almost.

Gazza was out on the stroke of lunch. I was at the non-striker's end and closest to the pavilion, so I started walking ahead of him. I was so wrapped up in the match I didn't think for a moment. Then it dawned on me. All week we'd been teasing him saying things like 'This is you last net, Gazza, enjoy it,' and 'This is your last team dinner,' - that kind of thing. Now it really was the end. I stopped immediately and waited for him to pass me. I didn't even walk close to him. The team had come out to greet him. I suddenly felt extremely emotional.

We still needed 20 or so runs to win after lunch, so I had to try and keep myself together, but I saw Jacques lurking in the corner of the change room with tears in his eyes and poor old Hersch's eyes were just blood red. Once again I was reminded that we had lost someone very, very special. Irreplaceable, in fact. It's not until someone

The final day

like Gary is actually gone that you truly realise how good he was. It'll be hard without him. But at least he'll still be around and involved. That could make a massive difference to how we evolve as a team in the two or three years after his retirement.

GAZZA'S BEST

(The nickname 'Gazza' is a version of 'Gary'.)

BEST SA TEST XI:
Graeme Smith
Herschelle Gibbs
Kepler Wessels
Jacques Kallis
Daryll Cullinan
Brian McMillan
Mark Boucher
Shaun Pollock
Nicky Boje
Brett Schultz
Allan Donald

BEST SA ONE-DAY XI:
Andrew Hudson
Herschelle Gibbs
Jacques Kallis
Hansie Cronje
Jonty Rhodes
Mark Boucher
Shaun Pollock
Lance Klusener
Pat Symcox
Makhaya Ntini/Fanie de Villiers
Allan Donald

**BEST BATSMEN
PLAYED AGAINST:**
1. Brian Lara
2. Sachin Tendulkar
3. Matthew Hayden
4. Ricky Ponting
5. Steve Waugh
6. Rahul Dravid

BEST BOWLERS FACED:
1. Glenn McGrath
2. Courtney Walsh
3. Curtly Ambrose
4. Wasim Akram
5. Shane Warne
6. Muttiah Muralitharan
7. Shoaib Akhtar

BEST HOTELS EVER STAYED IN:
1. Stanford Plaza, Melbourne
2. Oberoi, Calcutta
3. Pearl Continental, Lahore
4. Sandton Sun, Johannesburg
5. The Bay Hotel, Montego Bay
6. The Savanah, Barbados
7. The Hyatt Regency, Birmingham

**FUNNIEST CRICKETERS
PLAYED WITH:**
Meyrick Pringle
Dave Rundle
Neil Johnson
Fanie de Villiers
Steven Jack
Herschelle Gibbs

**MOST COMPETITIVE
CRICKETERS PLAYED WITH:**
Shaun Pollock
Jonty Rhodes
Mark Boucher
Garth le Roux
Brian McMillan

BEST LUNCHES:

1. Lord's (only menu in the cricketing world)
2. Eden Park, New Zealand
3. MCG, Melbourne
4. Adelaide Oval
5. Goodyear Park, Bloemfontein
49. Any curry, anywhere, served in 35-degree heat
99. Ahmedabad

BEST CHANGE ROOMS:

1. Lord's
2. Newlands
3. SCG
4. Wanderers
5. Faisalabad (biggest in the world).

STATISTICS

Gary Kirsten: Career Record – *As at 30 June 2004*

Tests

By series

Against	Country	Season	M	Inns	NO	Runs	HS	Avg	SR	100	50	Ct
Australia	Australia	1993/94	3	5	0	174	67	34.80	30.63	0	1	2
Australia	South Africa	1993/94	3	5	0	162	47	32.40	38.94	0	0	4
England	England	1994	3	6	0	190	72	31.66	43.67	0	2	1
New Zealand	South Africa	1994/95	3	6	1	226	66*	45.20	49.88	0	2	6
Pakistan	South Africa	1994/95	1	2	0	104	62	52.00	49.76	0	1	1
New Zealand	New Zealand	1994/95	1	2	0	92	76	46.00	51.39	0	1	1
Zimbabwe	Zimbabwe	1995/96	1	2	0	14	13	7.00	26.92	0	0	1
England	South Africa	1995/96	5	7	1	303	110	50.50	39.04	1	2	2
India	India	1996/97	3	6	0	322	133	53.66	54.57	2	0	2
India	South Africa	1996/97	3	6	0	137	103	22.83	45.51	1	0	1
Australia	South Africa	1996/97	3	6	0	82	43	13.66	30.82	0	0	1
Pakistan	Pakistan	1997/98	3	4	1	258	100*	86.00	36.64	1	2	2
Australia	Australia	1997/98	3	6	1	279	108*	55.80	43.93	1	2	2
Pakistan	South Africa	1997/98	3	6	1	130	44	26.00	42.34	0	0	3
Sri Lanka	South Africa	1997/98	2	4	1	165	75*	55.00	36.83	0	2	3
England	England	1998	5	8	1	257	210	36.71	37.19	1	0	4
West Indies	South Africa	1998/99	5	10	1	336	134	37.33	40.43	1	2	4
New Zealand	New Zealand	1998/99	3	4	1	245	128	81.66	45.03	1	1	1
England	South Africa	1999/00	5	7	0	396	275	56.57	40.61	1	1	4
India	India	1999/00	2	3	0	149	79	49.66	37.25	0	2	1
Sri Lanka	Sri Lanka	2000	3	6	0	131	55	21.83	27.93	0	1	3
New Zealand	South Africa	2000/01	3	5	1	138	49	34.50	43.12	0	0	5
Sri Lanka	South Africa	2000/01	2	3	0	266	180	88.66	41.17	1	1	2
West Indies	West Indies	2000/01	5	10	0	250	150	25.00	35.41	1	0	6
Zimbabwe	Zimbabwe	2001/02	2	3	1	316	220	158.00	63.32	1	1	1
India	South Africa	2001/02	2	4	1	112	73	37.33	52.58	0	1	4
Australia	Australia	2001/02	3	6	0	245	153	40.83	42.09	1	0	1
Australia	South Africa	2001/02	3	6	0	192	87	32.00	48.24	0	2	2
Bangladesh	South Africa	2002/03	2	2	0	310	160	155.00	68.88	2	0	2
Sri Lanka	South Africa	2002/03	2	3	0	77	55	25.66	40.74	0	1	5
Pakistan	South Africa	2002/03	2	2	0	75	56	37.50	49.66	0	1	1
England	England	2003	4	7	0	462	130	66.00	44.68	2	2	4
Pakistan	Pakistan	2003/04	2	4	1	271	118	90.33	50.18	1	2	0
West Indies	South Africa	2003/04	3	4	1	173	137	57.66	60.91	1	0	1
New Zealand	New Zealand	2003/04	3	6	1	250	137	50.00	48.63	1	1	0
Total			101	176	15	7289	275	45.27	43.45	21	34	83

Bowling by series

Series	Venue	Season	Balls	Runs	Wkts	Avg	RPO	BB	5I
v Australia	Australia	1993/94	138	62	1	62.00	2.69	1-62	0
v Australia	South Africa	1993/94	109	50	0	-	2.75	-	0
v England	England	1994	12	10	0	-	5.00	-	0
v New Zealand	South Africa	1994/95	30	11	1	11.00	2.20	1-0	0
v England	South Africa	1995/96	36	2	0	-	0.33	-	0
v Zimbabwe	Zimbabwe	2001/02	12	6	0	-	3.00	-	0
v West Indies	South Africa	2003/04	12	1	0	-	0.50	-	0
Total			349	142	2	71.00	2.44	1-0	0

Versus each opponent

Opponent	M	Inns	NO	Runs	HS	Avg	SR	100	50	Ct
Australia	18	34	1	1134	153	34.36	39.58	2	5	12
Bangladesh	2	2	0	310	160	155.00	68.88	2	0	2
England	22	35	2	1608	275	48.72	41.11	5	7	15
India	10	19	1	720	133	40.00	47.87	3	3	8
New Zealand	13	23	4	951	137	50.05	47.31	2	5	13
Pakistan	11	18	3	838	118	55.86	43.85	2	6	7
Sri Lanka	9	16	1	639	180	42.60	36.47	1	5	13
West Indies	13	24	2	759	150	34.50	41.68	3	2	11
Zimbabwe	3	5	1	330	220	82.50	59.89	1	1	2
Total	101	176	15	7289	275	45.27	43.45	21	34	83

By continent

Continent	M	Inns	NO	Runs	HS	Avg	SR	100	50	Ct
Africa	55	93	9	3714	275	44.21	45.38	9	17	53
Americas	5	10	0	250	150	25.00	35.41	1	0	6
Asia	13	23	2	1131	133	53.85	41.84	4	7	8
Australasia	16	29	3	1285	153	49.42	42.52	4	6	7
Europe	12	21	1	909	210	45.45	42.08	3	4	9

Home and away

Where	M	Inns	NO	Runs	HS	Avg	SR	100	50	Ct
Home	52	88	8	3384	275	42.30	44.33	8	16	51
Away	49	88	7	3905	220	48.20	42.71	13	18	32

At South African venues

Venue	M	Inns	NO	Runs	HS	Avg	SR	100	50	Ct
Bloemfontein	2	4	1	135	73	45.00	51.72	0	1	4
Cape Town	11	19	2	648	103	38.11	45.76	1	5	12
Centurion	7	10	1	276	134	30.66	38.22	1	1	4
Durban	11	18	2	1048	275	65.50	42.49	3	4	9
East London	1	1	0	150	150	150.00	67.26	1	0	1
Johannesburg	12	21	1	569	110	28.45	43.20	1	3	12
Port Elizabeth	7	14	1	398	69	30.61	39.76	0	2	8
Potchefstroom	1	1	0	160	160	160.00	70.48	1	0	1

Centuries

Season	Against	Venue	Runs	Mins	Balls	Fours	Sixes
1995/96	England	Johannesburg	110	353	241	16	0
1996/97	India	Calcutta	102	244	171	15	0
1996/97	India	Calcutta	133	317	196	18	0
1996/97	India	Cape Town	103	290	204	15	0
1997/98	Pakistan	Faisalabad	100*	298	208	15	0
1997/98	Australia	Adelaide	108*	235	159	17	1
1998	England	Manchester	210	650	525	24	1
1998/99	West Indies	Centurion	134	448	305	15	0
1998/99	New Zealand	Auckland	128	361	282	15	0
1999/00	England	Durban	275	878	642	26	0
2000/01	Sri Lanka	Durban	180	574	461	20	0
2000/01	West Indies	Georgetown	150	447	338	13	1
2001/02	Zimbabwe	Harare	220	442	286	33	1
2001/02	Australia	Sydney	153	437	359	20	0
2002/03	Bangladesh	East London	150	326	223	14	0
2002/03	Bangladesh	Potchefstroom	160	372	227	17	1
2003	England	Lord's	108	283	244	15	0
2003	England	Leeds	130	457	323	17	0
2003/04	Pakistan	Faisalabad	118	316	232	11	1
2003/04	West Indies	Durban	137	275	218	20	0
2003/04	New Zealand	Hamilton	137	306	213	18	1

Opening partnerships

Partner	Inns	Unb	Runs	Best	Avg	100	50
HH Gibbs	52	0	2303	256	44.28	5	11
AC Hudson	41	2	1289	236	33.05	3	5
AM Bacher	25	1	814	140	33.91	3	2
PJR Steyn	6	0	295	106	49.16	1	1
HH Dippenaar	8	0	183	81	22.87	0	1
GFJ Liebenberg	8	0	170	89	21.25	0	1
ND McKenzie	6	0	143	58	23.83	0	2
GC Smith	1	0	133	133	133.00	1	0
DJ Cullinan	1	1	15	15* -		0	0
PN Kirsten	2	0	2	2	1.00	0	0

Limited Overs Internationals
By year

Year	M	Inns	NO	Runs	HS	Avg	SR	100	50	Ct
1993	2	2	0	11	7	5.50	22.00	0	0	1
1994	20	20	2	610	112*	33.88	58.71	1	3	4
1995	7	7	1	362	87	60.33	68.95	0	3	2
1996	29	29	4	1442	188*	57.68	83.49	6	4	12*
1997	16	16	1	593	89	39.53	67.08	0	7	6
1998	18	18	1	561	103	33.00	75.60	1	3	5
1999	20	20	2	465	82	25.83	59.76	0	3	7
2000	36	36	3	1467	115	44.45	73.20	2	13	11
2001	13	13	1	638	133*	53.16	79.94	2	4	4
2002	18	18	1	463	102*	27.23	67.59	1	2	7
2003	6	6	3	186	69	62.00	85.71	0	3	2
Total	185	185	19	6798	188*	40.95	71.94	13	45	61

* Also one stumping

Bowling by year

Year	Balls	Runs	Wkts	Avg	RPO	BB	4I
1994	6	8	0	-	8.00	-	0
1996	24	15	0	-	3.75	-	0
Total	30	23	0	-	4.60	-	0

Versus each opponent

Opponent	M	Inns	NO	Runs	HS	Avg	SR	100	50	Ct
Australia	39	39	2	1167	112*	31.54	62.84	2	5	14
Bangladesh	1	1	1	52	52*	-	162.50	0	1	0
Canada	1	1	0	0	0	0.00	0.00	0	0	0
England	17	17	0	381	116	22.41	65.57	1	0	2
Holland	1	1	0	83	83	83.00	84.69	0	1	1
India	26	26	4	1377	133*	62.59	76.58	4	9	12*
Kenya	5	5	1	286	124	71.50	80.56	1	2	2
New Zealand	31	31	4	1180	103	43.70	71.34	2	8	9
Pakistan	24	24	5	1054	118*	55.47	73.60	2	8	8
Sri Lanka	17	17	0	460	76	27.05	72.44	0	5	6
United Arab Emirates	1	1	1	188	188*	-	118.23	1	0	0
West Indies	13	13	0	346	72	26.61	63.25	0	4	4
Zimbabwe	9	9	1	224	66	28.00	75.67	0	2	3

* Also one stumping

By continent

Continent	M	Inns	NO	Runs	HS	Avg	SR	100	50	Ct
Africa	76	76	9	2547	133*	38.01	74.21	6	17	22
Americas	6	6	0	189	72	31.50	66.31	0	2	2
Asia	45	45	7	2265	188*	59.60	77.64	5	16	15*
Australasia	42	42	3	1476	112*	37.84	66.96	2	9	16
Europe	16	16	0	321	82	20.06	52.53	0	1	6

* Also one stumping

Home and away

Where	M	Inns	NO	Runs	HS	Avg	SR	100	50	Ct
Home	63	63	7	2068	133*	36.92	71.63	5	14	19
Away	122	122	12	4730	188*	43.00	72.08	8	31	42*

* Also one stumping

Centuries

Season	Against	Venue	Runs	Mins	Balls	Fours	Sixes
1993/94	Australia	Melbourne	112*	199	137	8	0
1995/96	England	Centurion	116	163	125	11	0
1995/96	United Arab Emirates	Rawalpindi	188*	210	159	13	4
1995/96	India	Sharjah	106	182	116	9	0
1995/96	India	Sharjah	115*	212	142	4	1
1996/97	Pakistan	Nairobi	118*	170	127	16	0
1996/97	Australia	Indore	105*	202	139	9	0
1997/98	New Zealand	Brisbane	103	148	116	9	0
1999/00	India	Kochi	115	175	123	12	0
2000/01	New Zealand	Kimberley	101	144	107	10	0
2001/02	India	Johannesburg	133*	205	155	13	0
2001/02	Kenya	Cape Town	124	163	130	12	2
2002/03	Pakistan	Paarl	102*	183	118	9	0

First-class
By Season

Season	Country	For	M	Inns	NO	Runs	HS	Avg	100	50	Ct
1987/88	South Africa	WPB	6	11	4	424	163*	60.57	1	2	11
1988/89	South Africa	WP/WPB	11	17	2	512	159	34.13	1	2	8
1989/90	South Africa	WP/WPB	7	12	1	751	175	68.27	2	4	10
1990/91	South Africa	WP	11	21	1	724	189	36.20	2	3	2
1991/92	South Africa	WP	8	16	2	525	91	37.50	0	3	3
1992/93	South Africa	WP	7	14	1	512	109	39.38	2	2	3
1993/94	Zimbabwe	WP	1	2	0	75	75	37.50	0	1	2
1993/94	South Africa	WP/SA	7	12	0	650	192	54.16	2	2	9
1993/94	Australia	SA	4	7	0	207	67	29.57	0	1	2
1994	England	SA	11	19	3	751	201*	46.93	2	5	5
1994/95	South Africa	WP/SA	9	15	1	664	150	47.42	1	5	10
1994/95	New Zealand	SA	1	2	0	92	76	46.00	0	1	1
1995/96	Australia	WP	2	4	0	172	130	43.00	1	0	1
1995/96	Zimbabwe	SA	1	2	0	14	13	7.00	0	0	1
1995/96	South Africa	WP/SA	10	16	3	812	244	62.46	3	4	5
1996/97	India	SA	5	10	1	404	133	44.88	2	0	6
1996/97	South Africa	WP/SA	8	16	0	305	103	19.06	1	0	4
1997/98	Pakistan	SA	4	6	1	346	100*	69.20	1	3	2
1997/98	Australia	SA	6	12	1	627	201	57.00	2	3	2
1997/98	South Africa	WP/SA	6	12	2	334	75*	33.40	0	2	7
1998	England	SA	12	19	5	892	210	63.71	4	2	8
1998/99	South Africa	WP/SA	8	15	2	758	194	58.30	2	4	6
1998/99	New Zealand	SA	5	8	2	436	137	72.66	2	1	8
1999/00	South Africa	WP/SA	9	13	1	590	275	49.16	1	3	6
1999/00	India	SA	3	5	0	209	79	41.80	0	3	1
2000	Sri Lanka	SA	3	6	0	131	55	21.83	0	1	3
2000/01	South Africa	WP/SA	6	10	1	496	180	55.11	1	2	8
2000/01	West Indies	SA	7	14	0	368	150	26.28	1	1	7
2001/02	Zimbabwe	SA	2	3	1	316	220	158.00	1	1	1
2001/02	South Africa	WP/SA	7	13	1	710	244	59.16	1	5	7
2001/02	Australia	SA	5	10	0	454	153	45.40	1	2	3
2002/03	South Africa	WP/SA	11	14	1	733	160	56.38	3	3	13

First-class
By Season

Season	Country	For	M	Inns	NO	Runs	HS	Avg	100	50	Ct
2003	England	SA	7	12	2	713	130	71.30	2	4	5
2003/04	Pakistan	SA	2	4	1	271	118	90.33	1	2	0
2003/04	South Africa	WP/SA	5	7	1	412	137	68.66	2	1	1
2003/04	New Zealand	SA	4	8	1	280	137	40.00	1	1	0
Total			221	387	42	16670	275	48.31	46	79	171

Bowling by season

Season	Country	For	Balls	Runs	Wkts	Avg	RPO	BB	5I
1987/88	South Africa	WPB	36	17	0	-	2.83	-	0
1988/89	South Africa	WP/WPB	30	21	0	-	4.20	-	0
1989/90	South Africa	WP/WPB	30	14	0	-	2.80	-	0
1990/91	South Africa	WP	48	38	0	-	4.75	-	0
1993/94	Zimbabwe	WP	60	26	3	8.66	2.60	3-26	0
1993/94	South Africa	WP/SA	535	213	9	23.66	2.38	6-68	1
1993/94	Australia	SA	192	99	3	33.00	3.09	2-19	0
1994	England	SA	137	97	0	-	4.24	-	0
1994/95	South Africa	WP/SA	307	115	2	57.50	2.24	1-0	0
1995/96	Australia	WP	22	16	1	16.00	4.36	1-7	0
1995/96	South Africa	WP/SA	174	82	2	41.00	2.82	2-35	0
1996/97	South Africa	WP/SA	54	41	0	-	4.55	-	0
1997/98	South Africa	WP/SA	36	25	0	-	4.16	-	0
2000/01	West Indies	SA	12	6	0	-	3.00	-	0
2001/02	Zimbabwe	SA	12	6	0	-	3.00	-	0
2002/03	South Africa	WP/SA	30	19	0	-	3.80	-	0
2003/04	South Africa	WP/SA	12	1	0	-	0.50	-	0
Total			1727	836	20	41.80	2.90	6-68	1

For each team

Team	M	Inns	NO	Runs	HS	Avg	100	50	Ct
South Africa	135	236	26	9985	275	47.54	28	48	107
Western Province	73	128	11	5671	244	48.47	15	26	43
Western Province B	13	23	5	1014	163*	56.33	3	5	21

By competition

Competition	M	Inns	NO	Runs	HS	Avg	100	50	Ct
Test	101	176	15	7289	275	45.27	21	34	83
SuperSport Series	64	112	11	4891	244	48.42	13	24	35
UCB Bowl	13	23	5	1014	163*	56.33	3	5	21
Other First-class	43	76	11	3476	205*	53.47	9	16	32

Limited Overs
By competition

Competition	M	Inns	NO	Runs	HS	Avg	SR	100	50	Ct
Limited Overs Ints	185	185	19	6798	188*	40.95	71.94	13	45	61#
Standard Bank Cup	76	73	7	1825	104*	27.65	69.45*	2	10	24
Nissan Shield	17	15	0	470	103	31.33	45.14*	1	2	5
Other Matches	16	16	1	493	141*	32.86	82.05*	2	1	7
Total	294	289	27	9586	188*	36.58	71.42*	18	58	97

* Strike-rates are based on matches where details of balls faced are available. An asterisk indicates that details of balls faced are not available for all matches in the competition
\# Also one stumping.

The numbers

Bowling by competition

Competition	Balls	Runs	Wkts	Avg	RPO	BB	4I
Limited Overs Ints	12	14	0	-	7.00	-	0
World Cup	18	9	0	-	3.00	-	0
Standard Bank Cup	78	52	2	26.00	4.00	1-25	0
Other Limited Overs	30	37	1	37.00	7.40	1-37	0
Total	138	112	3	37.33	4.86	1-25	0

Miscellaneous

Most Test runs as an opener

Name	Team	Inns	NO	Runs	HS	Avg	100	50
SM Gavaskar	Ind	203	12	9607	221	50.29	33	42
G Boycott	Eng	191	23	8091	246*	48.16	22	42
GA Gooch	Eng	184	6	7811	333	43.88	18	41
MA Taylor	Aus	186	13	7525	334*	43.49	19	40
CG Greenidge	WI	182	16	7488	226	45.10	19	34
MA Atherton	Eng	197	6	7476	185*	39.14	16	45
DL Haynes	WI	201	25	7472	184	42.45	18	39
L Hutton	Eng	131	12	6721	364	56.47	19	31
G Kirsten	SA	149	12	5726	275	41.79	14	28
MJ Slater	Aus	131	7	5312	219	42.83	14	21

Most century partnerships in Tests

Name	Team	Tests	100 Parts
SR Waugh	Aus	168	64
AR Border	Aus	156	63
SM Gavaskar	Ind	125	58
SR Tendulkar	Ind	114	54
BC Lara	WI	108	52
Javed Miandad	Pak	124	50
G Boycott	Eng	108	47
R Dravid	Ind	78	47
ME Waugh	Aus	128	47
CG Greenidge	WI	108	46
G Kirsten	SA	101	45

Centuries versus all 9 Test opponents

Name	Team	Match in which set was completed
G Kirsten	SA	v Bangladesh (East London) 2002/03
SR Waugh	Aus	v Bangladesh (Darwin) 2003

Longest Test innings

Mins	Name	Team	Against	Venue	Season	Score	Balls	Fours	Sixes
970	Hanif Mohammad	Pakistan	West Indies	Bridgetown	1957/58	337	?	24	0
878	G Kirsten	South Africa	England	Durban	1999/00	275	642	26	0
799	ST Jayasuriya	Sri Lanka	India	Colombo-RPS	1997/98	340	578	36	2
797	L Hutton	England	Australia	The Oval	1938	364	844	35	0
778	BC Lara	West Indies	England	St John's	2003/04	400*	582	43	4
777	DSBP Kuruppu	Sri Lanka	New Zealand	Colombo-CCC	1986/87	201*	548	24	0
766	BC Lara	West Indies	England	St John's	1993/94	375	538	45	0
762	RB Simpson	Australia	England	Manchester	1964	311	743	23	1
753	RS Mahanama	Sri Lanka	India	Colombo-RPS	1997/98	225	591	28	0
740	R Dravid	India	Pakistan	Rawalpindi	2003/04	270	495	34	1

Most Test runs for South Africa

Name	M	Inns	NO	Runs	HS	Avg	100	50
G Kirsten	101	176	15	7289	275	45.27	21	34
JH Kallis	78	129	21	5840	189*	54.07	16	29
HH Gibbs	59	100	5	4693	228	49.40	13	17
DJ Cullinan	70	115	12	4554	275*	44.21	14	20
WJ Cronje	68	111	9	3714	135	36.41	6	23
B Mitchell	42	80	9	3471	189*	48.88	8	21
AD Nourse	34	62	7	2960	231	53.81	9	14
HW Taylor	42	76	4	2936	176	40.77	7	17
SM Pollock	83	116	29	2903	111	33.36	2	13
MV Boucher	74	100	12	2715	125	Ω30.85	4	16

Highest Test scores for South Africa

Score	Name	Against	Venue	Season
277	GC Smith	England	Birmingham	2003
275*	DJ Cullinan	New Zealand	Auckland	1998/99
275	G Kirsten	England	Durban	1999/00
274	RG Pollock	Australia	Durban	1969/70
259	GC Smith	England	Lord's	2003
255*	DJ McGlew	New Zealand	Wellington	1952/53
236	EAB Rowan	England	Leeds	1951
231	AD Nourse	Australia	Johannesburg	1935/36
228	HH Gibbs	Pakistan	Cape Town	2002/03
222*	JA Rudolph	Bangladesh	Chittagong	2002/03
220	G Kirsten	Zimbabwe	Harare	2001/02
211*	HH Gibbs	New Zealand	Christchurch	1998/99
210	G Kirsten	England	Manchester	1998
209	RG Pollock	Australia	Cape Town	1966/67
208	AD Nourse	England	Nottingham	1951
204	GA Faulkner	Australia	Melbourne	1910/11
201	EJ Barlow	Australia	Adelaide	1963/64
200	GC Smith	Bangladesh	East London	2002/03

Two Centuries in a Test for South Africa

Name	Scores	Against	Venue	Season
A Melville	189 & 104*	England	Nottingham	1947
B Mitchell	120 & 189*	England	The Oval	1947
G Kirsten	102 & 133	India	Calcutta	1996/97

Carrying bat in a Test for South Africa

Name	Score	Total	Against	Venue	Season
AB Tancred	26*	47	England	Cape Town	1888/89
JW Zulch	43*	103	England	Cape Town	1909/10
TL Goddard	56*	99	Australia	Cape Town	1957/58
DJ McGlew	127*	292	New Zealand	Durban	1961/62
G Kirsten	100*	239	Pakistan	Faisalabad	1997/98

Most catches by a fielder off the same bowler in a Test innings (excluding wicket-keepers)

Cts	Fielder	Bowler	Team	Against	Venue	Season
4	AEE Vogler	GA Faulkner	South Africa	England	Durban	1909/10
4	AL Wadekar	BS Bedi	India	New Zealand	Christchurch	1967/68
4	Y Goonasekera	VB John	Sri Lanka	New Zealand	Wellington	1982/83
4	G Kirsten	AA Donald	South Africa	England	Cape Town	1999/00
4	KC Sangakkara	M Muralitharan	Sri Lanka	Bangladesh	Colombo-PSS	2002

Note: Younis Khan held 4 catches as a substitute off Danish Kaneria for Pakistan v Bangladesh at Multan, 2001/02.

Most Test catches for South Africa (fielders)

Name	M	Cts
G Kirsten	101	83
JH Kallis	78	73
DJ Cullinan	70	67
SM Pollock	83	64
B Mitchell	42	56
BM McMillan	38	49
TL Goddard	41	48
HH Gibbs	59	45
AW Nourse	45	43
WR Endean	28	41

Most consecutive Tests for South Africa

Matches	Name	From	Until
73	MV Boucher	1997/98	2003/04
60	JH Kallis	1997/98	2002/03
53	G Kirsten	1993/94	1998/99
45	AW Nourse	1902/03	1924
42	B Mitchell	1929	1948/49

Highest World Cup scores

Score	Name	Team	Against	Venue	Season
188*	G Kirsten	South Africa	United Arab Emirates	Rawalpindi	1995/96
183	SC Ganguly	India	Sri Lanka	Taunton	1999
181	IVA Richards	West Indies	Sri Lanka	Karachi	1987/88
175*	Kapil Dev	India	Zimbabwe	Tunbridge Wells	1983
172*	CB Wishart	Zimbabwe	Namibia	Harare	2002/03
171*	GM Turner	New Zealand	East Africa	Birmingham	1975
161	AC Hudson	South Africa	Holland	Rawalpindi	1995/96
152	SR Tendulkar	India	Namibia	Pietermaritzburg	2002/03
145	PA de Silva	Sri Lanka	Kenya	Kandy	1995/96
145	R Dravid	India	Sri Lanka	Taunton	1999

Note: Kirsten's 188* is also the highest score in all Limited Overs Internationals for South Africa.

Most Limited Overs International runs in a calendar year

Name	Team	M	Inns	NO	Runs	HS	Avg	SR	100	50	Year
SR Tendulkar	Ind	34	33	4	1894	143	65.31	102.21	9	7	1998
SC Ganguly	Ind	41	41	3	1767	183	46.50	75.96	4	10	1999
R Dravid	Ind	43	43	5	1761	153	46.34	75.22	6	8	1999
SR Tendulkar	Ind	32	32	2	1611	137	53.70	82.31	6	9	1996
Saeed Anwar	Pak	36	36	5	1595	115	51.45	91.56	3	10	1996
SC Ganguly	Ind	32	32	4	1579	144	56.39	82.80	7	6	2000
ME Waugh	Aus	36	36	3	1468	106	44.48	75.51	2	11	1999
G Kirsten	SA	36	36	3	1467	115	44.45	73.20	2	13	2000
G Kirsten	SA	29	29	4	1442	188*	57.68	83.49	6	4	1996
Yousuf Youhana	Pak	32	30	5	1362	141*	54.48	84.91	5	6	2002

Most Limited Overs International runs for South Africa

Name	M	Inns	NO	Runs	HS	Avg	SR	100	50
JH Kallis	196	187	35	6977	139	45.90	71.15	12	47
G Kirsten	185	185	19	6798	188*	40.95	71.94	13	45
JN Rhodes	245	220	51	5935	121	35.11	81.05	2	33
WJ Cronje	188	175	31	5565	112	38.64	76.51	2	39
HH Gibbs	149	148	11	4726	153	34.49	81.76	12	19
DJ Cullinan	138	133	16	3860	124	32.99	70.39	3	23
L Klusener	164	131	49	3493	103*	42.59	90.37	2	19
AC Hudson	89	88	1	2559	161	29.41	64.47	2	18
HH Dippenaar	77	65	10	2322	110*	42.21	65.27	1	19
MV Boucher	171	119	30	2198	70	24.69	79.23	0	14

Most First-class runs for Western Province

Name	M	Inns	NO	Runs	HS	Avg	100	50
PN Kirsten	133	236	19	9087	204*	41.87	21	47
G Kirsten	73	128	11	5671	244	48.47	15	26
L Seeff	96	179	16	5250	141	32.20	7	30
AP Kuiper	107	179	25	5214	161*	33.85	6	32
EJ Barlow	82	146	6	5024	163	35.88	12	21
HD Ackerman	74	124	17	4700	202*	43.92	14	24
AJ Lamb	66	115	15	4316	206*	43.16	9	29
A Bruyns	73	130	7	4184	197	34.01	10	18
HM Ackerman	76	132	15	3668	179*	31.35	5	19
EO Simons	88	134	23	3202	157*	28.84	2	20

Score of 150 or more and 6 wickets in an innings in same South African First-class match

Name	Batting	Bowling	Team	Against	Venue	Season
JP Duminy	168*	6-40 & 1-21	Transvaal	Border	Durban	1928/29
DPB Morkel	150*	0-17 & 8-13	South Africans	Western Australia	Perth	1931/32
GL Hayes	167*	6-27 & 2-37	Border	Griqualand West	East London	1979/80
G Kirsten	192 & 5	dnb & 6-68	Western Province	Northern Transvaal	Verwoerdburg	1993/94
EA Brandes	165*	7-38 & 2-55	Zimbabwe Board XI	Griqualand West	Kimberley	1994/95
P de Bruyn	202 & 20	0-13 & 6-56	Northerns B	Griqualand West B	Centurion	1998/99

Conversions rates from 100 to 150 in First-class cricket

Name	Over 100	Over 150	Perc
KS Ranjitsinhji	72	37	51.38
DG Bradman	117	58	49.57
VS Hazare	60	29	48.33
BC Lara	54	26	48.14
WH Ponsford	47	22	46.80
VM Merchant	45	21	46.66
G Kirsten	46	21	45.65
E Paynter	45	20	44.44
SM Gavaskar	81	35	43.20
SR Tendulkar	57	24	42.10

Minimum: 40 centuries

Consecutive First-class innings without a duck

Kirsten finished his career without getting a duck in any of his last 72 first-class innings. Innings numbers 69,70 and 71 of that sequence were all scores of 1 in his last 2 Tests.

The numbers

Index